A Nation at Thought

A Nation at Thought

Restoring Wisdom in America's Schools

David M. Steiner

ROWMAN & LITTLEFIELD
Lanham • Boulder • New York • London

Published by Rowman & Littlefield
An imprint of The Rowman & Littlefield Publishing Group, Inc.
4501 Forbes Boulevard, Suite 200, Lanham, Maryland 20706
www.rowman.com

86-90 Paul Street, London EC2A 4NE, United Kingdom

British Library Cataloguing in Publication Information Available

Library of Congress Cataloging-in-Publication Data

Names: Steiner, David M., author.
Title: A nation at thought : restoring wisdom in America's schools / David M. Steiner.
Description: Lanham, Maryland : Rowman & Littlefield, 2023. | Includes bibliographical references and index. | Summary: "This is a book about the education America owes to its children, why its education system is in poor condition, and what might be done to give that system both energy and quality"—Provided by publisher.
Identifiers: LCCN 2022045850 (print) | LCCN 2022045851 (ebook) | ISBN 9781475867084 (cloth) | ISBN 9781475867091 (paperback) | ISBN 9781475867107 (epub)
Subjects: LCSH: Education—Aims and objectives—United States. | Educational change—United States.
Classification: LCC LA217.2 .S75 2023 (print) | LCC LA217.2 (ebook) | DDC 370.973—dc23/eng/20221123
LC record available at https://lccn.loc.gov/2022045850
LC ebook record available at https://lccn.loc.gov/2022045851

For Evelyne

Contents

Preface   ix

Acknowledgments   xiii

Introduction   xv

Prolegomenon: The Collective Good of Education   xix

Chapter 1: The Unmet Goals of American Schooling   1

Chapter 2: The Great Distractors   31

Chapter 3: What Works—and Why We Don't Do It   55

Chapter 4: Basic Skills: The "Main Idea" in K-12 Education   83

Chapter 5: Learning to Think   105

Notes   135

Bibliography   155

Index   185

About the Author   197

Preface

Buffalo had long been on our watch list. Students' academic performance in Buffalo Public Schools was unremittingly dismal—even by the standards of the economically depressed Mohawk Valley in western New York. As the car turned the corner to approach the next school on our itinerary, a surprise: The building was pristine, and the principal was eager to show it off. The extensive tour began with firm handshakes, smiles, and optimism. Then, the high point: a lesson on Shakespeare's *Hamlet*. As the lesson unfolded, students began writing on one side or the other of a piece of paper with a vertical line drawn down the middle.

What was going on? Was some kind of creative assessment in progress? How were students engaging with the text and the eternal questions it raises about the human condition? After forty-five minutes, the answer was clear. The students had been asked to think about their families and create lists of those for whom they felt anger and those they considered supporters and allies. There was no discussion of the text of *Hamlet*. There wasn't any discussion at all. The students appeared detached and bored.

There were inevitably low points during my time as New York State commissioner. I was once called "the worst person in the world" on national television, but the visit to that classroom remains the saddest hour of my tenure.

I was accompanied on that trip by my most valued colleague in the state education department, Senior Deputy Commissioner John King—later my successor as New York State commissioner and subsequently the US secretary of education. When I looked over to John, I was surprised to see anger. Surprised, because John has a remarkable capacity to stay calm in the direst of circumstances. As a former social studies teacher, principal, and manager of the urban charter organization Uncommon Schools, John had seen a great deal of teaching—good, bad, and indifferent. But this utter betrayal of responsibility by the educator infuriated us both.

After our visit was over, he and I agreed that his team would open an in-depth investigation of the entire Buffalo school system. We uncovered immense neglect, including the fact that principals and teachers alike—undermined at every step by an incompetent district leadership—were, on average, out of school more than four weeks of instructional days every year. Eventually, after excruciating delays, the worst among the leadership were nudged, pushed, and cajoled out of the district. A decade later, the academic results very modestly improved.

Two years later, I found myself visiting another high school during another lesson on Shakespeare—this time, on *Macbeth*. While the urban context of Newark shared much with Buffalo, the experience promised to be vastly different. The high school, North Star Academy, was part of Uncommon Schools, a network of high-performing charter schools in New York, Massachusetts, and New Jersey. My host was Norman Atkins, the founder and former CEO of the network. Never seeking the limelight, Norman is one of the most forward-thinking educational leaders in the United States. Due to his unremitting insistence on quality and his ability to spot talent and build superb teams, Uncommon Schools were among the highest-performing urban public schools in the country. At North Star Academy, students—many of whom had incarcerated family members—were excelling.

I knew I would see no repetition of the Buffalo catastrophe. Facing one another, students used the text to engage in focused, conscientious, and polite discussions about the play. Moreover, they asked each other questions, and, where points of view diverged, differences were treated with respect. On first impression, it was difficult to find fault. Critics of high-performing charters like Uncommon Schools point to rigidities of the behavioral code and the directive behavior of the teachers, but in this classroom, the teacher was very much the supportive coach lauded by progressive education theory. Learning was largely student led. At the same time, the content couldn't possibly disappoint the most traditional of English teachers—it was Shakespeare, after all.

I can't recall exactly the scenes discussed, but I am confident the lesson wasn't in any way introductory, or about the famous opening. The plot was familiar to the students, who named the characters, their roles, and relationships with confidence. Students measured each character for honesty or dishonesty: Who was telling the truth, who was lying? In each case, the students referenced a piece of the text that gave evidence for their conclusion.

For readers unfamiliar with the Common Core State Standards (CCSS) in English Language Arts—the standards used (under different names) in over forty states—it is worth adding that citing the text as evidence for the student's argument is one of the most important requirements. For decades, E. D. Hirsch has argued that in the case of, say, a Shakespeare play, the understanding of plot, and the contributions to it of each major character, amount to the kind of knowledge that is key to closing the reading achievement gap. In other words, these students' ability to master the vocabulary of their more affluent peers would enable them to become more fluent readers and put them on a far stronger trajectory to better life outcomes.

We watched the lesson for some time, and then quietly left. Norman was enthusiastic about what we had witnessed. Once again, however, witnessing a class about Shakespeare left me distressed. With little reflection and still fewer good manners, I told Norman why. *Macbeth* digs into some of the most fundamental tensions of the human condition: freedom and predestination, ambition and guilt, gender relations and family loyalties, courage, and death. The classroom exercise on mendacity, at a stretch, could have served as an introduction to some of these eternal questions, but using the text to show who was and who was not telling the truth had kept the conversations at a surface level. Trivializing the play in this way, I argued, patronized the students—and limited their potential learning.

Norman was understandably angry. I was a misguided, naïve snob, forever the unreflective product of my elitist education. Where did I get off demanding of an extraordinary inner-city high school that it duplicate the niceties of an Oxford college tutorial? Did I not realize what I had witnessed, namely an astonishing educational achievement that would be sending all but a handful of these students through to a well-earned graduation? Implicitly, Norman asked me to compare what I had seen at North Star to what I had experienced in Buffalo—definitely a night and day comparison.

The new high school in Buffalo and the charter high school in Newark embody for me the bookends of what American public education currently offers not only its underprivileged students of color but the great majority of all of its students. Buffalo checked every box of failure: The tens of millions spent on the building, however, should have gone to support effective professional development for teachers, curriculum-based tutoring, and academic learning in the summers.

The goal of so many in the education reform movement—the state chiefs, the district superintendents, the school principals, the academics with their empirical studies, the parents of modest means hoping for the best from their local public school—would be to replace every instance of what I saw in Buffalo with something like the classrooms in North Star Academy.

There is no question that an America in which low-income children have access to the kinds of schools Norman and his teams were building would represent a quantum leap in educational opportunity. Success in moving our education system in this direction has proved maddeningly elusive. The data show that, in many ways, modest progress has stalled, leading not only to deep frustration and cynicism but even to an increasingly widely held belief that serious progress is inherently impossible. As school leaders, academics, and policymakers, it seems that we are at an impasse, increasingly loathe to offer solutions with much serious optimism.

My career in education policy and academia has given me a front seat both to the contentious discourse about—and the voluminous research on—the state of US public education. The following chapters offer a diagnosis of the largely stalled efforts to raise learning outcomes for all and close achievement gaps between less privileged and more affluent students. As I hope to show, by letting go of corrosive distractions and consistently implementing some key changes, we could raise the quality of teaching and thus the level of basic skills of literacy and numeracy in our elementary schools.

But as we set our sights on middle and high school, a deeper failure comes into view, a failure that is embodied in our very model of what education should be. In diagnosing that failure, I will stubbornly—and perhaps foolishly—refuse to let go of my reaction that morning in Newark. Our collective disinclination to aim higher, far from adding to the demoralization of our education system, has solidified it. For the sake of America's children and the future of our country, we need to imagine what aiming higher means—and then get back to work.

Acknowledgments

John Silber (Boston University), Dana Gioia (National Endowment for the Arts), Jennifer Raab (Hunter College, CUNY), Merryl Tisch (NYS Board of Regents) and David Andrews (Johns Hopkins University) each enabled a key professional opportunity in my journeys through the world of American education. Chancellor Silber is now deceased, but I am grateful for the opportunity to say a public thank you to each of the others—exacting leaders who in each case made an unconventional choice in bringing me on board. With some there were inevitable frictions, but always extraordinary invitations to be creative, and to learn about new domains of education policy and practice.

In each professional home, I have been blessed by the good luck of remarkable colleagues. At Boston University, Charles Glenn posed fundamental questions about the purpose of public education that still resound. At the NEA, Wayne Brown taught me what public service at the highest level of professionalism can achieve (no matter how small the budget). The NEA also introduced me to Mark Bauerlein. Mark and I differ in political persuasion, but his keen intelligence and deep convictions have been a source of abiding friendship ever since.

At Hunter College, Provost Vita Rabinowitz embodied a synthesis of humanity and insight that modeled what a senior administrator should be. She set a standard impossible to reach, but always valued. Those years also brought me into Norman Atkins' orbit. The most innovative creator I have encountered in the field, Norman's invitation to work together to re-think how teacher preparation could be designed and delivered was exacting and exhilarating. His friendship since has been a treasure.

The privilege of serving as Commissioner of Education for NYS was greatly enhanced by John King—my successor in that role and subsequently the U.S. Secretary of Education. John's work ethic, exactitude of focus, and commitment to underprivileged students are remarkable. Working in partnership with John, often under great pressure, was a rare experience.

During my last years at Hunter College, I met Ashley Berner, who then agreed to partner with me to create the Institute for Education Policy at Johns Hopkins University. Without Ashley's sharp intellect, passion for the work, and astonishing capacity to make everyone she meets feel treasured and understood, the Institute would never have grown to what it is today, eight years later. No "thank you" can possibly be enough.

In preparing this book for publication, Dominique Dureau undertook the thankless task of a first reading along with creating innumerable footnotes. Miriam Merin and Mark Bauerlein read the manuscript, pressing me toward greater clarity in language and argument. The standard author's statement that all remaining faults are his responsibility needs to be underlined in this instance.

There are so many more who have been colleagues, friends, and advisors (often all three) on my privileged professional journey. John White (who shares with me the experience of having managed a state education system), Robert Hughes, Checker Finn, Robert Pondiscio, Tim Cloyd, and mentors and friends no longer living: Storm Jamerson, Wallace McCaffery, Susan Rothstein.

Above all my parents, who died ten days apart in 2020, both scholars and teachers of world renown. My mother was a proud product of NYC public schools, my father (home schooled in the great texts of European culture) was deeply skeptical about the aspirations of democratic education. Lessons from both are, I hope, reflected in this book. My sister Deborah is a professor of classics at Columbia University. To my great good fortune, she has inherited wonderful qualities from both of our parents, and has become an ever-dearer confidant since their deaths.

Ashley Berner, John White, and Deborah each read earlier drafts of this book. If there are persuasive passages in the pages ahead, they each deserve a share of the credit. The same applies to Evelyne Ender for the final chapter. Finally, I am most grateful for the superb work of my editor, Tom Koerner.

Evelyne Ender, consummate scholar, wonderful teacher, and companion in my thoughts or in person for over forty years, was not only a highly insightful final reader but endured many months of the author's moodiness. I knew Evelyne first as my father's brilliant doctoral student, then as a magical girlfriend during halcyon days at Oxford University, and many years later when I became her husband. I dedicate this book to her in acknowledgement of the often-difficult journey she has travelled to enable us to be together, and in endless love.

Introduction

A strong academic education for all American students is—alongside of their health—the most crucial gift a society can provide to the next generation. Today, the United States fails to provide that education to millions of its children. Even before the onset of COVID-19, academic outcomes had been flat for the preceeding twenty years: More than half of all American children—and the great majority of African American and Latinx children—fail to achieve proficiency in core academic subjects.

How did we arrive at this outcome? Fewer students in our public schools speak English as their native language, confronting teachers with ever greater challenges. At the same time, the education system has put the mechanistic repetition of basic skills at the heart of schooling. Bored with what they are studying, students, especially in middle and high school, disengage with their studies and learn less every year. To avoid the resulting perception of failure, we keep lowering achievement standards in schools and colleges alike, handing out increasingly meaningless grades and diplomas.

In the last decade, new trends have arisen that further undermine academic learning. Educators have invented a rhetorically enticing set of goals that invite teachers to become coaches of students' emotions and of their metacognitive skills. With this new focus, the central mission of academic learning has further eclipsed.

It could all be otherwise. The goal of well-educated seventeen-year-olds with thoughtful choices in front of them cannot be realized unless our nation grasps why academic learning is so precious and acts to release American schooling from the reductionist models of education that now dominate the system. This rescue mission requires acts of recovery and courage—recovery of wisdom about the human condition and the courage to bring that wisdom into classroom practice.

The displacement and hollowing-out of academic learning can and should be stopped. Rather than framing the mastery of academics in multiple subject-matters as reproducing the nineteenth-century factory model of education, we need to recognize that academic study, encompassing new fields and provoking energizing cognitive challenges, can be the demanding, empowering, and indispensable path to human flourishing.

There are some modest signals that this mission has begun. Schools of education are now under pressure to concentrate on preparing teachers to be more effective in the real world of the classroom. As a result, a few preparation programs are no longer actively undermining effective strategies of academic instruction. In the domain of student assessments, there are a handful of new designs that are less mechanistic than our current tests and probe for deeper understanding. Such alternative models encourage a focus on the intensive study of academic content. Finally, there has been progress in the world of curriculum design and use—with new models that support cognitively demanding instruction.

Promising as they seem, taken in the overall context of American K-12 education, these positive efforts nevertheless stand out as fragmentary and fragile. To break the hold of the status quo, the case needs to be made for a necessarily jarring shift in educational values, with a compelling model of learning at its core. That model must be consistent with our key goals for K-12 education. It must be engaging to students and galvanizing for a new generation of teachers.

So much has gone wrong in the American school system, and this in spite of so much labor and such good intentions. We have driven ourselves into a systemic trap that leaves most teachers and students struggling to make schooling an intellectually enriching experience. The central purpose of this book is to lay out what brought us to this impasse and to suggest what an escape would require.

At a time of lively but also contentious arguments that reinterpret the public good as embodying the private preferences of parents, this book begins by arguing that there remains a vital public interest in the quality of schooling for all American children.

Chapter 1 lays out four core goals for America's schools that still enjoy widespread support—but it argues in each case that we fall far short of achieving them and explains why this is so. The second chapter engages with the new silver bullets in American education and argues that research supporting their efficacy is greatly overstated.

The third chapter rehearses what we know about education policies that result in effective instruction; it then offers an account of why this country ignores what we know. Chapter 4 focuses on the core of current education—an instruction in basic skills. The purpose here is to suggest that this pedagogical approach is soul-destroying for teachers and teenage students alike.

Finally, chapter 5 lays what the three pillars of an education worthy of its name. If readers have reached this point in the book, they deserve to discover what is argued there without my revealing it here.

Prolegomenon

The Collective Good of Education

This is a book about the education America owes to its children, why its education system is in poor condition, and what might be done to give that system both energy and quality. In diagnosing the current practices and priorities of American education, the book presupposes a collective public interest in creating a well-educated next generation. While focused on public schools, the book addresses the education of all of America's children. What should well-educated future citizens learn in school?

The assumption that education embodies a collective public interest is today seriously debated. There is a strong push—both from certain political theorists and from powerful libertarian political forces—that would move the country in a very different direction. In their vision, public funds would continue to support the education of America's children, whereas establishing the content and the values embedded in that education would rest with parents and their schools of choice.

How might one defend the idea that there is such a thing as a collective interest in the content of K-12 education? There are at least two ways the defense could proceed. The first is to define a public interest in education as stemming from our joint political commitment to a pluralist democratic society. The second is to suggest that all children, whether educated in private or in public schools, deserve an education that carries the same fundamental commitment to learning.

Disentangling our public interest in the content of schooling from our political structures and their values is no easy task. The best-known effort to do so comes from Amy Gutmann, president of the University of Pennsylvania. Gutmann's voice as both a theorist and a senior administrator has given her a unique vantage point in considering educational theory and politics.

According to Gutmann, a democratic society requires more of its citizens than merely voting. Citizens who value the democratic way of life, she argues, must also value and support public debate and decision-making; without these two core elements, democracy withers. As a result, we must value, provide, and protect an education that enables future citizens to participate as equals in the activity of debate and public decision-making. In short, democracy presupposes the skills and virtues of deliberation. What do those skills and virtues consist of? "Literacy, numeracy, and critical thinking, as well as contextual knowledge, understanding, and appreciation of other people's perspectives. The virtues . . . include veracity, nonviolence, practical judgment, civic integrity, and magnanimity."[1]

This is quite a mouthful—and asks a great deal of our schools. Unsurprisingly, Gutmann's critics accuse her of overreaching. They present a very different interpretation of what our democracy entails—an interpretation grounded on parental choice. One such critic is the political theorist, Michael McConnell. In his view, Gutmann's argument starts in the wrong place—with political structures rather than with citizens. What a democratic state should most value, in McConnell's view, is the maximal exercise of individual rights and of free choice. He contends that one of the most fundamental rights is the parental right to decide how their children are to be educated. He argues that this choice should be minimally constrained by parental income and state policy.

The democratic goal, McConnell argues, is "a free and liberal society in the face of cultural, ideological, and religious differences."[2] Just as the United States rejected a national church, so McConnell argues, it must reject a state-run school system. Why? Because such a system imposes an illegitimate uniformity over a pluralist society and necessarily provokes acrimonious arguments over what should or should not constitute the substance of public education. He further argues that public schools cannot be run without the illegitimate requirement to establish an official set of values and ends for the education system. Why is establishing such requirements illegitimate? In his view, Americans just disagree too deeply about issues such as morality, gender, and justice, among many other key issues, to pretend that a public-school system can find some neutral common approach to educating our children. McConnell's answer is to take education out of public hands. If parents are empowered to choose "schools consistent with, or responsive to their convictions. . . . then there is no need for differences of opinion to break out into conflict."[3]

Notice the key difference of emphasis. Gutmann starts with what she intends to be the most basic human capacities that a democracy depends on—those that enable citizens to deliberate in public. Without such capacities, she argues, democracy would be a sham. Then she derives the core content of public education from what it takes to teach public deliberation. McConnell starts from the reality of lived politics, stating that we do as a matter of fact substantially disagree about the content of education. He then adduces that this disagreement is illegitimately adjudicated by any public authority, since that authority that will necessarily rule some parents' educational preferences as unacceptable.

Contra Guttmann, and pointing to rising support (especially among minority parents) for various school-choice models, McConnell argues that there is no widespread support for the need to establish a single, uniform set of educational aims. Even if a majority of the public happens to support a state monopoly over public education, McConnell isn't convinced: "Why not allow families to choose their own educational philosophy (at least within certain limits), just as we allow them to choose their own religion?"[4] He points out that since public funding is (largely) kept from religious schools, religiously minded parents' educational preferences are excluded from the start. Finally, in a direct response to Gutmann, McConnell argues that that there is no agreement about what values are definitive for democratic citizens, unless they are defined so vaguely as to be meaningless.[5]

These two visions represent vastly different models of educational goals. Gutmann asks schools to go far beyond teaching "the three r's." Rather, the goal is to create empathetic, reflective, well-informed "magnanimous" adults whose deliberations about politics will then further the public interest. Gutmann is forceful in pursuing these principles. She tells us, for example, that the state should not be funding a Jewish Yeshiva school, because the education it offers will not adequately prepare students for participation in civic debate. They won't know enough about the world, and their forms of argument, grounded in religious doctrine, will be too private to offer the kind of evidence appropriate in a contemporary civil society.

For McConnell, these claims amount to sheer imposition and philosophical arrogance. If individual freedom doesn't include the right to choose schooling for one's children that reflect the values of their parent, that freedom has been fatally abridged, and the results are a coercive state. If an orthodox Jewish family chooses that Yeshiva education for their child—an education that minimizes conventional studies in favor of close textual study of a canon of ancient and medieval texts central to Jewish life—then the state should fund that parental choice, just as it would fund a fundamentalist Protestant school, a Montessori school, or a school based on the radical model of the Summerhill School in England.

Neither theory is unproblematic. Whereas Gutmann might be vulnerable to the criticism of overreading what a democratic polity demands of education, with McConnell, the problem is where to put any limit on what kind of education parents might choose, given that their choice would be supported by public funding. Gutmann pushes on just this point: "Parental choice plans must satisfy some standard of mandatory schooling to be publicly defensible. . . . To avoid being empty, the minimum must be given content. Once given content, it establishes values to be imposed on schools."[6]

In a pragmatic concession, she acknowledges that when regular public schools fail to provide the education that she believes future democratic citizens require, some public funding for private schools might be legitimate. Guttmann would make that funding conditional on schools agreeing not to discriminate in their admissions policies and on their providing children with some civic education.[7] For his part, McConnell acknowledges that to count as an allowable school that school must be subject to "quality control." But just what Gutmann means by "adequate" or McConnell by "quality control" is left largely undefined.

Is there a way forward from this impasse? A third political theorist, William Galston, tries to split the difference, arguing that it would be appropriate to fund schools with religious values provided they teach what is minimally necessary for students to function in a modern secular world.[8] Ashley Berner, an education historian at Johns Hopkins and a colleague, has written extensively about the many democratic countries that do choose to publicly fund a wide variety of schools (thirty-six different types in the Netherlands, for example) so as to secure the public interest. In these educational systems, which she calls "pluralist," that public interest is protected by requiring that schools receiving public funds submit their students to a common, state-established set of public assessments, and in many cases to the teaching of a core curriculum.[9]

This is a compelling model that synthesizes parental choice with an education that is both funded by the taxpayer and protective of a nation's need for well-educated citizens. It is hard to predict if something close to this model can ever find strong political support in the United States. In many states, we currently find a very different model: The majority of students are in traditional public schools, some 10 percent in private schools, and a smaller group still in public charter schools. Only a tiny percentage of private school students are today funded by public dollars.

How fragile is this current system? Pointing to Supreme Court decisions and to the growing use of public funds for use in private schools in states such as Florida, libertariansincluding McConnell have little incentive to settle for less than the complete privatization of K-12 schooling, supported by education vouchers for all parents. The arguments of liberal Democrats remain dominant in states such as New York, where the current public-school system is supported by the vast majority. With states such as Texas and Florida pressing hard and quickly to support expanded parental choice, what may be ahead is an increasingly divided nation.

This would mean the unravelling of unified public vision for American schooling. As it stands, the American public-school system today still attempts to teach a curriculum that is premised on an interpretation of what the "public interest" requires. The entire edifice of federal education law over the last decades, from No Child Left Behind to the Every Student Succeeds Act, is grounded on the assumption that public-school students are to be tested by common, public, state-wide tests in ELA, math, and science; that schools (and in rare cases teachers) can be held accountable for those test results; and that (with the exception of vouchers, educational savings accounts, and tax credits) public funding must be restricted to such schools. In short, the governing assumption is that the state has a right to monitor the educational practices that it funds.

THE AMERICAN PUBLIC

While it is important not to overdramatize, there is evidence of a slowly moving tide against the status-quo model of public education. In 2020 alone, some eighteen states passed seven new school-choice programs and expanded twelve preexisting ones.[10] Choice options now affect some 4.5 million students. While it is difficult to interpret the competing polling, recent events suggest that COVID-19 and its exacerbation of the education culture wars are putting the public-school system as we know it under further pressure.[11] Robert Pondiscio, a conservative-leaning writer on education policy, argues that America's historical model of public schooling is in serious jeopardy.[12] Even before COVID-19, signs of declining public support for the status quo education system were evident.

- The PDK 2017 poll on education showed that traditional public schools don't command vast loyalty. If cost and location were not issues, just one-third of parents say they'd pick a traditional public school over a private school (31 percent), public charter school (17 percent), or a religious school (14 percent).
- Only slightly more than half of public-school parents (54%) say they'd stick with a public school if they were offered public funds to send their child to a private or religious school, assuming they received full tuition coverage.[13]

The current Supreme Court is also pressing choice models forward, weakening the previously rigid separation between public funding and private schools.[14]

But what would the educational landscape look like if the public education system turned into a publicly subsidized market governed by parental choice? What kind of schools would parents choose? American Federation of Teachers (AFT) polling shows that, beyond wanting safe and secure school environment, more than 90 percent of parents would seek out schools that focus on career and technical education.[15] There is evidence that minority parents, especially, would press for strong academics, but among all parents, many other competing educational values would come to the surface.[16] For instance, as *Forbes* Magazine journalist Nick Morrison argues, "millennial parents want their children to learn in schools that are creative, flexible and have a global outlook. . . . And parents increasingly value soft skills and personal attitudes above proficiency in academic subjects."[17] But there is no way to predict with any certainty what the educational landscape would look like, or which models of schooling would be ruled out as undeserving of public funds.

Moreover, those who support the breakup of the current state monopoly on the administration of publicly funded schooling argue from two very different directions: McConnell's argument is all about maximizing available educational choices. To see what this would mean in practice, consider a recent paper from the American Enterprise Institute (AEI) on early childhood education. The paper argues that the state should stop trying to run or contract-out the management of programs. Instead, it should incentivize the market to deliver the widest possible range and choice of programs.[18] The key point, however, is the article's disdain for educational quality: The word itself appears in scare quotes every time it is used. Clearly choice itself is the paramount value.

Proponents of expanding parental choice include Patrick Wolf. A professor of education at the University of Arkansas, he may agree with McConnell's theoretical arguments, but he is primarily concerned with educational justifications; he argues for the goal of choice in education policy because, on balance, he believes it brings higher academic outcomes.[19] The accuracy of this belief is the subject of a fierce and unsettled debate. A 2020 summary of research on the impact of vouchers reveals largely negative outcomes.[20] Another senior education researcher concludes that "the average effect of school choice on student outcomes is very close to zero."[21] Just as we can't predict what kind of schools the market would produce, we have no capacity to prejudge their academic quality. There is simply no current evidence that the widespread creation of schools that depend on parental choice would raise America's K-12 academic outcomes.[22]

Meanwhile, advocates for maintaining the monopoly of state authority over publicly funded schools in the name of democratic values face a different set of challenges. First, they must defend the current structure of public education despite tragically large achievement gaps between student populations and despite very modest overall academic outcomes. Second, wealthy parents have educational options (paying for expensive private schools) that poor parents don't.

This review of the research suggests that largely unfettered parental choice is not a convincing proposition for those who believe that the public interest (supported by taxpayer dollars) requires that schools be held accountable for providing students with a minimum level of skills and knowledge. Parents *should* be presented with a wider array of different schools to which they can send their children, but their private values cannot fully dictate the content of public schooling. Gutmann may have overreached, but she is fundamentally right. Democracies rely on a majority of citizens being capable of well-informed reasoning. That is a demanding goal that will require major changes in America's public schools.

But in the end, Gutmann's model, too, is inevitably insufficient as a full guide to what education should offer. Gutmann is concerned with public schools only, but education, as suggested above, is ultimately about all children, and about a universal good. Deriving the content of education from our political structure cannot provide an adequate foundation for the content of education. A K-12 education, wherever it takes place, should be grounded on the fundamental human right to the freedoms afforded by thought. An education worthy of the name must emerge from our understanding of human beings—their capacities, their emotions, their nature. This book will discuss both the impediments to providing a basic level of universal education and argue for the core of an education that we owe to every child.

Chapter 1

The Unmet Goals of American Schooling

"The real seriousness of our situation is revealed when we recognize how uncertain Americans have become as to what the proper goals of education are."[1]

What do Americans collectively expect of our public schools? Perhaps that they teach students some basic math and literacy, impart some knowledge of science and social studies, and provide some exposure to the arts. Perhaps also that this schooling prepares the great majority of students for gainful employment and/or college studies, that high-school graduates leave ready to participate thoughtfully in democratic decision-making, and that students leave the K-12 system motivated to be life-long learners.

Even within this broad set of expectations, the consensus is limited. There is no agreement as to what counts as academic competence. The nation is uncertain about which subjects beyond the core five (ELA, math, science, social studies, and the arts) are worth teaching. There is no accord on what teaching for democratic citizenship requires, nor as to whether it should be done at all. While few oppose the goal of "life-long learning," that is because the phrase happens to be devoid of content.

In an education system that enrolls some fifty million children, disagreements about what to teach and how to teach it are inevitable. Because education is in part about transmitting cultural values, American's clashing beliefs about which values should be passed on to the next generation inevitably produce discord in regard to the concrete the purposes of schooling.

But schools must provide specific and concrete answers to these questions. When they hire a teacher, select a curriculum, establish disciplinary codes, and choose extracurricular offerings, schools enact their understanding of educational purposes. No matter the disagreements between American citizens over the best ways to educate children, schools must operate with a set of ongoing assumptions about their mission—assumptions that are then integrated into their policies and practices.

How do public schools find their goals and ground their choices? They are subject to state accountability, public funding, elected school boards, and to an educational "thought world" that impacts teacher preparation and practice. Additionally constrained by legal requirements and sensitive to political pressure, schools try to deliver practices that are minimally controversial. Meanwhile, private schools try to match the values and expectations of their students' parents.

However, schools also exist in specific geographies. While the broadest goals of education may be consensual, the immediate expectation of their communities will differ, formed as they are from different histories, hopes, and assumptions about what is possible. Moreover, schools must operate in vastly different contexts: children enter schooling with widely disparate levels of health, vocabulary, and levels of home support.

A key portion of funding for most public schools—the dollars generated by local property taxes—also contributes to the radically different fiscal contexts within which schools operate. In the 2022–2023 school year, there were public schools on the North Shore of Long Island that spent $22,000 per pupil, while other schools just a few miles away could afford $45,000.[2] Private school tuition varies just as greatly.

Given the differences in expectations, student readiness, and funding, is it still meaningful to speak of shared educational goals? At least when it comes to America's public schools, the answer is a firm yes. Aware of the deep differences between public schools and districts, most Americans share some basic hopes for the education of the next generation, hope that have often been disappointed:

- Parents says that schools should teach core academic knowledge to children, yet teachers are convinced that there are more important goals for their work.
- Twelfth-graders intent on college attendance should not have to settle for unemployment or dead-end jobs, but American public schools don't provide most children with career and technical learning opportunities that lead to strong employment outcomes.
- Americans largely agree that the color of a child's skin or the income of that child's parents shouldn't be the controlling factor in that child's academic achievement. Even before COVID, however, the modest progress American schools had made in closing achievement gaps that separate African American and Hispanic students from their white peers had stalled, and in the case of high-school students, had started to widen.

- There is a widespread support for teaching students about the structure of their government and the values of a democracy, but, civic knowledge is at an all-time low.

In this chapter, each of these four elements, and the challenges that beset them, will be addressed in turn.

HANDWAVING AT ACADEMIC ACHIEVEMENT

It may strike the reader as obvious that teaching children how to read fluently, learn mathematics to at least the level of precalculus, understand the core elements of the nation's history, gain some scientific knowledge, and be exposed to the arts together embody the core purpose of our K-12 schooling. Isn't this akin to saying that the core purpose of medicine is to cure illness?

A preliminary glance at federal education policy seems to confirm that academic achievement is indeed the focus of our K-12 system—particularly since the passage of the No Child Left Behind Act (NCLB) in 2001 and Every Student Succeeds Act (ESSA) in 2015. The nation has been pressing for stronger academic results for decades, requiring measurements of student progress, annual student testing, and intervention in underperforming schools.

However, while most parents share the assumption that the teaching of academic skills and knowledge is the most fundamental purpose of American education, their children's teachers believe otherwise. While both parents and teachers are keen that students make progress, parents are more focused on their children's achievement levels than their teachers are.[3] More striking still, almost two-thirds of America's teachers put another priority ahead of academics, namely readiness for "democratic citizenship."

As discussed below, it isn't clear what exactly this phrase means, or how it is translated into classroom teaching, though it is clear is that the nation's schools are not focused on teaching civics content.[4] Rather, the phrase seems to be a catch-all for a number of disparate pedagogical goals, including teaching "social and emotional skills," "the whole child," "critical thinking," and child-based (or "constructivist") education.[5] We know that teachers devote a large percentage of their instructional time to social and emotional learning. In high schools, this constitutes an average of five-and-one-half hours a week, greater than the average time spent teaching math or English language arts.[6]

When two-thirds of the teaching profession doesn't believe that students' academic learning is their primary educational goal, one would expect to see evidence for their convictions in the operating practices of K-12 education.[7] One crucial piece of evidence that this is occurring is to look at what's happening to graduation tests in the United States. States have been steadily abandoning the use of such tests: an ever-increasing number no longer require students to pass any tests to graduate. The most recent pre-COVID data indicate that just eleven states required high-school graduation tests for the high-school class of 2020, down from twenty-seven that either had or were planning to have such tests. Seven states—Alaska, Arizona, California, Georgia, Nevada, South Carolina, and Texas—decided retroactively to grant high-school diplomas to students who had previously failed their required graduation assessments.[8]

What about the states that still require graduation tests? Here all is not what it seems. There is a plethora of "alternative" pathways to graduation. For example, in Maryland, students who fail the state tests can still graduate if they complete a "Bridge Project"—an independent study project supervised by their school. The numbers of students involved is not trivial: in Baltimore, typically more than 30 percent of students graduate thanks only to this route.[9] In response to a press inquiry, the Maryland Department of Education responded that it doesn't collect data on passing rates.[10] It is thus unclear if any student ever fails a Bridge Project. These "alternative" low (or nonexistent) gateways to graduation are not exclusively a Maryland problem.

While different states offer different alternative routes (in Massachusetts, it is the "Educational Proficiency Plan"), the most common are known by the name of "credit recovery"—a pathway to high-school graduation that involves the student making up for a failure on the state test or required coursework. The use of these pathways is especially prevalent in urban public schools. While once again data on any failure rates are hard to come by, there are plenty of indications that these practices are being used in shoddy ways.[11]

In short, one important measure of academic achievement has been removed or substantially diluted in almost all states. To be clear, no one announced that tests were being eliminated or bypassed to rid education of a critical metric. Despite strong evidence linking test scores to long-term life success,[12] the usual argument made by teachers and policy today is that tests are a poor way to evaluate student work. Most specifically, they point instead to the importance of grades.

Teachers have a point: While tests and grades both correlate with long-term life outcomes, grades may be the stronger predictors of important education outcomes, such as the choice to apply to college.[13] Perhaps instead of worrying about the disappearance of test-based graduation standards, one should better focus on GPA and high-school graduation rates. Here the news looks much better: A casual observer of average US GPAs will find plenty to celebrate. First, the percentage of high-school seniors who successfully graduate is steadily rising across the country, from 79 percent in 2010–2011 to 86 percent in 2018–2019.[14] Second, these results are a consequence of steadily rising GPAs, as figure 1.1 clearly demonstrates:

Overall grade point average ⇄

Grade point averages earned by high school graduates in 2019 increased compared to 1990.

Average grade point average earned by high school graduates, overall and by course type: Various years, 1990–2019

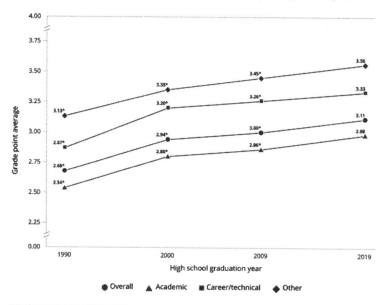

* Significantly different (*p* < .05) from 2019.

Figure 1.1. The Inflation of GPA. *https://www.nationsreportcard.gov/hstsreport/#home/.*

Could it be that, despite having doubts about the centrality of academic learning, teachers are teaching academic material ever more effectively in their classrooms? The answer is no, because GPA and graduation statistics are deeply unreliable measurements of academic achievement. If we compare high-school graduation rates with two other external measures of achievement—the SAT/ACT scores and the National Assessment for Educational Progress (NAEP)—it becomes clear that the same academic performance that would have previously indicated failure now counts as success.

First, as grades and graduation rates have risen, ACT scores have decreased.[15] Perhaps one should dismiss ACT data because the demographics of students taking the test have changed considerably over time, making comparisons difficult. The NAEP, which *is* an assessment of math and ELA proficiency, is thus arguably the better measure. The NAEP collects data that confirm that "high school graduates are earning more credits, especially in academic subjects" and that "grade point averages are climbing."

However, its results reveal that in recent years, even before COVID, scores have been flat or modestly declining—with a marked decrease in performance between 2009 and 2019.[16] In reading, NAEP tells the same story. The percentage of twelfth-grade students performing at or above the ELA NAEP proficiency level in 2019 was three percentage points lower compared to 1992, the very first year in which the ELA assessment was given.[17]

In short, even as students receive higher grades in their math and ELA course work, they are becoming less proficient in both subjects. Imagine the NAEP and GPA as two measuring scales. The NAEP is calibrated via a fixed measure of performance that represents proficiency in the tested subject.[18] The second scale—the GPA—is a more mysterious instrument. This scale tells us that more and more of our twelfth-graders are being better educated, but this is an illusion: the scale is constantly being recalibrated as a result of grade inflation. As a result, an increasing number of students who would in the past have been judged as underperforming are today declared proficient.

There is a possible objection to attributing any importance to high-school grade inflation. So long as GPA continues to roughly predict college performance, grade inflation does no harm. Perhaps students are simply being measured more accurately in terms of what counts most—their ability to do college work. But this objection misses the point: the main reason that GPA scores and college achievement continue to correlate is that *both* our K-12 system and our colleges and universities have been adjusting their standards downwards. The GPA inflation in higher education is the mirror image of what we find in the K-12 system.[19] The Woodrow Wilson National Fellowship Foundation reported that in 1969, 7 percent of students at two- and four-year colleges reported a grade-point average of A-minus or higher. In 2009, that number was 41 percent. In the same period, the percentage of students with a GPA of C had gone from 25 to 5 percent.[20]

At the community college level, no amount of grade inflation can cover up the fact that students can't manage freshman-level course work. The National Center for Education Statistics shows that just 13 percent of community college students graduate in two years. Within three years, approximately 22 percent of students graduate, and within four years, 28 percent.[21] Certainly, one reason for these very low percentages is that students in community colleges are often trying to balance schoolwork with family responsibilities, including the need to earn a living.

The more fundamental explanation lies in the insufficient level of preparation for college work that is a feature of so many schools. Research shows that while across both two- and four-year colleges, almost half of all high-school graduates took remedial courses, the figure for community colleges alone (in 2015–2016) is 63 percent. In community colleges situated in high-poverty locations, it is much worse: At the Baltimore City Community College, just

13 percent of freshman are ready to take credit-bearing courses.[22] Recall that all these students are high-school graduates or have GEDs—high-school equivalent diplomas. As a nation, we are handwaving at strong academic outcomes for most of our students.

AMERICA'S K-12 EDUCATION OUTCOMES

In August 2022, the results of the long-term NAEP assessment in math and ELA for nine-year-old children were released. Demonstrating the impact of COVID, the results were the lowest in twenty years. Minority students were especially impacted, with nine-year-old black students' math performance in 2022 about a year behind where they were in 2020.[23] But what the resulting headlines missed was that, as referenced earlier, the academic performance of America's students had already stalled: 2019 results for nine- and thirteen-year-olds on the same long-term NAEP assessments were statistically identical to those in 2004.[24]

Decades of flat results are rightly depressing. After nearly two decades of failing to show gains on independent tests such as NAEP and PISA (Program for International Student Assessment), there is deep frustration and fatigue. Some have blamed failures in education policy,[25] while others have gone much further and decided that academic outcomes are just the wrong thing to care about. When the governor of Oregon announced that Oregon was no longer going to ask its high-school graduates to demonstrate any level of academic skills or knowledge, her spokesman provided a statement that this change would greatly help "Oregon's Black, Latino, Latina, Latinx, Indigenous, Asian, Pacific Islander, Tribal, and students of color."[26]

Will it really do so? Does the governor of Oregon believe that abolishing standards will help students who can't meet them? This would seem to entail the supporting conviction that the educational failure of underprivileged children is inevitable. If this isn't racism, it is an acknowledgment that the education system in her state is unable to provide basic academic competence to a quarter of its children. By abolishing standards, perhaps that fact can be hidden in plain sight, and the uneducated children's failure to learn can be softened by not publicizing it. Conveniently forgotten, however, is the price those children will pay for the rest of their lives.

The Oregonian policy may be an extreme example, but it illustrates a general trend of devaluing measures of educational outcomes. Why are so many educators who do not for a moment share the beliefs of Oregon's governor no longer prioritizing a focus on academic outcomes? One answer is that teachers want their students to succeed even when they are falling short. When students from low-income families—often students of color—fail to graduate, teachers understand that financial implications may be lifelong.[27] The easiest way to try to prevent the cycle of poverty from repeating itself is to pass students on to the next stage of life with little education, but without the public stigma of failing to graduate high school.

In 1999, George W. Bush famously spoke about the "soft bigotry of low expectations" in American education.[28] America continues to require students to pass various courses to graduate from high school but continues to lower the level of academic knowledge and skills required to do so. The result is an ever-higher percentage of students who graduate with, on average, lower and lower academic achievement. Arguably, this is the only dimension on which American K-12 education has reached widespread consensus.

Today, high-school graduation in most states requires students only to show up to school on a fairly regular basis and engage in some minimal academic effort. Grade inflation is steadily lowering the academic signaling value of grades.[29] In the words of one teacher: "When half the grades average in the A range, teachers and students can avoid feedback. It sends the message that knowledge can be finished and left behind."[30]

Of course, there are thousands of teachers who do everything they can to support the learning of their students, but theirs is an increasingly lonely task. Many of their peers disdain the tests that would offer an external measure of that learning; students' parents demand better grades for their children regardless of actual learning (this is discussed later in this chapter); and politicians are often disinclined to take responsibility for poor educational outcomes.

Whether one thinks academic outcomes aren't that important or, alternatively, is embarrassed by an inability to alter the weak academic outcomes of less advantaged students, the result is the same. The United States increasingly gives students an easy pass by eliminating or rendering increasingly meaningless the objective measures of their individual achievements. Can one assert that the devaluation of metrics of academic performance in turn *causes* less focus on, and less effective teaching of, academic content?

That's a complex question, but common sense suggests an affirmative answer. If one is serious about achieving a goal, what is required are reliable measures by which to judge success. To suggest an analogy: Working hard to lose weight, the discovery that the weight measuring scale wasn't accurate would be infuriating. In fact, our teachers, schools, and policymakers have been steadily changing the calibration on the academic scale. As a nation, we still talk a lot about achievement and the achievement gap, but there is plenty of evidence that we aren't serious about ensuring meaningful academic proficiency for our children.

In a country in which pragmatism—the "can do" pioneer spirit—has always had more grip on the public imagination than intellectualism or academic prowess, a commitment to "bookish" learning should never be assumed.[31] There are, however, more proximate systemic causes pressing the education system in general and teachers in particular to turn away from prioritizing academic knowledge. These include our rote skills-oriented standards in domains such as ELA, the flawed designs of most of our state tests, and widespread calls to focus on nonacademic goals for education. The following chapters will discuss each of these issues, but what is clear that the case for the centrality of academic learning cannot be taken for granted—it must be made anew.

WHAT IS CAREER AND TECHNICAL EDUCATION?

It has become almost a cliché in American education to say that our K-12 students should be "college and career ready." Fulfilling the first part of this goal requires effective instruction in the academic disciplines, but what about the second?

When taking the perspective of the overall economic well-being of the United States, there is strong evidence that we shouldn't split our goals between academics and career readiness. Eric Hanushek, among the most influential American educational economists of the last twenty years, has argued that the best way to maximize a nation's economic wealth is to raise the overall level of education achievement. From analyses of economic outcomes, he points out that national education levels—measured by *cognitive* skills—have powerful economic effects. In other words, what children learn matters.[32] The data show that "relatively small improvements in the skills of a nation's labor force can have very large impacts on future well-being."[33]

Hanushek's key point is reinforced by PISA director Andreas Schleicher, who concludes that "high-income non-OECD countries, as a group, would see an added economic value equivalent to almost five times the value of their current GDP—if they equipped all students with at least basic skills."[34] The key here is the word "skills." Both Hanushek and Schleicher are talking about academic skills, specifically in math and science, not technical skills of the kind young adults would learn, say, during an apprenticeship.

Hanushek's argument may be surprising. If educational levels are so important to national economic outcomes, how can it be that the United States has so long been among the world's most productive economies while its educational results have sagged? Hanushek's response is two-fold. First, America's capital and labor markets were for many years more efficiently structured than those abroad and were able to attract and keep global top talent.

But that advantage has atrophied as other countries have more closely copied these structures, and thus America's competitive advantage is shrinking.[35] Second, Hanushek argues that critics confuse years of schooling with actual

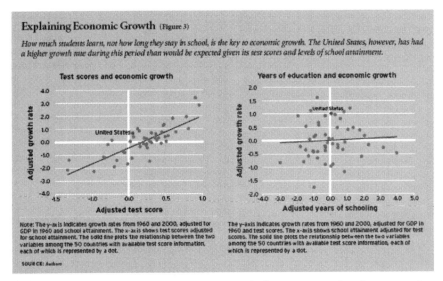

Explaining Economic Growth (Figure 3)

How much students learn, not how long they stay in school, is the key to economic growth. The United States, however, has had a higher growth rate during this period than would be expected given its test scores and levels of school attainment.

Figure 1.2. Learning Levels and Economic Growth. *https://www.educationnext.org/wp-content/uploads/2020/03/ednext_20082_62_fig3.gif.*

educational outcomes—it is the second that counts when trying to measure economic impact. Hanushek's data can be seen as figure 1.2.

STEM Education

As the figure above shows, from the point of view of national economic growth, the argument for focusing on raising the level of academic skills is very strong. At the level of schooling, this would specifically imply an urgent need to better prepare students for careers in STEM (Science, Technology, Engineering, and Math) by providing them with strong academic instruction in science, computer science, and math while at school.[36]

The United States is not close to making this happen. The numbers of American high-school students studying STEM subjects at a freshman college level (as reflected in those taking STEM subject AP exams) has increased in recent years, especially in computer science (from 16,600 in 2009 to 166,000 in 2019),[37] but these are still very modest numbers. Even in the top performing states, not even one in six high-school graduates had passed a single AP STEM assessment. In many states, the figure is less than 5 percent.[38]

Within these weak results, racial disparities are clear. There are two available AP assessments in computer science—the AP "computer science principles" exam and the more advanced "computer science A" assessment. Of all test takers of the AP principles exam in 2020, just 7 percent were African Americans.[39] The figure for the Science A exam was 3 percent.[40] A similar pattern appears in high-school course work in general. In New York State, in 2017–2018, some 27,750 white high-school students took the Regents exam (the state assessment for high-school students) in physics, while 96,400 took English (28.8 percent).[41] By contrast, just 3,450 African American students took the Regents exam in physics, and 44,600 the English Regents exam (7.7 percent).

These data are doubly troubling, because in addition to the national economic interest in raising the level of access and success in the STEM academic disciplines, STEM study makes future financial sense for individual students. College graduates of STEM programs achieve higher earnings than those with degrees in other fields. The majors that generate the highest future earnings are aerospace engineering, energy and extraction, the chemical and biological fields, computer software, and electrical.[42]

If the case for stronger STEM education is so compelling at both the national and individual levels, why are we failing so badly? The answer takes us back to the first part of this chapter. Our ever-dropping high school graduation requirements explain the low level of STEM course taking. New York is one of the dwindling number of states that requires a series of subject-based high-school exit assessments, including in science, but the science requirement can be satisfied by taking the "earth science" assessment instead of the more rigorous tests in specific science subjects such as physics or chemistry.

When states enable students to earn the same credential (in this case, a high-school diploma) by choosing an easier pathway, it should come as no surprise that most students take that option. Using the same 2017–2018 data cited above for English and physics Regent test takers, we find that some 80,000 white students and 23,300 black students chose this less rigorous science assessment route to their graduation.

CAREER AND TECHNICAL (CTE) PROGRAMS

When most people think about career readiness, academic study is not what they have in mind. Rather, they are talking about opportunities—as early as middle school but certainly in high school—for students to gain experience and proficiency in preprofessional skills. These CTE opportunities span a wide array, from the traditional options of woodworking and car repair to new fields such as robotics. No matter what the specific career option, the key issue is the breadth and caliber of what the public education system provides—through such means as industry partnerships for on-the-job training or apprenticeships—while students are still in school.

What the American education system offers in these domains is very modest indeed. In the United States, CTE has been the default option usually and deliberately assigned to underprivileged students, who either lacked the academic preparation to benefit from a precollege track or whose families couldn't bear the economic hardships of postponing workplace earnings during college years. A high proportion of those who are today put onto "career track" are still minority students shunted into a pathway to dead-end jobs.[43] The most common CTE options available across the United States match the expectation of modest academic skills—cosmetology being a ubiquitous example.

It doesn't have to be this way. A revamped, national CTE initiative would maximize students' choices, offering opportunities that would provide excellent jobs and life-time earnings that can rival those of college graduates. In fact, there are American public schools that do just that, for example, the Anderson Institute of Technology (AIT) high school in Anderson, South Carolina. Supported by partnerships with industrial giants such as Bosch and Michelin, AIT offers some twenty CTE programs, including aerospace engineering (supported by advanced flight simulators on the school campus), digital and visual art development, and medical technology.[44]

Each program combines hands-on training with supporting course work designed to teach the required cognitive skills so that students not only know what they are doing but also know why. To use the aerospace example, students will study the science of aviation materials and structures with the requisite math skills, having already successfully completed Algebra 1.

The offerings that AIT provides are rare indeed. Given the historical legacy of regarding CTE as a track for the underprivileged, and that many CTE programs are of poor quality, it is not surprising that far fewer American high-school students choose this option than do their international peers. A study from the Johns Hopkins Institute for Education Policy shows that about 6 percent of US students concentrate in CTE *pathways*. While most high schools (94 percent) in the United States offer one or more CTE *courses*, most of them are housed in traditional high schools, with just 4 percent of them placed within specialized career/technical high schools.[45]

Contrast this with our international peers: In European countries, more than 50 percent of students enter what is called vocational training, with Switzerland topping the list at 64 percent. A further challenge is the gender distribution within the American CTE universe. In the United States, the CTE tracks with higher earnings potential are heavily male dominated. Information technology has a three-to-one male-to-female ratio, while human services is four-to-one female-to-male.[46] As currently structured, young women are heavily overrepresented in CTE fields with the lowest earnings potential.

What would it look like to transform our CTE programs to match, say, the Swiss model? Stripping away nuances, the basic idea of the Swiss model is a universal education focused on academics through ninth grade, at which point students choose between a rich array of CTE options or a college track, with about two-thirds of the students choosing the first option. These students must pass an academic test—the "multicheck" assessment—before they can enter the CTE track, and those that choose the university track face a rigorous assessment in their first year of college that some 50 percent don't pass.[47]

Should the United States try to emulate Switzerland by providing AIT-type career-training options to a far greater percentage of American students? Answering this question isn't simple. One way of looking at it is to ask if students abroad who choose CTE programs in countries like Switzerland and Germany do as well for themselves in the long run as those who choose college options. Hanushek's research suggests a complex reality: It all depends on the economy of the specific country. Examining the data from eleven countries, he finds that "individuals with general education initially face worse employment outcomes but experience improved employment probability as they become older relative to individuals with vocational education."

But while this was the case in Denmark and Germany, it wasn't true of other countries where economic acceleration isn't as rapid. In Switzerland, for example, life-time earnings favor those who chose vocational training over college.[48] A review of other research on CTE programs in Europe finds similar mixed results: The comparative economic advantages of choosing a vocational versus a college track vary among countries.[49] The important point to keep in mind is that even in countries where the choice of a vocational track doesn't quite produce the future earnings of the college option, the gap in future earnings between an academic and a technical track is far smaller than it is in the United States.

Assuming that our goal is to maximize strong educational options available to our high-school students, given what we know about Europe, and considering the uncertainties of the future job market, how should this country deliver on the goal of a robust CTE option for American school students?

On balance, the evidence suggests that a national education goal should be a rough approximation of the Swiss model.[50] In the United States, even students with some community college education have extremely modest income potential. This is not the case in Switzerland, where students who undertake the equivalent of our associate in arts (AA) degree do so while already in a well-established, industry-supported CTE track. By contrast, the economic prospects for American students who enter community college and never graduate—more than 70 percent of community college students—is much bleaker.

Even a completed American college degree is no longer a guaranteed ticket to a strong economic future. While college graduates in the current American education system earn more than those without a degree, the relationship isn't linear.[51] Moreover, adjusted for inflation, average hourly wages for recent college graduates have barely budged since 2000, while the bottom 60 percent of college graduates earn less than that group did in 2000.[52] A college diploma is no longer a sure passport into the middle class.

Furthermore, there are already data from the United States showing that a student doesn't have to choose between a well-designed CTE track and doing well in college. It turns out that when students are enrolled in high-quality CTE programs, they also do better in terms of high-school completion rates and employment while still holding open their college options.[53] Vocational programs can be designed so that they do not permanently block a subsequent choice to go to college.

In Switzerland, vocational programs offer coursework to prepare students for the "federal vocational baccalaureate" that enables entry into eight Swiss Universities of Applied Sciences.[54] Finally, implementing a strong, nation-wide CTE option in the United States would enjoy deep public support. According to the 2017 PDK Poll of the Public's Attitudes Toward the Public Schools, some four out of five Americans support job or career skills classes even if that means students might spend less time in academic classes.[55]

There has been some modest progress in developing stronger CTE programs in the United States, with efforts to synchronize learning and credentials across high schools, community colleges, and industry. In Delaware, for example, the state has worked to integrate the state's labor market needs into academic instruction using a combination of private and public funding to seed programs in thirty-eight of forty-four Delaware high schools (California and New York have also made major investments in CTE programs).[56]

But to reach anything close to the Swiss model, the United States will have to confront an enormous obstacle: Most American students aren't academically prepared to choose most of the offerings that a strong set of CTE options would provide. To make this point clear, let's return to the AIT high school in South Carolina. To apply for the biomedical sciences CTE option, students must already have demonstrated competency in algebra and biology. Both computer-related CTE pathways as well as "mechatronics" require algebra competency, which students demonstrate by passing that school's rigorous courses in math and science.[57]

The possibility of adopting these programs in the United States thus takes us back to where this chapter started—academics. Explicitly attempting to mimic a key element of the Swiss education structure, the Maryland Commission on Innovation and Excellence (the "Kirwan Commission") recommended to the Maryland legislature that the state focus on a tenth-grade assessment in the core academic subjects. If students can pass that test, the commission said, they may choose from a wide array of CTE options or a college track. If they fail it, then they will have two years of high school in which to pass it.[58]

But if one takes Maryland's current eighth-grade NAEP results as any indication of students' academic readiness for high-school studies, it is a safe prediction to say that almost three-quarters of these students would fail the anticipated tenth-grade tests. Under the current plan, that would mean that instead of choosing between a CTE program and a college track, the great majority of Maryland's students would spend eleventh grade trying to pass the tenth-grade assessment. Maryland could (and probably will) design a test that will be easier to pass—but then many Maryland students won't be academically equipped for the more demanding CTE pathways that AIT offers.

In short, our goal of providing a world-class CTE option for our high-school students means taking a program historically directed to academically underprepared students and transforming it into one in which most of the pathways require a far higher level of academic readiness than most American students possess.[59] It's a tall order—one that requires a deep commitment to a more effective academic education than we currently provide.

THE LIMITS OF CTE

While the United States needs a complete redesign of its CTE offerings, enabling students to benefit from this redesign would necessitate much stronger academic preparation, particularly in math and the sciences. Stronger academic skills—no matter if they lead to technical or postsecondary employment—will benefit both individual citizens and the country's overall economic growth. But there is one final challenge: With some exceptions (for engineers and chemists, for example), the economy would currently lack enough jobs for all such well-prepared students—and might not have them in the future.

A review of the most recent Bureau of Labor report on occupational outlooks shows that the jobs in the United States with the highest number of job openings require only modest educational achievement, coupled with on-the-job training that requires neither a sophisticated CTE program nor a community college degree.[60] The highest absolute number of new jobs that will be available from 2020 to 2030 are in the following occupations (sorted by numbers of jobs from high to low):

1. Home health and personal care aides (1,129,900)
2. Cooks and restaurant workers (563,500)
3. Fast-food and counter workers (517,500)
4. Software developers and software quality assurance analysts (409,500)

5. Waiters and waitresses (407,600).

Taken together, these professions provide approximately three million new jobs. Of these, only the software developer openings require a BA degree, with recent data showing that this, too, is changing.[61] Other summaries of the largest employment openings over the 2020–2030 period show lower demand for computer specialists, with not one of the ten highest-employing occupations requiring more than a high school diploma.[62] Our most recent data reinforces these predictive metrics.[63]

From 2020 to 2030, the number of jobs requiring a BA or higher degree is expected to grow somewhat more rapidly than those requiring a high-school diploma or less. However, the largest proportion of the total number of available jobs in 2030 will require less than an associate degree. In terms of absolute numbers of jobs for each level of education, the picture is not expected to change dramatically. See figure 1.3.

These numbers raise awkward questions. In economic terms, one can argue that our K-12 education system is operating rather efficiently. We have the (low-paying) jobs for the roughly 40 percent of our high-school students who are not college ready. In Europe, by contrast, the education system is arguably overeducating for the job market. According to the European Centre for the Development of Vocational Training's (CEDEFOP) skills and jobs survey, 20

Typical entry-level education	Employment 2020	Employment 2030	Employment distribution, 2020
Master's degree	2,782.8	3,238.9	1.8%
Associate degree	3,274.8	3,617.2	2.1%
Bachelor's degree	36,407.8	40,009.1	23.7%
Post-secondary non-degree award	9,542.7	10,469.3	6.2%
No formal educational credential	34,302.1	37,345.0	22.3%
Doctoral or professional degree	4,204.0	4,579.4	2.7%
High school diploma or equivalent	59,150.7	62,170.0	38.5%
Some college, no degree	3,868.9	3,985.0	2.5%
Total, all employment	**153,533.8**	**165,413.9**	**100.0%**

Figure 1.3. Project US Employment. *https://www.bls.gov/emp/tables/education-summary.htm.*

percent of young Europeans are employed in jobs that require a lower level of qualifications than what they have earned.[64] But this isn't just a European problem. According to data from the Federal Reserve Bank of New York, about a third of all American college graduates are working in jobs that don't require a college degree.[65]

It is possible that there are fewer high-skilled jobs available in the United States because companies adapt their expectations to what the educational system offers them. Given the sheer scale of the demand for minimally educated workers, however, it is more likely that there is an irreducible tension between a model of an education that is designed to fit the current economic needs of the country and the aspirations of most individuals to maximize their economic and social opportunities through education and/or advanced skill sets.

What could be done to ameliorate the circumstances of those workers doing the lowest-skilled, lowest-paying jobs? Perhaps more of these jobs be taken by younger adults while they are still gaining education. Such jobs could be supported by learning opportunities that would be designed to enable workers to move on to other, more rewarding opportunities. The state could provide a stronger support system that would render these jobs less economically debilitating. Perhaps a greater percentage of them will be automated than current forecasts suggest.

But the honest response is that raising educational outcomes will almost certainly lead to more students being overqualified for the jobs they will occupy. The right answer, and the focus of the final chapter, is that a higher level of education is desirable because it represents an absolute good.

SOCIAL JUSTICE AND RACIAL EQUITY

There is no question about the centrality of race to any consideration of America's K-12 education system. To put the matter bluntly, our school system leaves black and brown children far behind their white and Asian peers. As Pedro Noguera puts it in *City Schools and the American Dream*, "Rather than serving as the 'great equalizer' as envisioned by Horace Mann, one of the early architects of American public education . . . schools in the United States more often have been sites where patterns of privilege and inequality are maintained and reproduced."[66]

For Noguera and most of those involved in educational policy, the acute disparities of educational outcomes between student populations in the United States is the single most pressing issue in education policy.[67] To make the scale of the crisis clear, it is important to look at the data. The focus here will be on African American students because the research literature is so far much more extensive for that population. Hispanic students' academic achievement scores show a wide variation depending in part on their country of origin—but, on average, they are only very modestly stronger than their African American peers.

The results of the most recent twelfth-grade NAEP math assessment showed that 32 percent of white students achieve proficiency, compared with 8 percent of African American students and 11 percent of Hispanic students.[68] To put it another way, in math, the average academic performance of an African American twelfth-grader is equal to that of white students performing at the nineteenth percentile. The figures in reading are barely better: The average score for African Americans matches that of the white students at the twenty-second percentile. Reducing the gap between the academic outcomes of white and African American students has been so slow that at our current rate of progress, it would take over 150 years to close it.[69]

These data show that teachers work with a deeply divided population of students. In the average public-school district in the United States, white students are between one-and-a-half and two grade levels more advanced than their black peers.[70] This gap is found at all income levels. Children of affluent African American families underperform their affluent white peers by about as much as the gap between underprivileged black students and underprivileged whites (although this measurement depends to some extent on how income is measured).[71]

Today, the "achievement gap" is often reconceived as the "opportunity gap"—a shift in nomenclature made to emphasize racial differences in access to high-quality teaching and the strong instructional materials that are indispensable for educational success. In "The Opportunity Myth," a study of teaching practices across the United States, The New Teacher Project (TNTP) reports that in the average American public school African American students will spend twice as much time on underdemanding academic work as will white students.[72] Perhaps the most damning data reported is that in classrooms in which the majority of students in a class are of color, 38 percent of those students will never receive a grade-level assignment—for these students, schooling involves learning every day with dumbed-down materials.

Explanations for achievement/opportunity gap abound. The continued segregation of American schools; the underfunding of majority minority schools; too few minority teachers; students afraid of doing well and being accused by their minority peers of "acting white."[73] But researchers agree that the most powerful explanation of all is found in the vast inequalities in the background family circumstances—the economic, social, and medical disparities that separate black and brown America from their fellow citizens.[74] Although this book focuses on education itself, there can be no question of deciding where more blame resides—outside or inside America's schools, there is vast work to be done in both domains.

The many factors that produce achievement/opportunity gaps, both inside our schools and in our society, interact in a myriad of ways. To take just one example, many Baltimore public schools (with a population made up of 75 percent African American and 15 percent Hispanic students) close on the hottest days of the summer because they have no working air-conditioning. Why? Because those schools are in locations predetermined by red-lining housing policies from another century, and because the school district is struggling with half-empty school buildings due to a declining city population beset with racial violence and a shrinking economy.

John Valent, a senior fellow at the Brookings Institution, points to the historical legacy of racism and the resulting challenges faced by minorities in our inner-cities: zoning policies that kept black families out of high-performing schools, tax policies that prevented them from accumulating wealth, and mass incarceration.[75] Every one of those factors impacts Baltimore—and many other American urban centers—today.

REDUCING THE ACHIEVEMENT/OPPORTUNITY GAP

What can be done—in Baltimore and across the country—to reduce the gap? In recent years, something approaching a consensus has emerged.

First, the nation must focus on its teachers. America needs far more well-prepared teachers of color. Indeed, strong research indicates that African American students simply do better when taught by African American teachers.[76] To ensure that minority teachers from modest educational backgrounds are able to teach, the country would also need to ensure that their teacher preparation programs are free,[77] that teacher certification tests don't unnecessarily keep minority would-be teachers out of the classrooms,[78] and that salaries are competitive with other college-based professions.

Second, the nation's schools must implement strong literacy programs. Underprivileged minority children arrive at kindergarten with a smaller vocabulary than their more affluent peers. They face from the outset a vocabulary gap that translates into a reading comprehension deficit that rarely closes. This can be remedied, as shown recently in Mississippi. That state launched a policy initiative in early reading that included large-scale professional development for teachers, outreach to parents, and major revisions to instructional materials—all of which have produced substantial gains in reading performance.[79]

Third, the K-12 system must stop or at least greatly reduce remediation. Because minority students enter public-school classrooms already behind, the national policy has been to remediate them—that is, try to teach these students the material they previously missed. But this strategy as failed, not only because remediation stigmatizes the children who are put into the remedial tracks and/or because it involves material to read that is absurdly simple in subject matter (because it was designed for younger children). These children also face an inherent contradiction: They can never catch up, since their peers are moving ahead while they move backward.

The solution can only be a concerted effort at pre-K and kindergarten to overcome the reading gap, and then a policy of accelerating these students' learning so that they can be taught grade-level–material along with their peers.[80] Due to compelling research from the late Robert Slavin of Johns Hopkins University, policymakers also know now that they need to provide mentoring and tutoring at a far-larger scale than is currently the case. Tutoring is simply the most powerful method we know of boosting the learning of K-12 students, and it is a critical component of effective acceleration.[81]

Finally, as students progress through their years of schooling, the country owes all of them the best possible curricula. Louisiana has set an example here, replacing poor math and reading programs with high-quality instructional materials. Chapter 4 will discuss this issue further, showing why this is so important. For now, it is enough to say that a strong math curriculum provides the conceptual understanding that is vital to long-term competency, while a strong ELA curriculum is replete with texts worth reading, not summaries or chunks of texts that deprive children of the knowledge they need to become fluent readers and informed citizens.

TOO HARD, TOO SLOW

While these five strategies, if implemented at scale, would reduce the achievement/opportunity gap, they depend on major changes to current policy, on shifts in funding priorities, and on a deep adjustment of the mindsets of many teachers. Many critics of our current education inequities either don't believe these changes can occur or, at best, see them as offering only wretchedly slow improvement. Some reject any education-based reforms from within the current K-12 system.

At the risk of oversimplifying, these critics fall into three broad groups: those who believe that no real progress will be made as long as the disparities in housing, employment, and health of minority families are not addressed; those who argue that we can create schools—usually charter schools—that can reduce or eliminate the achievement/opportunity gap using the right school-based strategies; and those who regard America's educational challenges as a product of historical and current racism—a racism so deeply ingrained in our system that it must be challenged from the ground up before any educational equity is possible.

There has been a very active debate between the first two groups. For Richard Rothstein, a leading progressive analyst of educational inequities, it is clear that until the background conditions of African American and Hispanic families more closely match those of white Americans, any effort to equalize educational outcomes will largely fail.[82] By contrast, leaders of high-performing urban charter schools that enroll almost exclusively children of color believe that the crucial work of equalizing educational opportunities for minority students can be done today in their classrooms. While these charter school leaders are certainly supportive of the social and economic reforms that Rothstein espouses, they don't think they will happen soon enough to rescue today's underprivileged students.[83]

The debate about charter schools is so bitter because there are plausible arguments on both sides.[84] On the one hand, Stanford University researchers' CREDO 2015 report on urban charter schools has shown that these schools, when run by strong charter management companies such as KIPP, Achievement First, and Uncommon Schools, produce far stronger academic instruction than regular public schools in the same geographies.[85] Based on this data, African American parents desperate to get their children out of failing urban public schools and into these charters are doing right by their children.

Critics of these same schools point to their funding advantages (their budgets in cities such as New York are often supplemented by large private donations).[86] They also invoke the processes by which charter schools manage to insert selectivity into lotteries to recruit stronger students, the demands top-performing charter schools make on parental involvement that many parents or guardians cannot provide, the fact that charter schools churn through teachers, and the regimented cultures of discipline that critics regards as inhumane.[87]

The debate is also bitter because critics of charter schools see them as a threat to the public-school system. While charter schools are subject to state-level accountability, they are exempt from the authority of publicly elected school boards. Their success suggests that local political control is a hindrance to effective schooling. Instead of enabling charter schools to pull students away from regular public schools, critics want to fund those same regular schools at higher levels to show that they, too, could be more successful. Defenders of charter schools point out that while no doubt higher funding would be helpful, the level of funding of our urban public schools has risen far faster than inflation, but the performance of these schools has remained flat.

African Americans are deeply divided on the issue. While black parents in their thousands are on waiting list to get their children into inner-city charter schools, the NAACP has called for a moratorium on the expansion of charter schools, arguing that they maintain segregation and employ unacceptable disciplinary policies.[88] Others in black communities point to white-dominated charter school governance and to the predominance of white governance in schools that are serving African American children.[89]

Deep Disagreements

The debate about charter schools is born of deep disillusionment about the tragically persistent racial disparities in K-12 education, but that debate sits in the context of a much deeper dispute that now underpins—and threatens to implode—any consensus on how to move forward in addressing the racial achievement/opportunity gaps. That debate goes to the most fundamental question—the purpose of public education in contemporary America.

The most visible manifestation of this debate has centered on the presence (real or imagined) of critical race theory (CRT) in our classrooms, and what should be done to "protect" our children from exposure to it.[90] But the debate about CRT is only a symptom of the fundamental disagreements over the nature of racial identity, over the legacy of American history, and the place of institutional racism in our nation's education system. Within these disagreements are beliefs that can render the entire goal of reducing academic achievement gaps redundant, irrelevant, and indeed racist.

For some critics of the current system and the resulting outcomes for children of color, school reform must start with a full-scale acknowledgment of the systemic racism built into the American polity—dating back to the country's founding.[91] The controversial *New York Times* 1619 Project, for example, "aims to reframe the country's history by placing the consequences of slavery and the contributions of black Americans at the very center of our national narrative."[92] For the author of the project and her many supporters, the idea that we should aim to be "color-blind" or "race-neutral" in our educational policies is itself a manifestation of structural racism.

A second group of critics of the K-12 system go further. Ibram X. Kendi, a recipient of the National Book Award and a Guggenheim Fellowship, writes in his book *How to Be an Antiracist*, "There is no such thing as a nonracist or race-neutral policy. Every policy in every institution in every community in every nation is producing or sustaining either racial inequity or equity between racial groups."[93] In her bestselling and multiple award–winning book *White Fragility*, Robin DiAngelo argues that "white identity is inherently racist," and "a positive white identity is an impossible goal."[94]

How do these views translate into specific policy recommendations for our education system? One clear implication is that the metrics we use to evaluate academic achievement are "white"—and must themselves be abandoned. Taken to its logical conclusion, such a view implies that we stop treating learning as something that enables recognizable progress from ignorance to knowledge in any way that we currently recognize or reward. Frederick Hess, director of education policy studies at the conservative American Enterprise Institute, summarizes:

> Cornelius Minor, a leading "Grading Equity Advocate," has worked with Columbia Teachers College and the International Literacy Association. He seeks to dismantle "pernicious" grading practices, such as teachers reserving A's for students who demonstrate understanding of the subject matter. This, he explains, is because one "cannot separate grading practices" from "the history of classism, sexism, racism, and ableism in the United States. [95]

This isn't simply the view of Minor alone. It is found codified in education policy documents that have become widely circulated. As Williamson Evers and Ze'Ev Wurman from the Independent Institute report, this view includes the teaching of mathematics. They illustrate the point by quoting from "A Pathway to Equitable Math Instruction: Dismantling Racism in Mathematics Instruction," which has become a key document in math curriculum controversies in Oregon and California:

> The manual provides indicators of "white supremacy culture in the mathematics classroom," including a focus on "getting the right answer [and] "Upholding the idea that there are always right and wrong answers perpetuates 'objectivity.'" According to the "Pathways" manual, teachers should investigate and oppose ways in which math is used "to uphold capitalist, imperialist, and racist views."

Hess, Evers, and Wurman are all conservative educational commentators who seem intent on trying to ridicule (in part by cherry-picking from) the texts they are citing. For these critics, the language of Kendi, DiAngelo, and Minor are anathema. A favorite target of these critics is Nikole Hannah-Jones, head of the 1619 Project, especially her (uncharacteristic) Twitter statement in November 2019 that "The 1619 Project explicitly denies objectivity"—an assertion that is unfathomable for those who reject the charge that American is fundamentally a racist country.

There are efforts to bridge the gap between those who call the system irredeemably racist and those for whom that claim is a large overreach. For example, the *New York Times* has made modest changes in the 1619 Project in response to the critics,[96] but Kendi and DiAngelo are trying to reframe the entire direction of education for black children. The 1619 Project was intended as a seismic jolt to the entire edifice of the accepted American historical narrative—to create no less than a fundamental reframing. In a speech commemorating the twenty-fifth anniversary of Teach For America, Professor Jeff Duncan-Andrade argues in the same spirit that the only useful purpose of current American textbooks is to serve as door stops or as materials in which to look for lies.[97]

The critique is fundamental. Take the following statement about education policy, which was endorsed by a major "mainstream" education reform organization (Education First). The statement calls for us to "redesign the design thinking process, mindsets and tools themselves to ensure they mitigate for the causes of inequity."[98]

We arc asked not just to acknowledge but to "re-design oppressive historical structures." Because racism is so baked into our history, the past cannot guide us: *"Because an equitable reality has never existed, we cannot look to our past to learn how to create an equitable future* [emphasis in the original]."[99] The argument made here is that with no guidance, we must think this equitable reality into existence. To write a different story, we have to create and use a new, postracist language.

Meanwhile, in African American communities, there is no agreement that the current educational structures need to be altogether dismantled. The NAACP, the National Urban League, La Raza, and nine other civil right groups have denounced antitesting efforts, which they tie to an effort to hide achievement gaps. Each of these groups has pointed out that test data are indispensable for understanding the extent of inequality of opportunity in our education system.[100] Charter school leader Ian Rowe argues that while racism remains a problem, arguments to the effect that structural racism undercut possibilities of African American educational gains are deeply counterproductive.[101]

The deepest divide is between those who don't see progress as possible, and those who would still work within the existing system to realize that opportunity for minority students. For the first group, the key question is just what is being claimed and demanded? What exactly is the scale and nature of social, ethical, and political reengineering needed to realize the new "equitable reality?" Having abandoned the lessons of the past and adopted the new mindset, what would be different about our fifth- or tenth-grade classroom, about the content of our curriculum, about the nature of any testing, about the management of schooling?

In other words, if the nation's schools are not to make their contribution to overcoming racism through raising the caliber of academic instruction for minority students, then what should the K-12 system be doing instead? What exactly is the message to African American parents who are today desperate for public schools that can prepare their children for good jobs or college?

How is teaching self-esteem as an end itself a means to providing students of color the tools to achieve social and political reforms? The revolutionary mindset must at some point take on the responsibility of answering this question; to date, it largely hasn't.

Meanwhile charges of systemic racism have created politically charged consequences. The demand for white Americans—and their children—to engage in soul searching together with the claim that racism is the defining characteristic of the American experiment have given powerful fodder to conservatives who are intent on pushing back on progressive policies.

When third-graders are "forced to discuss their racial identities and rank themselves according to their "power and privilege," or when parents in New York City are asked to choose among eight "white identities" which include "white supremacist" and are asked to commit to dismantling whiteness, a backlash is inevitable. The Arizona state department of education may believe that children should be instructed about racism before they have learned to speak, but many Arizona parents inevitably hear this as inflammatory rhetoric.[102]

These kinds of demands aren't common, but that fact is disregarded by those who are ready to rile up their base by highlighting them. Republicans, unsurprisingly, see a powerful wedge issue in crying foul. They have done so successfully in Virginia, where creating rhetorical hay out of the largely manufactured threat of critical race theory arguably tipped the 2022 governor's race to the Republican candidate. Further success has come in Florida, where math textbooks that included material intended (or judged) to support social and emotional health have been banned.[103]

The charged racial politics of education have now become part of the wider culture wars, characterized by incendiary language that leaves schools and teachers caught in the middle.

The impassioned and polarized rhetoric over the centrality of racism in America and American education today threatens to displace the urgent, granular task of overcoming the legacy and current strands of racism in the United States by providing minority students with outstanding academic instruction.

WHAT'S TO BE DONE?

Progressive critics of socioeconomic inequalities and the leaders of strong urban charter schools are both right: To ask that one take sides between a commitment to reducing the consequences of racism in housing, health, and welfare, on the one hand, and the effective education of underprivileged minority students, on the other, is misplaced—the country needs to do both. But the most essential point here is that policymakers and parents cannot give up pressing for the educational changes across the entire spectrum of public schools—change that would systemically redress the lack of learning opportunities for minority students.

It may be tough to find the funding to support more minority teachers, but it is vital—as vital as is reversing our national habit of teaching down to minority students, of giving them mediocre instructional materials, and of failing to provide the mentoring and tutoring that would change their life trajectories.

Above all, efforts to raise the level of teaching academic knowledge to our disadvantaged students must not be stamped out under the guise of riding American schools of racism. Luminary figures from the history of African Americans' anguished fight for racial equity chose to fight for an education in what is now dismissively termed the "hegemonic discourse." Or rather, they saw the necessity of such an education if their fight was to be effective. The twenty-year-old Malcom X was convicted of larceny and incarcerated in Charleston State Prison in Boston, Massachusetts. Face to face with his own lack of education, he made the choice to read about African and Asian history and oriental philosophy. He also read Nietzsche, Kant, Schopenhauer, Gandhi, and H. G., Wells along with Elijah Muhammad and the dictionary.

Martin Luther King's *Letter from the Birmingham Jail* is replete with learned theological and philosophical sources. Frederick Douglass learned to read, risking his life to study classic works, including Cato and John Milton. Anika Praether—a lecturer at Howard University, a school principal and now a colleague of mine—"discovered that the classics not only *influenced* the black intellectual tradition; they were *central* to it. Before black Americans found freedom from slavery, through classical texts they conceived of and engaged with ideas of virtue, liberty, and the public good."[104]

Given the large and static achievement/opportunity gaps, it is no wonder that some are crying foul on the American experiment and its education system, but the purpose of criticism must be to build better, and that requires a renewed commitment to the difficult but rewarding task of ensuring the best education for disadvantaged students. While there is every reason to debate its exact content, there is no justification for assaulting the knowledge that their schooling has failed to teach them.

To be clear: There is vital work to be done to enable all teachers to treat every student without bias, conscious or otherwise. It is absolutely right that instructional materials do not traffic in the rhetoric of nationalist triumphalism or present a white-washed narrative of the American experience. The full histories of African Americans—together with those of Native Americans and other persecuted groups—belongs in the curriculum of every school, as does exposure to the genocides committed in Europe, Asia, and Africa. So, too, there must be a place for the great achievements of discovery, governance, protest, and creativity, no matter the identity of those to whom humanity is indebted.

None of this implies the treatment of knowledge as racist "all the way down." That makes learning next to impossible. In the end, there is no short cut, no bypassing the hard work of improving, by orders of magnitude, the quality of schooling America provides for its students of color.

CIVICS EDUCATION

"We have to remind ourselves over and over again that the whole point of compulsory free public education was to make citizens, was to produce people capable of self-government."[105]

Even a cursory glance at civics education reveals a yawning gap between rhetoric and reality. As referenced above, a majority of teachers think that preparation for democratic citizenship is the primary purpose of schooling. Thirty-two states place preparation for citizenship as the highest goal of public education (the others don't articulate a position). A majority of Americans of both parties believe that civics education is the most positive tool available to strengthen a common national identity.[106]

Yet report after report on civics carry the same message—civics is regarded as an add-on in America's public schools; its teachers are among the poorest supported instructional staff with the largest class sizes. The results, as reported in the National Assessment of Education Progress are unsurprising: In the 2018 civics NAEP, just one in four eighth-grade students reached proficiency, a rate considerably lower than results in any other NAEP-tested subject. The proficiency rates for black and Hispanic students were 10 percent and 13 percent, respectively.[107] Meanwhile, the need is clear. The Center for Civic Education warns that just 30 percent of Americans born since 1980 believe it essential to live in a democracy.[108]

The low status and equivalently low outcomes of civics education are consequences of multiple factors. First, there is no consensus on the subject matter. In some classrooms, it means getting acquainted with the nation's founding documents and memorizing some facts about the three branches of government and their functions. Instruction in civics can also be considered from a dispositional and skills perspective, nurturing students' interest in civic participation and developing their capacities to do so effectively. A third possible content for civics education, evidence from the founding of the Republic onward, is to inculcate a strong allegiance to the basic values and structures of the American polity.

Finally, since the founding of the Republic, civics education is interpreted to involve character education, where the goal is to create citizens who take their duties to one another seriously, and their tolerance for individual differences as a foundational norm of political ethics. This is what President Roosevelt emphasized when insisting that creating "worthy citizens is the most important responsibility" placed on schools.[109]

The multiple purposes of citizenship education inside the classroom might be manageable if there was an underlying consensus about civic values.[110] Without it, the politics of a seismically divided national culture come home to roost at the schoolhouse door. As the previously introduced theorist William Galston points out, the content of civics education must be in synch with the prevailing political regime. As a result, when that regime is itself splintered, it becomes exponentially harder for teachers of civics to find any secure footing.[111]

In these circumstances, it is too easy for Rebecca Winthrop of the Brookings Institution to write that "While civic learning has been essential throughout American history, in this age of growing polarization and rising civic deserts, it should be considered an essential component of a 21st-century education."[112] Exhortations of this kind underestimate the profound difficulties involved: How can one demand that schoolteachers create consensus among children when this very domain is riven with active adult dissension?

Civics education is caught in a web of cultural discord. In 1995, the US Senate (in)famously voted down the proposed national history standards 99–1. In a nation that cannot decide what to call the 1861–1865 war (the "Civil War," the "War between the States," or "the War of Northern Aggression"), the Senate's negative vote was indeed never in serious doubt.

As the previous section of this chapter suggests, the intensification of polarized debate around the historical legacy of race and racism in this country has added a further toxic element to the teaching of history, an indispensable element of civic education. Since January of 2021, forty-one states have introduced bills or taken related steps that would limit the teaching of racial history and/or gender bias, with seventeen of those states imposing bans.[113] Meanwhile, the political polarization, which had already been on an upward trajectory in the United States, has now reached an unprecedented level.[114]

These factors constitute a fraught pedagogical environment. As the educational commentator Michael Rebell writes in *Kappan*, "Preparing students for civic participation in a society beset by ideological polarization, racial inequality, accelerating economic gaps, rapid demographic shifts, and changing social norms is a formidable challenge."[115] In other words, the task of the civics teacher has become one of the most difficult of all classroom assignments. But the demands are not only on the teacher. If civics instruction is to be anything but the most rudimentary acquisition of basic facts about American government, then the cognitive requirements on students are considerable.

First, students not only need to acquire a body of knowledge pulled from different domains while also grasping the complex interrelations and the interdependence between these fields. In a 2022 piece on civics for the Fordham Institute, the educational analyst Chester Finn notes that students will have to bring information drawn from their entire curriculum, from history to data analysis, to make sense of social and political debates.[116]

Second, students need to be able to understand and interrogate conflicting claims from sources as diverse as legal opinion, social and news media, academic scholarship, and political rhetoric to make thoughtful judgments about the respective merits of arguments couched in very different discourses. Third, these same students will think through all these materials and the value judgments that emerge from them within the context of their family belief structures and the ethos and beliefs of their peers, their community, and the culture of their respective schools.

A review of recent curriculum offerings in civics underlines the learning challenges that result from taking the subject matter of civics seriously. The Educating for American Democracy project is arguably the most ambitious and extensive source of instructional materials for school-level civics instruction. The curriculum is anchored by what the project calls "Driving Questions" for students. These questions include asking students how best to engage with "hard histories (e.g., religion, race, ethnicity)" that have "shaped our society"; the degree to which the "diverse people of the U.S" have "become one nation"; and how "race relations" in the United States compare with those "in other countries around the world."[117]

A lesson plan on the 9/11 attacks requires students to juxtapose contemporary world politics with the normative claims about liberty enshrined in America's founding documents. This is a task that the curriculum designers rightly suggest will involve "Analyzing Texts, Images, or Videos, Historical Thinking Skills, Building Evidentiary Claims, Engaging in Difficult Conversations, Understanding Diverse Perspectives."[118]

The challenge of providing a civics education should be seen as a magnifying glass held up to the entire K-12 system. For to take on the core responsibility of civics instruction means teaching the full gamut of academic skills and knowledge throughout the years of schooling, and doing so to a high level. It also entails preparing students to think though moral and ethical dilemmas, engage with issues of identity, and situate personal experience in the context of social and political history and contemporary politics.

No matter if the issue is the inflation of educational standards, the provision of world-class career and technical education, the duty to reduce the opportunity/achievement gap, or the fundamental requirement of delivering an adequate civics education, one arrives at the same conclusion: There is an urgent need to deliver a universally higher quality of K-12 education. To do so, the nation needs to grasp first why the challenge is so great and solutions seem so complex or difficult. This reckoning seems right now to be the only way to address the frustrations, disillusion, and resulting exhaustion and despair when it comes to teaching academic knowledge effectively to all America's children.

Chapter 2

The Great Distractors

Teachers must be prepared to teach and assess students in new skills of complex reasoning, socioemotional intelligence, and creativity. This includes more project-based learning, active learning, collaborative learning, and instilling a growth mindset in students.[1]

The previous chapter reviewed four core aims of American schooling—academics, career and technical education, racial equality, and civics education—showing why we fall short of realizing them. Teaching far more children to become proficient in the core academic disciplines is a necessary condition of reducing the achievement/opportunity gap, preparing children for the job market, and dealing head-on with the legacy of racism in the United States. Despite the overwhelming importance of academic learning, the majority of America's teachers don't rate the academic preparation of children as their highest aim, a view epitomized in increasingly inflated grades and steadily reduced academic demands.

If academic proficiency isn't the indisputable core aim of our teachers, what is? This chapter will review several alternative aims for K-12 schooling that have, in the last decade or so, become widely endorsed in the education community. It is fair to suggest that they can be collectively summarized as the goal of teaching "the whole child." The core idea is that the teacher should broaden and deepen the traditional conception of what education means. Instead of "just" teaching children the academic disciplines, the aim is to nurture the child's overall well-being. This means attending to children's social-emotional and cognitive capacities, including their self-regard, their creativity, and their physical well-being.[2]

Alongside heightened attention to teaching the "the whole child" is a second aim—providing children with "twenty-first-century skills." Given the discussion of career and technical education in the previous chapter, this could be confusing: Hasn't that aim been covered? Not so. In its most common education usage, the label of "twenty-first-century skills" doesn't refer to, say, robotics in high school. Although sometimes inclusive of specific

31

skills such as internet literacy, the phrase almost always refers to "soft skills," such as "critical thinking," teamwork, leadership, and "innovation" that are purported to be essential to success in the contemporary workplace.[3]

While nurturing the whole child and teaching twenty-first-century skills might look like two different enterprises, in both literature and practice, they tend to overlap. It turns out that the soft skills (skills of communication and cooperation, for example, rather than math skills) that help individuals navigate the demands of tomorrow's workplace largely duplicate the goals of educating the whole child. This overlap is important: It means that there is no deep tension or bifurcation between the two aims. Because they coalesce, they offer teachers a unified, persuasive model of pedagogy.

It's a model based on a new and much grander narrative about a teacher's profession: Compare "teaching fractions" to "nurturing the whole child." Can there be much doubt as to which model carries the more uplifting emotional appeal? Teachers become not academic instructors but coaches of the human psyche, charged with a task that combines responsibilities that might once have resided with priests, mental health professionals, and families.

This chapter will examine the key components that add up to this new goal for teachers. The title of the chapter gives away the conclusion: Because there is little evidence in the research record to support these new goals, they are most accurately termed educational "distractors." They are shiny objects that sound appealing, but they distract our teachers and schools from academic instruction. To be clear, this is not a critique of teachers themselves: They tend to do what schools and policymakers dictate. It is the tendentious thinking of politicians, theorists, and vendors that forces these distractions on teachers.

This chapter will analyze the following distractors:

1. Critical thinking: "The ability to think clearly and rationally about what to do or what to believe."[4]
2. Growth mindset: "Thinking that your intelligence or personality is something you can develop, as opposed to something that is fixed."[5]
3. Grit: "Perseverance and passion for long-term goals."[6]
4. Social and emotional learning: The "ability to seek out and form healthy strong relationships with family members and others."[7]
5. Metacognition: "Awareness or analysis of one's own learning or thinking processes."[8]
6. Twenty-first-century skills: "Leadership, teamwork, collaboration, cooperation, facility in using virtual workspaces."[9]
7. Creative thinking. No clear definition available.

CRITICAL THINKING

Perhaps the most ubiquitous phrase in current K-12 educational parlance is "critical thinking." Strongly supported by public opinion, the education system appears to be nearly unanimous in wanting to teach critical thinking and is equally convinced that much more needs to be done to do so effectively. In 2019, the Reboot Foundation found that 98 percent of the American public thought that critical thinking skills are either "extremely" or "very" important. All but 10 percent of those surveyed agreed that schools should make courses in critical thinking required, with 86 percent agreeing that their fellow citizens lacked this essential capability.[10]

Daniel Willingham, a leading educational psychologist, reports that the public thirst for instructing students in critical thinking is strongly supported by the business community, human resource officials, and a wide swath of education reform think tanks, including the National Center on Education and the Economy, the American Diploma Project, and the Aspen Institute. He adds that the College Board has redesigned the SAT to measure students' critical thinking more precisely and that the ACT offers a dedicated test of that skill.[11]

The fixation on critical thinking is no longer confined to the United States. The OECD took up the issue in 2019 and recently announced that it will add an assessment of these skills to the forthcoming PISA tests.[12]

What exactly is this skill that has attracted so much attention, the teaching of which is so universally regarded as an urgent task? That's surprisingly difficult to pin down. In fact, it's impossible to specify with any exactitude. As the *Stanford Encyclopedia of Philosophy* puts it rather succinctly, "its definition is contested."[13]

There is some agreement on what critical thinking *isn't*. It clearly isn't uncritical thought, meaning it is not thought that is undisciplined or irrational.[14] There is also some convergence in the literature on the view that critical thinking involves the ability to offer reasons for one's arguments. But dig any further, and the definition expands to cover just about anything. The Center for Critical Thinking creates a list that includes relevance, depth, breadth, clarity, consistency, and fairness.[15]

Some organizations push critical thinking as a synonym for scientific thinking, emphasizing that critical thinking is above all deductive. Others argue that critical thinking should involve seeing both (or many) sides to an issue.[16] Searching for some common denominator across the many elements results in very high-level wooly generalities, namely, that students should be able to give reasons or evidence rather than purely emotive statements for the arguments they make, and that they should be open to new ideas.[17]

When it comes to critical thinking, it is difficult to square the attention and urgency with the lack of specificity in defining the term. Given the heated rhetoric, one might have thought that America had discovered something powerfully new, that after a millennium of educating children, we finally understand that we were missing a vital ingredient. But this view cannot be sustained. After all, did earlier generations of teachers believe that thinking should be unclear, shallow, irrelevant, and unfair? Did teachers who hadn't yet discovered "critical thinking" champion the view that children should never be taught more than one perspective in an argument?

It's not only that on further examination the concept of critical thinking evaporates into bromides. More destructively, critical thinking has been held up as a pedagogical end-in-itself—something teachers should simply teach. But whatever definition of critical thinking you choose, you cannot teach it in isolation of actual content. To prove this, try thinking for the next thirty seconds about nothing in particular. Alternatively, think critically on something about which you know nothing. Unless you are in a trance, neither is possible. Thinking of any kind requires a content. Whatever critical thinking might mean, it cannot be content free.

Regardless of the definition of critical thinking, becoming better at it cannot be separated from learning and knowing more about what you are critically thinking about. Take, for example, General Robert E. Lee's key decision during the Battle of Gettysburg to order Pickett's fatal charge up the hill to the Union lines. To offer more than one explanation for that decision—as all definitions of critical thinking require—one needs to consider at least two different contexts: the military (perhaps Lee thought his artillery had sufficiently softened the enemy lines) and the psychological (perhaps Lee was simply exhausted and/or at this point he had an overly positive view of his own military instincts). To assess these hypotheses as carefully as possible would mean digging into the historical record, comparing Lee's actions at Gettysburg to those he took in other, earlier battles and being careful to distinguish factors that might have differentiated the later battle from the former. In short, one would need to study history.

Dan Willingham sums it up: "Can critical thinking be taught? Decades of cognitive research point to a disappointing answer: not really."[18] And why is that? Because one learns in the old-fashioned sense of studying an issue, a problem, or a text in order to think "critically" about it. As an abstract, decontextualized skill, critical thinking comes down to no more than being wary of accepting the first answer.

Every step beyond that requires substantive knowledge about the domain to which critical thinking is supposed to apply, be it history, science, literature, or any other discipline. Moreover, because critical thinking in itself is a mental stance and not a kind of knowledge, there is no transfer of "critical thinking" across academic domains. Learning to be a careful reader of the historical record has little impact on the ability to be an acute interpreter of scientific experiments.

In the end, it is not possible to distinguish critical thinking from considering more than one perspective when one is faced with a set of facts or ideas. Trying to squeeze deeper meaning out of the phrase is pointless. After a long discussion of the contested definition of critical thinking, the *Stanford Encyclopedia of Philosophy* leaves us with this: "'Critical thinkers' have the dispositions and abilities that lead them to think critically when appropriate."[19]

One might respond that while critical thinking lacks the heft one would expect given its ubiquity in our educational discourse, there is no harm. We have just given a new label to the valuable readiness to look at issues from more than one point of view. But that is a different matter than making critical thinking a holistic goal of education. Moreover, it would be an error to dismiss the issue as a harmless fad. As we will discuss below, the idea that critical thinking can be taught as a set of transferable skills relates to a wider set of beliefs that, in the age of Google, knowledge is secondary to metaskills.

AN INTERLUDE—UNDERSTANDING RESEARCH

Before analyzing further educational distractors, a brief exegesis about research terminology will be helpful for readers who may be unfamiliar with its basic research terminology (others can happily skip this section).[20]

There are essentially three models of empirical research, each associated with a different level, or strength, of persuasiveness. Of the three research models, correlational studies are the weakest in terms of the claims that they produce. In correlational research, the point is to link—or show a correlation between—an intervention and an outcome. But correlational studies cannot show causation. For example, consider a study that finds that married people are diagnosed with cancer at lower rates than unmarried people (being married is correlated with lower cancer risks). Such a study cannot establish that getting married is a good way to reduce cancer risk: The link between the two could be the result of other factors. Perhaps married couples are more likely to live in the suburbs than in polluted urban centers. If so, a single person could move to the suburbs and still reduce his or her cancer risk.

In the two more rigorous research models, quasi-experimental and randomized control trials (RCT), researchers divide those they are studying into a "control group" and an "intervention group." As the term suggests, the intervention group experiences an intervention, while the control group does not. In the context of education research, an intervention group may experience a new teaching strategy, new curricula materials, or some other change to their routine.

Quasi-experimental research creates more secure findings than do correlational studies. In a quasi-experimental model, researchers look at what happens when one group is subject to an intervention (say, extra math support) and the other is not. The two groups are then both evaluated on the outcome of interest (in this case, math results) to see if the intervention made the difference.

The research challenge here is to make the two groups as similar as possible (perhaps those who passed a math assessment versus those who failed it) and to try to make sure nothing else interferes with the study conditions (for example, the group without the extra support got a new math curriculum). Because ensuring both these things is difficult, the most we can say of a carefully executed correlational study is that the intervention *plausibly* created a difference in the outcomes, assuming we find a difference at all.

The third kind of research, the RCT, is the gold standard. A group of subjects is randomly assigned into two groups: One group is subject to an intervention, and the other is not. If nothing unexpected happens, researchers can claim that any difference in outcomes is due to the intervention: It *caused* the change in outcomes. The larger the group of subjects studied, the stronger this causal claim.

The most common measure of how large a difference an intervention makes is called the effect size, often stated in terms of a standard deviation (an effect size of 0.2 is the same as 20 percent of a standard deviation). Sparing the reader a discussion of exactly what this means, the important point is that the higher the effect size, the more compelling the results. There is a lot of discussion of how large an effect size needs to be for us to consider it significant, but few effect sizes in educational interventions register an effect size of greater than a 0.5. Effect sizes below 0.1 are usually not considered meaningful.[21]

For reasons we will not explore here, effect sizes from RCT studies tend to be lower than those from the other two methods. But one note of caution: Because American students, on average, have successively lower learning gains each year they remain at school, an intervention with a fixed effect size across grade levels will have a much higher impact on learning outcomes at higher grade levels than in the elementary school years.

Finally, researchers sometimes report their outcomes not in effect sizes but in points or in percentages. This is most common when a standard assessment is used as the measure of an outcome. Researchers will report that a certain group of students gained x points on the test, or that students previously scoring at, say, the thirty-fifth percentile now score at the forty-fifth.

In some cases, researchers helpfully report their results using multiple measures. For example, they might state the effect size of an intervention and then explain what that effect size means when translated into the real world of percentile gains on a test result, or when expressed as added months of learning. Readers are often surprised by how modest a change in percentiles is achieved by a given effect size.

GROWTH MINDSET AND GRIT

We return now to our review of contemporary teaching strategies. Teaching critical thinking has become almost a cliché, something teachers are expected to do as a matter of common sense. What links Growth Mindset (GMS) and grit to critical thinking is that, like the latter, they invite teachers to focus on mental habits that are distinct from academic disciplines. But in contrast to critical thinking, a teacher intent on incorporating GMS and grit into her pedagogical strategies is asked to adopt specific pedagogical approaches, approaches touted as "research based." Taking each strategy in turn, that claim collapses.

GMS is the idea that when students assume they can get better at a task or at learning an academic discipline (often math), they will. Putting the same point negatively, if students are convinced that their poor results in math are the consequence of "being bad at math"—which they take to be an unchangeable reality—then they will remain poor at math. If students believe that effort won't make any difference, no amount of exhortation on the part of the teacher will help.

GMS is an appealing idea. Students' academic potential can be unlocked by shifting their psychological stance. Once they do so, students will see that greater effort leads to more learning. Given the potential power of this shift, it is unsurprising that GMS has attracted wide-spread attention. Like critical thinking, it has become a recognized and widely accepted teaching strategy.

How strong, however, is the research base that supports the use of GMS? The most complete research review was conducted by Erin Harrison, who provides a summary of published studies since 2015. She reports that all but one of the studies she included used RCT methodology, and she concluded that all but one of these studies had small effect sizes (that one study found a positive impact from academic intervention in the control group and a "slightly negative" impact for the intervention group).[22]

In 2022, What Works Clearinghouse, the US Department of Education's collection of research findings, found only five studies of GMS that met its standards for inclusion. Three of these had a sample size of fewer than 300 students. While it concluded very cautiously "that implementing *Growth*

Mindset interventions . . . may increase academic achievement," all five of the included studies were done in college settings, not with K-12 students.[23]

What happens when one includes less rigorous, non-RCT studies? The most famous is from Carole Dweck, whose name is now synonymous with GMS. Her work is based on research she conducted in Chile. Using test scores and controlling for students' own views of their existing intelligence, Claro, Paunesku, and Dweck found statistically significant effect sizes of 0.171 higher performance in language use and an effect size of 0.119 in math. The authors correctly characterized these results in their article as very modest effects.[24] Consistent with other research, they also found that "students from the lowest-income families were twice as likely to endorse a fixed mindset as students from the top-income families and schools"[25]

More evidence of the efficacy of GMS comes from OECD data from the PISA 2018 assessment. This was a large-scale study: Surveying some 600,000 students in seventy-eight countries, PISA set out to test Dweck's thesis that "students with a growth mindset are more likely to be resilient, develop learning strategies to achieve complex objectives, are willing to try new learning strategies, capitalize on learning experience, and respond positively to feedback" (Yeager and Dweck 2012, 11).[26]

To test this hypothesis, PISA 2018 asked students to what extent they agreed with the following statement: "Your intelligence is something about you that you can't change very much."[27] PISA took disagreement with the statement as evidence of a growth mindset on the basis that if students believe that intelligence can change, they will be much more likely to challenge themselves to improve the quality of their own thinking.[28] The results of the study indicated some positive correlations. They found, as Dweck had done previously, that more disadvantaged students were much more likely to believe that their intelligence was fixed. The more unequal the country's economic structure, the more pronounced the difference between the poorer and wealthier students was when it came to their views of intelligence.[29]

Second, those who reported having a GMS as PISA defines it scored higher on the PISA reading, science, and math tests after controlling for the socioeconomic profile of the students.[30] But as the PISA report makes clear, there is no evidence of causation (that a focus on GMS *caused* the academic improvement). It simply shows that students exhibiting higher GMS were also more likely to be students with stronger academic results. Perhaps those who are stronger academically tend to believe, understandably, that they can learn more easily than those who struggle.

A study in the form of two meta-analyses from 2018 asks, "To What Extent and Under Which Circumstances Are Growth Mind-Sets Important to Academic Achievement?" The study reviews and summarizes primary research studies, which in this case collectively involve almost 366,000 students. Their meta-analyses had generous inclusion criteria (meaning that they included RCT, quasi-experimental, and correlational research studies in the first meta-analysis and subtracted correlational studies in the second). Their only requirement was that every study they included had used "a measure of academic achievement."[31]

The authors start by pointing out just how much attention GMS has garnered: The idea of GMS has led to the creation of major nonprofit organizations (e.g., Project for Education Research that Scales [PERTS]), for-profit entities (e.g., Mindset Works, Inc.), schools purchasing mindset intervention programs (e.g., Brainology!), and seven-figure grants to individual researchers. All this in spite of the fact that, in the first meta-analysis, the researchers conclude that the average correlation between growth mind-set and academic achievement was "very weak."

In the second meta-analysis, the researchers focus on differences in academic achievement between students who received a growth-mind-set intervention and students who didn't get the intervention. The results, given the extraordinary prominence of GMS, were surprising: "37 of the 43 effect sizes (86%) are not significantly different from zero."[32]

The meta-analysis concludes that the results of the examined research studies *do not support* claims that GMS leads to "large gains in student achievement." The most the authors are prepared to concede is that disadvantaged students might benefit from GMS, but they stress that this is a fragile conclusion based on very modest differences in the outcomes of poorer and wealthier students and with a very small sample size.

One can briefly summarize this evidentiary record. Unlike the case of critical thinking, there is at least a small research base for GMS. But we lack both RCT and even strong quasi-experimental research that would show which interventions raise GMS in ways that will make a sustained impact on academic learning. To summarize, the stronger the methodology used to demonstrate the positive impact of GMS, the weaker that demonstration turns out to be.

Dweck herself recently noted her worries about the misuses of her theory. Upon reviewing how GMS is being used in schools, she found that it serves more to flatter students than to help them put GMS into action. In other words, students are being told that they are all smart and that they are all trying hard—even when they aren't learning successfully. Worse, teachers are rationalizing children's failure to learn as a result of their having a fixed mindset.

Whereas Dweck had earlier assumed that GMS would counter the empty self-esteem movement, she has now discovered that it is being added as a powerful way of reinforcing that movement. GMS was supposed to open children's thinking to the idea that if they applied themselves to hard work, they would experience positive results. Instead, Dweck found that teachers were not following through with the support, encouragement, and demand for that work itself.[33]

A generous review of the research could conclude that GMS may cause some modest learning gains for underprivileged children, especially if we enlarge the target populations to include their parents so that they as well as teachers encourage their children to think of learning progress as dependent on effort.[34] But this points to a larger issue: It isn't children who are the key here but adults who believe that children can't grow academically, who label certain children as remedial cases, and/or who track them into noncollege pathways.

Belief creates a self-fulfilling prophecy: If one is convinced that students can't learn effectively, they are treated in ways that fulfill this expectation. It is our mindset that is fixed, and through our policies, we transfer that mind-set about the limited potential of underprivileged children to them. Unsurprisingly, once children are labeled as requiring academic intervention services, or a "Tier 3" response, they are very unlikely ever to exit these classifications.[35]

Is there something complex, new, and surprising about GMS that warrants all the fuss? When Dweck describes what teachers should do to inculcate GMS in their students, she recommends rewarding learning and progress, pointing the usefulness of seeking help, trying new strategies of learning, and trying to avoid getting discouraged when things don't go well.[36] These "new strategies," however, look simply like sensible advice that effective teachers have always used. Take, for example, the list of GMS strategies from the American University School of Education. The following are three examples from the website, presented in their entirety:

- Fixed mindset statement: "It's OK if you're having trouble. Maybe algebra isn't one of your strengths."
- Growth mindset statement: "When you learn how to do a new kind of problem, it develops your math brain."
- Fixed mindset statement: "Great effort. You tried as hard as you could."
- Growth mindset statement: "The goal isn't to get it right immediately. The goal is to improve your understanding step by step. What can you try next?"
- Fixed mindset statement: "Don't worry, you'll get it if you keep trying."
- Growth mindset statement: "That feeling you're experiencing of algebra being hard is the feeling of your brain developing."[37]

Is it unfair to suggest that in the end, GMS means something like "be encouraging of renewed effort when your students hit learning roadblocks"? It's not rocket science.

GRIT

The basic idea of "grit" is that self-discipline is an important habit: If children can be taught to strengthen their capacity for self-denial and increase their ability to withstand instant gratification, they will achieve stronger academic outcomes. Researcher Jennifer Bashant defines it this way: "Grit is the quality that enables individuals to work hard and stick to their long-term passions and goals."[38] Grit is often paired with "resilience"—the ability to bounce back from adversity.[39]

The research base for grit is even shakier than in the case of GMS. As with GMS, the claims for the efficacy of "grit" come most prominently from just a single researcher on the subject, Angela Duckworth. She argues that on just about every measure of academic performance—grades, test-scores, attendance, and admission to competitive high schools—adolescent students with high levels of self-discipline outperform their more impulsive peers. Moreover, she asserts that measures of self-discipline predict more variance in these multiple outcomes than does IQ.[40]

For many years, the most famous demonstration of the impact of "grit" was the marshmallow test. This test has been largely misunderstood: When first administered in 1972 it was designed to see if a child's level of self-control could be impacted by different kinds of distractions (yes, it could). Eighteen years later, a different team of researchers analyzed the relationship between preschoolers' delay of gratification and their subsequent SAT scores.[41] Researchers found a positive correlation between young children who were able to wait longest for their marshmallow rewards while being given no alternative focus of attention and their SAT test results years later.

But subsequent research found that this predicted effect was greatly exaggerated. Tyler Watts, a professor of psychology at New York University, replicated the marshmallow test in 2018. He found much weaker results than in the original study. Once he controlled for family background, ethnicity, gender, and cognitive ability, the difference in the capacity of children to delay gratification barely mattered. He found essentially no correlation at all between the ability to delay gratification and behavioral outcomes later in life.[42]

The overall research record on "grit" is equally negative. According to Martin Credé, a social psychologist at Iowa State University who has been particularly outspoken, schools shouldn't be wasting money or time trying to inculcate grit-like behavior, as he could find neither strong correlation to academic success nor identify strategies that were likely to strengthen grit-like habits.[43]

In a 2017 article titled "Much Ado about Grit: A Meta-Analytic Synthesis of the Grit Lliterature," Credé dug into the research asked if grit can be differentiated from well-established habits such as persistence, industriousness, self-control, determination, tenacity, and will-power, or if it simply is a new name for them? Credé and his coresearchers found that it was the latter, an appealing label that gestures at a slew of traits without being distinct from them. To put the matter in research parlance, "the construct validity of grit is in question."[44]

Duckworth's response to push-back from the research community has been to suggest—despite her earlier research—that schooling may be the wrong place to assess the efficacy of grit. Because schools are not the place where students are most passionate about their achievements, she argues, they are unlikely to apply much grit to their academic work.[45]

In short, just as Dweck now worries about the misuse of GMS, so has Duckworth been pushing back on the over-use of grit in education. She has explicitly criticized the use of any measure of grit or its associated characteristics as a metric for a judgment of teacher or school effectiveness.[46] But none of her concerns or her back-tracking, ends the story. As so often in American education, ideas that are intuitively attractive have long half-lives and refuse to die. Despite Duckworth's efforts to soft-peddle the educational use of grit metrics, they are still being used all over the country.[47]

SOCIAL AND EMOTIONAL LEARNING

The teaching of critical thinking, growth mindset, and grit each offers teachers specific strategies that are purported to contribute to students' doing better academically, even though they don't aim to develop knowledge in an academic discipline. As we have seen, the research base for making such claims is weak. Social and Emotional Learning (SEL), however, is even more pervasive in K-12 education, and far more ambitious in what it claims to offer. In a nutshell, a focus on SEL is said not only to impact students' overall well-being but to rival or even be superior to relying on traditional measures of student learning (like tests) when it comes to longer-term life benefits.

The teaching of SEL is offered not as a singular pedagogic strategy but as an entirely new approach to teaching itself. Showing that in the end it merits inclusion on the list of negative educational "distractors" will cause strong pushback. The commitment to SEL is widespread and passionate. Moreover, that commitment is supported by an often-cited study from one of the most prominent of America's current educational researchers.

The following treatment of SEL will focus mainly on the claims SEL proponents make for its impact on academics and long-term life outcomes, but first a quick point about teachers taking on substantial challenges with students' mental health. Here, caution is in order. Teachers are not mental health experts, and when they act as well-meaning amateurs, students are unlikely to benefit. Researchers in England analyzed more than thirty empirical studies since 2010 and found no evidence that teachers could successfully address serious mental conditions such as depression or anxiety.[48]

What exactly is the definition of SEL? As in the case of critical thinking, there is no clear answer. The core idea seems to be that if grit or a growth mind set alone don't have a major impact, combining them with other important habits and skills adds up to something more than the sum of their parts, a larger construct called "Social and Emotional Learning." This bundling has proved irresistible to the America's K-12 education system.

Perhaps the most widely used definition of SEL comes from the Collaborative for Academic, Social, and Emotional Learning (CASEL). CASEL identifies five domains of SEL: "Self-management, responsible decision-making, social-awareness, self-awareness, and relationship skills."[49] CASEL maintains that students should be exposed to and made aware of these skills from preschool onward, with exploration and engagement activities added from middle school onward. These are broad domains, which cover a potentially vast array of school-based interventions. The scope is daunting, including:

- Teaching students to integrate and apply SEL skills to prevent or reduce specific behavior problems
- Offering students the chance to contribute more actively in class, school, and community, and therby to sense of belonging
- Enabling the construction of safe and nurturing learning environments
- Working with peers and families to create whole-school communities that in turn support stronger classroom work habits.[50]

Putting these goals into in practice is more complex. The basic premise is that the right emotive states can support or undermine students' levels of engagement, commitment to studies, and their ultimate school success. Their sense of well-being, of experiencing positive relationships with teachers and peers, is critical to carrying a positive emotional effect into school each day. Without it, students will simply disengage.[51]

Researchers promise positive academic results from well-taught SEL programs. One meta-analysis of over 200 school-based SEL programs involving some 270,000 students found that, on average, students who engaged in these programs achieved an eleven-percentile point gain in achievement.[52] Once again, however, caution is in order. Any meta-analysis of multiple studies is only as good as the studies themselves. By definition, inclusion criteria for what studies are counted will greatly impact the reported outcomes. In the study just cited, for example, the inclusion criteria were extremely generous, accepting any research with some kind of control group.

As a recent report from Johns Hopkins University's Robert Balfanz and Vaughan Byrnes noted, if the research review is restricted to including only high-quality, randomized control trials, the measured outcomes would have been much more modest.[53] Balfanz and Byrnes also observe that most of the SEL studies involve small numbers of students, have extremely varied definitions of what SEL skills actually are, and use a wide number of measures of academic success.[54]

Perhaps unsurprisingly, individual research studies show a wide range of effects of SEL programs. Those that use student or teacher self-reported impact can only be suggestive. Other studies that rely on additional, more objective metrics, such as state assessments, are of greater value. Here too, however, the results are mixed. For example, a research paper that finds positive impact on self-reported measures concludes that when the impact on test scores was evaluated, there was no effect on reading and just a marginal effect on math.[55]

Another high-quality (RCT) study found that in relatively well-run schools with safe environments, SEL interventions had next to no impact. In schools that were chaotic, SEL made a difference.[56] In short, when basic norms of reasonable behavior have broken down, attention to fixing them is a good idea, no matter what you call the intervention.

As this last study suggests, it is difficult to tease apart what SEL interventions may themselves be producing from other aspects of school-level behavior. For example, students who attend high-performing charter schools evaluate themselves more negatively than their lower-performing academic peers on self-reported SEL measures. As the research on this phenomenon indicates, it is more likely that students who are in schools that are already academically strong and behaviorally demanding have higher standards of what is expected of them. These students thus rate their strong SEL skills more negatively for the same behavior than do students in a more chaotic school.

What to these charter students looks like modest self-discipline and conscientiousness would strike their peers as highly demanding behaviors.[57] In other words, in schools with higher expectations, students simply expect more of themselves, and are thus more self-critical of their own behaviors on their SEL surveys. This is why basing any conclusions about SEL impact on self-reported measures is dicey; such measures are just too context dependent. The same research paper that examined charter and noncharter schools is cautious about linking specific SEL interventions directly to higher academic outcomes, concluding by suggesting only that such efforts *may* in certain schools yield some academic benefit.[58]

The findings of the Johns Hopkins study by Balfanz and Byrnes are of special interest here. The research includes a large number of students (over 38,000 plus) from 326 schools. All the students studied were in schools with high rates of poverty and were academically challenged: Due to poor attendance, troubled behavior, and/or poor grades, they were not on the pathway to graduation.[59]

The results of implementing SEL interventions were very positive, with some of the effects equal to a full-year achievement growth in mathematics and ELA for students in grades 3–10. What is striking, however, is the form of the SEL intervention. It centered on the use of City Year volunteers, which are teams of eight to fifteen AmeriCorps members who served almost full-time in a variety of student support roles including tutors, mentors, and role models.[60]

In short, the core of the successful program was the fact that underprivileged, underperforming students were paired with a mentor, whose relationship was in part coach, friend, and tutor. Not coincidentally, we know that academic tutoring has one of the highest positive impacts on student outcomes of all educational interventions.[61]

The Balfantz and Brynes study concludes emphatically, "City Year's Whole School, Whole Child approach, shows that human-centered, relationship-driven approaches to social-emotional development may be as, if not more, impactful than curricular or programmatic approaches."[62] But we need to treat this conclusion very carefully. The City Year volunteers were doing many things with their students, of which only a portion (never defined) can reasonably be called SEL. Tutoring, for example, is an academic and not an emotional learning support tool.

Balfantz and Brynes found that students who scored high on something called DESSA (the Devereux Student Strengths Assessment)—their measure of SEL—also had stronger academic outcomes.[63] In other words, the two were strongly correlated, but what was causing both outcomes? It may well have been the tutoring that was the primary driver of the academic gains. One cannot easily separate out the impact of tutoring from aspects of mentorship and psychological support.

A commonsense assumption would be that they feed one other: Knowing someone really cares about your doing well in math raises your motivation to succeed; tutoring gives you the knowledge and skills to do so; better math results encourage you to come to school for the next tutoring session and attend your regular math classes; the ultimate result is that you feel better about yourself all around.[64] If, indeed, students experienced this positive feedback loop, they would unsurprisingly show higher levels of SEL.

This hypothesis is strongly supported by other passages of the Balfantz and Brynes report. When students were identified for academic support from their City Year partners, they did better academically in both the short and long run, improvements that were also correlated with increases in their school attendance—a measure often cited as evidence of higher SEL. Students who were identified for behavioral support, however, saw no such increase in academic outcomes.[65] While their attendance improved, their academic results did not."[66]

Headlines are often imperfect indicators of what research demonstrates. Take, for example, the conclusion of the Balfanz and Brynes report: "Human-centered, relationship-driven approaches to social-emotional development may be as, if not more, impactful than curricular or programmatic approaches."[67] This can be misleading: A core part of these human approaches was focused on providing academic support.

No review of the SEL research is complete without an analysis of "School Effects on Socio-Emotional Development, School-Based Arrests, and Educational Attainment," perhaps the most influential paper published in support of teaching SEL, by Northwestern University professor Kirabo Jackson.[68]

Jackson argues that improving ninth-grade students' SEL performance has a greater impact on several important student outcomes (high-school GPA, taking the SAT, graduating high school, and indicating an interest in attending college) than does an equivalent increase in student test scores. Put another way, teachers who successfully focus on SEL are of greater use to students than those who manage to raise their academic outcomes. Jackson's study also finds that teachers who are good at doing the former are not, on average, likely to be strong at doing the latter—and vice versa: Teaching SEL and teaching academics embody separate skill sets.

This sounds rather definitive, but yet again, caution is advised. First, the outcomes that Jackson uncovers are modest. He reports that the impact of teachers on students' SEL-related behavior is some ten times more predictive of high-school completion than are teachers' impact on student test scores. To put this differently, if high-school graduation is the metric of interest, then as a student you would do much better to be taught by a teacher with strong SEL-teaching skills than a teacher who focuses on your academic learning.

As ever, the full story is more complicated. Ten times more impact on graduation rates sounds very dramatic. In practice, however, the difference is very small. A teacher who is very strong (at the eighty-fifth percentile of all the evaluated teachers) at raising SEL levels increases a student's on-time graduation rate by 1.46 percentage points. The equivalent for the academically strong teacher (also at the eighty-fifth percentile) is 0.12 percentage points. So given a group of 100 students, the difference is that in the former case, one more student will graduate on time.

It is also very important to examine exactly what Jackson means by SEL. To measure SEL, he creates a basket of "noncognitive skills" that he then constitutes as a "behavior index." The key idea is then reformulated as follows: A teacher that positively impacts a student's behavior index rather than one who focuses on a student's cognitive skills will have the stronger impact on that student's GPA and likelihood of graduating.

What makes up this behavior index? We might expect to find social-awareness, self-awareness, and relationship skills—the typical components of SEL, but Jackson doesn't include such items in his metrics. Instead, he includes the number of absences and suspensions, grade point average, and on-time progression to tenth grade. The problem here is clear: GPAs and on-time progress have cognitive elements. Even if we concede that some elements of a strong GPA have behavioral elements (for example, a tendency to hand in work on time), it would seem implausible to argue that academic ability is irrelevant to GPA.

It may simply be the case that Jackson used the data that were available to him, but these measures are a limitation to the study. It is unclear what Jackson is capturing in his "noncognitive" measures, but they include metrics that clearly go outside SEL and omit many metrics usually included in SEL measures. At most, Jackson captures something different than test scores and finds that this something matters a little (ignoring the fact that we can't fully define whatever that something really is).

The research shows that, once again, there is risk of losing sight of the obvious. Underprivileged children with academic difficulties benefit from consistent attention from an adult who assists them with their academic work and makes efforts to be generally supportive and friendly. On average, children who receive targeted SEL *might* learn slightly more and are slightly more likely to improve their school behavior, including attending regularly and graduating.

There is no need for new vocabulary or for startling claims of a new science to understand and to support the idea of supportive teaching, to remind teachers that effective instruction should include giving students the sense that they matter, and that their successful efforts to learn are important to teachers, too. As well-known education researcher Jay Greene puts it, SEL has "educational priorities that are as old as education itself."[69]

Isolating SEL as a singular set of interventions—especially to the point of diminishing attention to academic learning—risks creating a whole new set of demands on teachers that the research doesn't (yet, at least) warrant.[70] Taken to an extreme, as Robert Pondiscio has argued, we risk trying to render education a kind of therapeutic enterprise. He quotes multiple examples of what is now expected of teachers—that, for example, they must "accept their responsibilities to ameliorate the consequences of trauma on youth."[71] Instead of sensibly arguing that teachers should model mutual respect and habits of hard work, we ask that teachers become experts in mental health and turn away from teaching English, math, and other academic subjects.

METACOGNITION AND
TWENTY-FIRST-CENTURY SKILLS

The interventions analyzed to this point are advocated mainly for their ability to raise academic outcomes—claims we have shown are exaggerated. But there is a second major set of demands on today's teachers, namely, that they prepare students for the new workplace of our increasingly automated, high-skills economy. The core of such a preparation is collectively known as promoting "metacognative" (thinking about thinking) skills.

Why are these skills needed? The usual argument is that our current K-12 education model is failing because it is stuck in a nineteenth-century "factory model" of teaching and learning. That model—so the argument goes—undermines our human capacities and fails to provide children with what our new economy demands.

While the vocabulary that describes metacognitive skills can be somewhat different from growth mindset and SEL, one of the most attractive features of metacognitive skills is that they are fully complementary with those described above. With a stroke of cosmic good luck, it turns out that the new skills of critical thinking, social awareness, and collaboration are the same as those required by the twenty-first-century economy. As one commentator in *Education Week* put it, we don't need to learn information any longer, but instead to process it and use it intelligently. As we transition from operating like machines to being creative problem solvers, learning will take us from the industrial to the automation age. "To succeed in the future will require rediscovering what it means to be truly human."[72]

Putting aside the equation of "truly human" with "information processing" (discussed at length in chapter 4), it is fair to say that the *Education Week* quote presents the predominant view in education circles. The influential RAND Corporation drives home the same message: Globalization renders urgent the need to teach students "to learn [how] to learn."[73] The Center for Global Education at the Asia Society calls for "Teaching and Learning the 21st Century Skills," arguing that we need to abandon the "transmission" model of learning and instead teach "higher order thinking skills."[74]

What exactly are the twenty-first-century skills for which this higher order thinking is so urgently required? As in the case of positive mindset and SEL, there are lots of definitions and a broad list of desired skills. The Glossary of Education Reform, aiming to offer an overview of twenty-first-century knowledge, skills and work habits, offers the following list of metacognitive skills:

- Critical thinking, problem solving, reasoning, analysis, interpretation, synthesizing information
- Research skills and practices, interrogative questioning
- Creativity, artistry, curiosity, imagination, innovation, personal expression
- Perseverance, self-direction, planning, self-discipline, adaptability, initiative
- Oral and written communication, public speaking and presenting, listening
- Leadership, teamwork, collaboration, cooperation, facility in using virtual workspaces
- Information and communication technology (ICT) literacy, media and internet literacy, data interpretation and analysis, computer programming
- Civic, ethical, and social justice literacy
- Economic and financial literacy, entrepreneurialism
- Global awareness, multicultural literacy, humanitarianism
- Scientific literacy and reasoning, the scientific method
- Environmental and conservation literacy, ecosystems understanding
- Health and wellness literacy, including nutrition, diet, exercise, and public health and safety.[75]

This is just a long list of utopian traits, much too encompassing to offer anything actionable or measurable. Other lists of metacognitive skills are typically this lengthy and thus rather vapid: The Metacognitive Awareness Inventory (MAI), developed by Schraw and Dennison in 1994, cited in multiple research papers, has fifty-two listed skills.[76]

As Daisy Christodoulou writes in her book *Seven Myths about Education*, the problem with the entire edifice of twenty-first-century skills is that the expectation to develop creativity or problem-solving skills is hollow; when pressed, the definitions collapse into synonyms for being curious. When advocates of these new skills also claim that they are unique to the new knowledge economy, she adds, they are wrong. Is anyone seriously going to claim that no one needed to solve problems, to collaborate, or to be innovative prior to the year 2000?[77]

If the list of twenty-first-century skills is hopelessly long, the effort to codify the cognitive processes that are supposed to animate those skills—higher order thinking or metacognition—suffer from the opposite problem: The definitions are parsimonious and vague to the point of meaninglessness.

One such effort is captured in the article "How to measure metacognition," written by researchers whose affiliations span the universities of Oxford, NYU, Columbia, and UCLA. The researchers define metacognitive sensitivity as the capacity to be confident when one is more likely to be correct. In this definition, the degree of correlation between accuracy and confidence is taken to be the quantitative measure of metacognition.[78] In other words, when one's confidence in being right is warranted, one has higher metacognition. This was once called being smart.

A second effort to define metacognition parsimoniously comes from a researcher at Vanderbilt University. Once again, the focus is on cognitive processes. In this case, the definition is "thinking about one's thinking."[79] The key idea here is introspection—the ability to interrogate one's own thought processes. As in the case of critical thinking, it turns out that simply asking oneself questions about thought outside of any substantive situation is of no use. Instead, the Vanderbilt paper asserts, the key is to interrogate one's own strengths and weaknesses of thought in a variety of different contexts such as solving specific academic or professional problems.

But to what end? On closer inspection, it turns out that it is not the interrogation per se that matters. Rather, what really matters is getting to the right answer. Take the case of Youki Terada's "How Metacognition Boosts Learning." The author suggests that students overestimate how well they will do in a test in part because they may have invested time in the wrong study strategies. Once they have learned the skills of metacognition, they will understand the gap between being casually familiar with a topic and truly understanding it and then invest energy to achieve the latter.[80]

But what Terada means by metacognition is that to be effective, "thinking about thinking" actually means asking a series of very explicit questions, all of which require a correct answer. His examples include asking and accurately answering the question: "What are the main ideas of today's lesson?" In other words, it is helpful to understand what one is studying.[81] "Thinking about thinking" without thinking about something in the right way turns out to be rather useless.

To be clear, none of this is intended to suggest that self-reflection is a bad idea. Rather, the point is that the entire edifice of metacognition has added next to nothing to this common-sense notion. Even the vocabulary of metacognition is not as new as the "twenty-first-century skills" vocabulary would lead us to presume. Forty years ago, the now infamous "Nation at Risk" report reprimanded American educators for not teaching seventeen-year-olds the "'higher-order' intellectual skills" that the country so clearly needed.[82] Then and now, these skills exist rhetorically, but lack substance.

CREATIVE THINKING

The last of the educational distractors is "creative thinking"—a concept that encompasses just about everything previously discussed, although it adds an appealing if vague allusion to artistic values. Creative thinking is not to be confused with the study of the creative or fine arts—a crucial educational endeavor that will be discussed in the final chapter. Rather, "creative thinking" is, once again, a label for something that sounds positive but turns out to be fuzzy and feel good, lacking any specific definition.

This hasn't, however, impededr the education world from taking the term very seriously, indeed. "Creative thinking" has recently been blessed by perhaps the most important international education authority. As noted above, in 2022, the OECD PISA assessment, arguably the world's education thermometer, started testing not only critical thinking but "creative thinking." The OECD is adding this new element to the PISA assessments because "creative thinking is a necessary competence for today's young people to develop. . . . It can help them adapt to a constantly and rapidly changing world, and one that demands flexible workers equipped with '21st century' skills that go beyond core literacy and numeracy."[83]

As we have seen with critical thinking, grit, growth mindset, SEL, and metacognition, the promises that come with teaching students the skills of creative thinking are dramatic. Inducing educational systems to deliver higher levels of "creative thinking," the OECD assures us, will "improve a host of other individual abilities, including metacognitive capacities, inter- and intra-personal and problem-solving skills, as well as promoting identity development, academic achievement, future career success and social engagement."[84]

Once again, we need to ask: What exactly does it mean to think creatively? By claiming that raising levels of creative thinking schools will also raise "a host of other abilities," OECD makes it clear that creative thinking isn't synonymous with those abilities. What, then, is creative thinking? The OECD's definition doesn't help: "It is a tangible competence, grounded in knowledge and practice, that supports individuals in achieving better outcomes, oftentimes in constrained and challenging environments."[85] What competence? The next part of the definition highlights "engagement in the thinking processes associated with creative work" (idem). What processes?

Then one reads that "*the competence to engage productively in the generation, evaluation and improvement of ideas, that can result in original and effective solutions, advances in knowledge and impactful expressions of imagination*" (emphasis in the original).[86]

The problem with this last definition is that it has shifted to a vastly generalized set of outcomes. Just what counts as the improvement of ideas, what defines original solutions, and on what basis are advances in knowledge to be determined? To make an obvious point, most would argue that some children can show unusual creativity, but we scarcely measure that creativity by the standard of contributing to "original and effective solutions"—solutions to what?

Perhaps realizing the problem, OECD in the very next paragraph defines the concept of creative thought quite differently. Here, they focus on the degree to which students can rework ideas until they reach a satisfactory outcome. But what ideas, and satisfactory to whom? Finally, the OECD suggests that creativity is actually two skills—a "big C" creativity—say, what Leonardo da Vinci had, and "little c" or everyday creativity (e.g., arranging family photos in a scrapbook; combining leftovers to make a tasty meal; or finding a creative solution to a complex scheduling problem at work). The OECD cites academic literature to the effect that creativity (without specifying whether they refer to small c or large C) depends on six different cognitive resources:

1. Intellectual skills (such as synthetic and analytical skills)
2. Domain-related knowledge
3. Particular "thinking styles" (such as a preference for thinking in new way)
4. Motivation
5. Specific personality attributes
6. An environment that is supportive and rewarding of creative ideas.

Throughout the remainder of their explanation for creative thinking, the OECD adds further discrete descriptors of this illusive skill, including:

1. Openness to experience
2. Persistence
3. Perseverance and creative self-efficacy
4. Collaborative engagement
5. Task motivation.

These eleven cognitive resources are so broadly defined that it is hard to imagine how a single test could assess them all, but the OECD adds yet more descriptors. The assessment will test "creative expression"—the communication of one's inner world to others—and "creative problem solving."

In demonstrating their abilities in the first of these two domains, students will be asked to show skills of originality, aesthetic appreciation, imagination, and something called "affective intention." In the case of creative problem solving, students will be asked to generate solutions that are original, innovative, effective and "efficient."[87]

It strains credulity to believe that a single test can assess such a large list of skills. PISA is putting together a test of creative thinking that will be used to compare national performance based not only on a very large number of performance indicators but of indicators that are most often extremely vague (what exactly is "creative expression?").

What is especially concerning, however, is to read the following: "According to the current PISA assessment design, students who take the creative thinking assessment will spend one hour on creative thinking items with the remaining hour assigned to mathematics, reading and scientific literacy items."[88] In other words, a large and inchoate set of good-sounding cognitive attributes will be assessed across the nations of the world through an hour of testing—equal in time and weight to measuring student learning in math, reading, and science. The PISA test in creative thinking will be one more powerful distractor from a focus on academic learning.

TAKEAWAYS

"Critical thinking," "Grit," "SEL," "growth mindset"—when correctly understood as common-sense terms, have all been taught for a long time. It's not that they had no place in schooling, just as it's not that they have no place in schooling today. But they aren't new, and the research support for putting them at the center of schooling is simply not there. It is difficult to keep one's balance, one's common sense, in the face of the barrage from advocates for this "new" learning. Despite every evidence that the terms used are vague or vacuous, that the supporting research is thin, and that proponents are putting new labels on familiar educational practices, the drumbeat goes on. But why?

At its heart, the new learning isn't new and it isn't about learning. Instead, it is a powerful effort and seductive effort to circumvent the tough challenge of providing effective, discipline-based academic instruction. Learning to learn, like critical thinking, is akin to a ship's propeller spinning above the water line—it doesn't propel the vessel forward. As Graham McPhail notes in his essay on twenty-first-century education, the hope is that by replacing the content of education with generic skills such as critical thinking and problem solving, deep learning will occur. But McPhail concludes that there is no hard evidence to support the claim.[89]

It is sobering to unpack the claims made for the new learning: To analyze the vocabulary, to pressure-test the evidence, and finally to discover how imprecise its definitions are and how modest is the evidence. Hebert Simon (who won the Nobel Prize for his work on decision-making) could be speaking for the forgoing review of the new learning when he writes: "New theories of education are introduced into school every day (without labeling them as experiments) on the bases of their philosophical or common-sense plausibility but without genuine empirical support."[90]

What is striking about the components of new learning is less their novelty or purported effectiveness as stand-alone interventions than their overall thrust. Collectively, they serve as major distractors—seductors from the work of academic instruction, which is constantly treated as beside the point and old-fashioned, or simply passed over in silence. If we can teach the skills of critical thinking themselves, why worry about learning math, or understanding a difficult novel?

If thinking about one's own thinking is the new educational mantra, then just studying geometry or music seems so twentieth century (or perhaps so fourth century BC). It is hard to escape the conclusion that all the research on these new goals for education represents a deep frustration with our failures to teach academic content to children. The result is a somewhat frenetic effort to find some alternative purpose for schooling.

To conclude with another quote from Hebert Simon,

> In every domain that has been explored, considerable knowledge has been found to be an essential prerequisite to expert skill . . . we have no reason to suppose . . . that one day people will be able to become painlessly and instantly expert. The extent of the knowledge any expert must be able to call upon is demonstrably large.[91]

Unfortunately for all those who embrace the language of "metacognition," there isn't a replacement for learning content and analyzing that content. Striving to teach cognitive skills in the absence of knowing something is a passport to ignorance. The honeyed invitation to do so is educational poison.

Chapter 3

What Works—and Why
We Don't Do It

"A system is defined as 'coherent' when the national curriculum content, textbooks, teaching content, pedagogy, assessment and drivers and incentives are all aligned and reinforce one another. For this to be the case a certain level of control is necessary."[1]

The previous chapters focused on the core aims and distractions that confront America's K-12 education system that drain energy, clarity, and confidence from teachers. The results are clear: These new goals have done nothing to make teaching more attractive. Schools continue to struggle in recruiting and retaining teachers and school leaders.

This isn't some new phenomenon. Headlines to the contrary, COVID hasn't been the key cause.[2] The problem is systemic and enduring: Between the 2008–2009 and the 2018–2019 academic years, the number of individuals who finished a college-based teacher preparation program went down by almost a third.[3] For their part, principals have found the challenge of running schools overwhelming. A recent study of public-school principals found that about 18 percent leave their school after a year—a figure that rises to 31 percent in schools with high poverty rates.[4] Higher up the ladder of educational administration, the picture is no different: About a quarter of district superintendents changed jobs in the 2021–2022 school year.

But what about the educators who are in our classrooms, who every day tune out the noise, manage the distractions, and focus on teaching? They may worry about how much time to spend on teaching social and emotional skills; they may be concerned about the social climate in schools, about the departure of their colleagues, and constant changes in district policy. At the same time, however, they do their best to teach the children in their classrooms. This chapter will discuss what we know about optimizing the conditions for their daily work and why creating those conditions has proved so elusive.

This entails examining the key elements of successful instruction—a strong curriculum, sound teaching practices, and content-based assessments. In each case, the focus will fall on how our K-12 system has undermined the efficacy of these key elements of learning.

It is not as if we started educating just yesterday. There is considerable knowhow about creating schools that achieve strong educational outcomes in numeracy, literacy, and a foundational knowledge of history and science. Much of that knowledge is little more than good common sense. Tony Bryk and his colleagues at the Consortium on Chicago School Research have been studying public-school performance for years and have honed-in on key elements of success. They have found the following shared elements of strong schools:

- School leadership: Schools work when principals are instructional leaders.
- Parent-community ties: Schools thrive when there are tight connections between that school, the parents of its students, and local institutions.
- Professional capacity: Teacher efficacy is maximized when teachers share a set of teaching values and beliefs about necessary change; are supported by high quality professional development; and have the habit of active and mutual collaboration.
- Strong student learning climate: Are schools safe and welcoming while focused on learning for all students?
- Instructional guidance: Success is achieved when a coherent rigorous curriculum is in place.[5]

The Consortium found that schools that performed strongly in all five of these domains were ten times as likely as schools with one or two positive measures to achieve substantial learning gains. By contrast, a major weakness in even a single area undermined almost all efforts to improve academic outcomes."[6] Other analyses of successful schools and strong school districts offer similar findings. In her book, *Districts That Succeed*, Karin Chenoweth reiterates Bryk's finding about the importance of collaborative teachers, strong instructional leaders, a supportive safe environment, and rigorous instruction.[7]

David Kirp, a professor of public policy at the University of California, Berkeley, studied the success of schools in Union City, New Jersey, and concludes that among a few key elements were a strong curriculum with high academic expectations, good parental communication, and close attention to test data about students' academic performance. He found that "when boiled down to its essentials, what Union City is doing sounds so obvious, so tried-and-true, that it verges on platitude. Indeed, everything that is happening in Union City should be familiar to any educator with a pulse."[8]

At the school district level, Kirp observed that successful policies were equally unglamorous. Because of high mobility rates of students between district schools, he found that when districts insisted on teachers teaching the same material, in the same curriculum, in the same sequence, across all districts, students did better. That finding applied to all students—English language learners (ELLs), special needs students, and the gifted and talented.[9]

Rigorous academic content taught by teachers with high expectations emerges as a strong, shared component across these empirical findings—no matter if the focus is the school or the district. But there is a missing element here—namely strong assessments that are integrated with curriculum content, that is, assessments that test the knowledge students are supposed to learn in the curriculum that they have studied. Twenty years ago, after a close study of America's performance on the TIMSS international assessment, Michigan State University researcher Bill Schmidt concluded that "curriculum coherence"—the alignment of curriculum, instruction, and assessment—was both essential to strong learning gains and fundamentally absent from American schooling.

Schmidt points out that the highest-performing countries often have an assessed national curriculum against which all the other aspects of education are normed. First, a national or regional core curriculum is established. Then teachers are trained to teach that curriculum and given professional development throughout their careers to improve their teaching. Finally, assessments of student learning are integrated with that national curriculum. These assessments matter to students, because they enable access to further education.[10] In sum, countries that establish this triangular frame of curriculum, instruction, and assessment have a coherent education system and have established the necessary foundation for strong education outcomes.

International test results affirm Schmidt's findings. Perhaps the most telling contemporary example is Estonia. A close analysis of Estonia's rise to strong PISA results shows that a granular national curriculum with very detailed descriptions of exactly what teachers should teach in their subjects, plus assessments directly linked to their curriculum, were critical to their success.[11] The tight relationship between the curriculum and national assessments was codified in the Estonian Basic Schools and Upper Secondary Schools Act 2010, which also established goals for learning outcomes at each stage of the curriculum.[12]

The Estonian experience is mirrored in multiple countries. When they embrace a rigorous curriculum and test it, students do better; when they abandon that curriculum, they fall. As E. D. Hirsch points out in his book, *Why Knowledge Matters*, France, once the proud proponent of a national curriculum, decided to drop it in 1989. Instead, the state directed teachers to choose their own instructional materials.

The result was that over the following years, every subgroup of French students suffered worse reading outcomes, with the most disadvantaged students suffering by far the most.[13] When countries reverse these failing policies and instead institute a rigorous knowledge-rich curriculum (curriculum that explicitly lay out the information students are expected to master) with integrated assessments, as England did in 2014, results rise.[14]

The findings of volumes of research on effective schooling show that at a national level, successful school systems are those in which teachers consistently teach a knowledge-heavy curriculum to all students, assess students on their mastery of that curriculum, use metrics carefully to pinpoint where individual attention is needed, and do so with the strong support of a positive leader and in regular communications with students' families.[15] *In terms of delivering the foundations of an effective education, that's about it.* That what works is so familiar and mundane *should* make that finding both actionable and a relief. We know what to do, and it isn't especially complicated.

STRONG ACADEMIC CONTENT

At the heart of the international findings is the evidence that the teaching of a high-quality, externally designed curriculum is crucial for students' academic success. This commonsense, empirical finding is not welcomed in America's K-12 system. The American teaching profession instead endorses student-centered learning and teachers' "authentic autonomy"—meaning that teachers should design their own learning materials to suit their particular students.[16] As the previous chapter detailed, the United States also believes that a new approach to education (teaching "critical thinking," etc.) will solve our educational problems.

Strong rhetorical support for the conviction that teacher-designed curricula materials are the best way to teach has come from the OECD itself. The organization has prominently stated that curriculum-centered instruction should be regarded as passé, while learner-centered teaching is the wave of the future.[17] This message is so often repeated and so influential that it's worth explaining, using the OECD's own data, why it's wrong.

The argument originates in the success of Finland on the OECD's PISA tests. Once the results became familiar, researchers raced to Finland to report on its educational policies. They found that the country had moved away from "traditional" models of centralized curriculum and instruction in favor of teacher autonomy and student-centered learning and they assumed that this policy shift led to strong PISA results. But their conclusions were based on a basic misunderstanding of how instructional models and results interact.

As Tim Oates, the director of assessment research at Cambridge Assessments in the United Kingdom points out, a key problem in using test results as a measure of a country's education policy is time lag. In the Finnish case, care had to be taken to treat the outcomes of PISA tests as indicative not of the up-to-the moment policy but rather the policy that was in place in the years leading up to when they took the PISA assessment in question.[18]

In fact, the high level of curriculum autonomy in Finland witnessed by educational tourists had been a very recent development. Finland had had a national curriculum in place since 1881, and in the years before their PISA success, the state exercised tight control over school textbooks and teaching materials.[19] Finland's success on PISA was wrongly attributed to its move away from "old-fashioned" instructional measures. Once it did, in fact, abandon them, scores started to decline.[20]

In short, Finland's success was due to a hierarchical educational culture, traditional teaching methods, and a shared curriculum. The abandonment thereof led not only to a single, poor PISA result but also a steady slide in Finland's PISA scores.[21] As Andreas Schleicher, the head of PISA testing at the OECD acknowledged, "Finland has gone overboard . . . ideas became ideologies [the country was convinced that] we no longer learn in subjects [but that] doesn't actually work, subject matter and knowledge is in fact quite important."[22]

THE FRAGMENTED ACADEMIC CORE

At the heart of what "should be familiar to any educator with a pulse" is a clear strategy: the teaching of shared high-quality materials.[23] If the national and international research supporting this common-sense approach is clear, why aren't we following it in the United States? In a nutshell, the reason is because the dual impact of progressivism and cultural heterogeneity undermines any shared agreement on the content of education and thus on the traditional role of the teacher.

An introduction to progressivism in American education must start with an (all-too-brief) discussion of John Dewey, its best-known proponent. Across many decades and a vast output of writings, Dewey undertook a wholesale critique of Western philosophy and simultaneously sought to build a new vision of education. Dewey directly challenges the idea that knowledge in a particular domain can be codified and is slow to change through time. He argues the reverse: that knowledge is a "liquified" entity that is constantly in a state of re-creation.[24]

Dewey maintains that Plato and his followers have wrongly bequeathed to the West a division between a higher realm of fixed realities and an inferior world constituted by change, experience, and human practices.[25] The link between Dewey's metaphysics and his pedagogical theories is direct: Because knowing is not an act of recognizing something that is fixed but of the act of constantly creating meaning, the teacher is there to activate students' work of creation, not to instill a body of information into their minds.[26] Dewey argued that the material to construct knowledge comes out of common experience, which generates its own methods, standards, and values.[27]

The translation from Dewey's complex philosophy to the condensed summaries that find their way into contemporary teacher training inevitably simplifies and even misreads his body of writings.[28] But that translation has been immensely significant for the content taught to American school children and the training of their teachers. Laying this impact out in some detail through analyzing America's curricula, teacher preparation and assessments will reveal just how forceful Dewey's progressivist legacy has been in this country.

THE CURRICULUM

Access to public schooling wasn't widely available until late in the nineteenth century. There were almost no public schools for African American children before the Civil War, and as late as 1910, only 14 percent of Americans twenty-five and older had completed high school.[29]

For those students who *were* able to attend school, the United States had something close to a national curriculum—the McGuffey Readers, of which more than 150 million copies were sold. In 1879, The "Sixth Eclectic Reader" from McGuffey lays out what we would now call the ELA content reading for grammar and high-school grades. It contains 138 text selections, including short stories, poems, and excerpts from novels.[30] The content selection is explicit, the authors are largely British, and the academic demands rigorous (see the "supplementary reading" list, which is not included in the 138 count, in figure 3.1).

While no American school was expected to teach all of this material, the focus on what we would call the liberal arts tradition was common across all high schools, no matter if they were private "academies" or public high schools.

In urban school districts, a curriculum heavy on content was matched with a clear and even rigid set of pedagogical expectations for teachers. The editors of *The American Curriculum* give the example of Chicago's curriculum in 1862. Nothing was left to chance: How much time to spend on specific material, which exercises students should undertake, the exact subject matter to be taught—all was all laid out in detail. As *The American Curriculum* make

SUPPLEMENTARY READING FOR

GRAMMAR AND HIGH SCHOOL GRADES

ECLECTIC ENGLISH CLASSICS.

Arnold's (Matthew) Sohrab and Rustum
Burke's Conciliation with the American Colonies
Carlyle's Essay on Burns
Coleridge's Rime of the Ancient Mariner
Defoe's History of the Plague in London
De Quincey's Revolt of the Tartars
Emerson's The American Scholar, Self-Reliance and Compensation
Franklin's Autobiography
"George Eliot's" Silas Marner
Goldsmith's Vicar of Wakefield
Irving's Sketch Book (Ten Selections)
Irving's Tales of a Traveler
Macaulay's Second Essay on Chatham
Macaulay's Essay on Milton
Macaulay's Essay on Addison
Macaulay's Life of Johnson
Milton's L'Allegro, Il Penseroso, Comus Lycidas,
Milton's Paradise Lost, Books I and. II
Pope's Homer's Iliad, Books I, VI, XXII, XXIV,
Scott's Ivanhoe
Scott's Marmion
Scott's Lady of the Lake
Scott's The Abbot
Scott's Woodstock.
Shakespeare's Julius Caesar
Shakespeare's Twelfth Night
Shakespeare's Merchant of Venice
Shakespeare's Midsummer-Night's Dream
Shakespeare's As You Like It
Shakespeare's Macbeth
Shakespeare's Hamlet,
Sir Roger de Coverley Papers (The Spectator),
Southey's Life of Nelson
Tennyson's The Princess,
Webster's (Daniel) Bunker Hill Orations,

Sent, postpaid on receipt of price.

COPYRIGHT, 1879, BY VAN ANTWERP, BRAGG & COMPANY COPYRIGHT, 1896, BY AMERICAN BOOK COMPANY.
COPYRIGHT, 1907 AND 1921, BY HENRY H. VAIL.

M'G REV. 6TH EC.
EP 118

Figure 3.1. Supplementary Materials: McGuffey's Sixth Eclectic Reader. *https://www.gutenberg.org/files/16751/16751-pdf.pdf.*

clear, "what is most striking about Chicago's 'graded course of instruction' is the large number of subjects taught . . . by teachers following an elaborate and rigid set of directions."[31]

Perhaps the "high-point" of America's effort to establish a national curriculum was marked by the 1893 Report of the Committee of Ten on Secondary School Studies. The documents that made up this report included subcommittee reports in Latin, Greek, mathematics, English, other modern languages, natural history, geography, physical science, and a combination of history, civil government, and political economy.[32]

Above all, the recommendations embodied the convictions of the committee's chair, Harvard University president Charles Eliot. Condemning the underteaching occurring in America's schools, he pointed out that "we shall not know till we have tried what proportion of children are incapable of pursuing algebra, geometry, physics, and some foreign language by the time they're 14 years of age . . . We Americans habitually underestimate the capacity of pupils at almost every stage of education."[33]

In the early decades of the twentieth century, Dewey and his allies (building on a body of European thought that dated back to Jean Jacques Rousseau and Johann Heinrich Pestalozzi in the eighteenth century) attacked this entire educational edifice, especially the prescriptive nature of curriculum models and their embedded assumption that there was a fixed body of material that American students should study. In 1918, William H. Kirkpatrick, who inherited the leadership of the progressive movement from Dewey, published *The Project Method*. Grounding his model in his understanding of child psychology, Kirkpatrick argued that "most people get into trouble by choosing what children should learn." Instruction should be centered on students' interests and practical needs.

He maintained, for example, that anything beyond the most simple mathematics shouldn't be taught since it was useless for most citizens.[34] Above all else, Kirkpatrick explains, the child's tendency is "to grow," and thus the most important function of education is to nurture that growth.[35] Kirkpatrick was supported by a third influential progressive, G. Stanley Hall, who argued that the Committee of Ten was trying to force children into a "sedentary, clerical, bookish and noetic education," a policy made worse by coaching, cramming, and examinations.[36]

For these thinkers collectively known as progressivists, the focus on educational "growth" came with natural limits. They argued that children shouldn't be pressed beyond their "given" talents or probable station in life. To do otherwise, it was argued, would doom children to failure and would thus be an act of cruelty. William D. Lewis, principal of a Philadelphia high school, argued that a modern school had to recognize that its students can't all become doctors, lawyers, or members of the professional classes.[37]

The superintendent of Cleveland's public schools declared that an academic curriculum was suited only to those with a "strong mental capacity" and "of bookish tastes." In a high school in Los Angeles in the 1930s, so little academic rigor was required of those from whom it couldn't be expected that failure was abolished.[38] (Readers may recall the previous chapter and reasonably ask if we are steadily abolishing it once again.)

A final legacy of the progressive movement was a new faith in IQ testing to establish what was assumed to measure the natural limits to learning. By the 1920s, there were more than seventy-five separate tests of mental ability, tests taken by some four million students. School administrators used the results of these tests to track students into a variety of academic paths.[39]

It is striking that progressives, often grounding their arguments in appeals to freedom and a liberation from what they identified as the dead weight of intellectual authoritarianism, nevertheless created a model of education that condemned millions of the less privileged children to an inferior place in a fixed social-economic structure, all justified by aptitude or IQ tests. Instead of testing students to discover how effectively they have mastered a body of academic knowledge (a notion that Dewey had done much to undermine), the progressivist joined with Eliot and his fellow university presidents in endorsing aptitude tests—including the SAT—that closely correlated with IQ scores and cut off millions of children from advanced academic studies.

In both the short and long run, the legacy of the progressivist attack on academic knowledge was powerful. As Richard Hofstadter summarizes, during the forty years after 1910, the number of students studying a whole range of academic subjects fell precipitously. In the typical American high school, the percentage of students enrolled in modern languages fell from over 80 percent to 22 percent, Algebra from 57 percent to 27 percent, and science from 82 percent to 54 percent.[40] But it is the more enduring legacy of the progressivists that matter to American education today, and it is to that which we now turn.

THE FRAGMENTED CURRICULUM

In the long run, the progressivists' arguments undermined much of what we know about effective schooling. First, they helped to ensure that no consensus around a core educational content would be possible. Dewey's deeply impactful conviction that knowledge was fluid and couldn't be taught as a body of information saw to it that there would be no twentieth-century version of the McGuffey Readers. The possibility of agreement over educational content was undermined further as the once compelling metaphor of the "melting pot"—the Americanization of immigrants into a singular cultural conception—gave way to the "salad bowl": Different populations claimed an educational space for their own unique cultures, values, and histories.[41]

The definition of what being an American means is always in flux, and the widespread dissatisfaction with a singular, collective identity goes far beyond schooling. That dissatisfaction encompasses deep anger over the nation's history of racial, ethnic, and gender discrimination. The education system is but a component of that larger shift in the national debate. Defining themselves less as "Americans" and more through their cultural traditions, practices, and beliefs, Americans have inevitably become more siloed in their educational demands, with less tolerance for the claims of a single historical narrative or of the value of reading universally important or canonical texts.

As Stanford University historian David Tyack wrote two decades ago, "Some find new history standards unpatriotic; others find them insufficiently multicultural. The field of English seems in perpetual deconstruction. The New Math wars with the Old Math."[42] Tyack attributes the endless battles over what we should teach to efforts by group after group to claim its place in the national narrative—an effort that undermines our ability to find common ground.[43]

It is the joint legacy of progressivism and the educational identity politics that has undermined efforts to create a state-wide curriculum, still less a national curriculum in the United States. That undermining has been bolstered by our system of education governance, where some 13,800 individual school districts set much of the education policy for their students.

What has happened instead? Despite efforts at the public-school district level to provide teachers with a shared curriculum, most teachers concoct a brew of disparate instructional materials. As recent RAND survey data attest, more than 95 percent of American public-school teachers curate these materials from the internet (primarily Google, Pinterest, or Teachers pay Teachers), mix it with some elements of their district curriculum, and teach the unique curriculum that results.[44]

When given a new curriculum, even one deemed "high-quality," this practice largely persists; teachers usually combine small pieces of the new formal curriculum to their own play-list of preferred materials.[45] The practical result is that children—even within the same large school—receive different instruction from those in other classes, and certainly from students in other schools, districts, and states. *What a child learns in the public schools of the United States is largely a consequence of her or his individual teacher, and the instructional materials that teacher happens to favor.*

Furthermore, social inequalities have an outsized influence on the materials American teachers select for their students. Faced with students who enter their classrooms often a year or more behind in their grade-level skills, teachers try to "reach students where they are" by remediating them—attempting to teach the material students haven't mastered in prior years. The direct result is that across the United States, some 80 percent of the instructional materials teachers assemble for use in their classrooms are less rigorous than grade-level standards require.[46]

The consequence is a downward spiral. The students, already depressed by the awareness that they are being remediated, are clumped into classes taught by teachers with few expectations that these children will ever catch up. In this self-fulfilling prophecy, students are given material to study that cannot possibly bring them up to grade-level knowledge. The result is that, in the great majority of cases, achievement gaps not only persist but deepen. Students fall ever further behind.[47]

INEFFECTIVE TEACHER PREPARATION

The second progressivist legacy has been its impact on pedagogy. The belief that instruction should be centered on nurturing the natural instincts and preferences of individual children has become a deep-rooted conviction among teachers, in part because the schools of education that prepare them have been bastions of progressive beliefs.[48] These schools have long provided would-be teachers with the message that authentic teaching cannot be based on conveying information but rather in guiding children in acts of authentic learning.[49] Genuine teaching, in this view, occurs only when teachers create classroom content focused on children creating their own meaning and producing their own knowledge.[50]

In its most radical form, constructivist pedagogy has its foundation in encouraging children to pursue whatever interests them. The most famous example is Summerhill School in the United Kingdom, where what students study is almost entirely left to their whims.[51] In practice, constructivism usually means that the teacher tries to create learning experiences such that students arrive at learning through their own efforts, experiments, successes, and failures. This can be done very effectively—as Deborah Meier showed in her school Central Park East in Harlem in New York City.[52] But as Meier's own account makes clear, if students are to learn this way, the demands on teachers multiply. They require inexhaustible wells of patience, high energy, imagination, detailed planning, and a deep knowledge of their subject matter.

There is no evidence that we can expect this level of pedagogy from a profession of millions. What is clear is that when the great majority of teachers try for constructivist pedagogy, the results are negative. PISA data provides strong evidence that strong learning gains occur only when teachers' main task lies in conveying information—albeit with sensitivity to providing timely feedback and giving students extra learning support as needed.

Take the domain of science. If any academic subject should support a constructivist, child-discovery-based approach to teaching, it would be science, where experimentation is clearly intrinsic to the academic discipline itself. So, what does the record show? In 2018, some 700,000 fifteen-year-old students from seventy-nine countries took the PISA test. An analysis by the OECD of the reason for differences in the science scores clearly indicates that teacher-directed instruction has a highly positive impact on results, whereas "inquiry-based instruction" was heavily negative.[53] Scholars analyzing the PISA results as a whole have also found no evidence supporting student-centered teaching.[54]

One important clarification should be noted. As will be discussed in the final chapter, there is no claim here that teachers should blandly deliver content at their students with no interaction or opportunity for active dialogue and independent work. The key point is that the teacher has an indispensable role in instructing children in a predetermined body of academic knowledge.

Besides the fact that schools of education denigrate traditional teaching methods, they also embrace the progressivist conviction that teachers should create their own curricula. Teaching effectively and designing a strong curriculum are two different skills. Most American models of teacher preparation espouse the view that teachers should do both, emphasizing the importance of the self-curation of instructional materials (the only "authentic" curriculum is a teacher-created curriculum).

Future teachers are taught to regard published curricula with skepticism. One of the most frequently assigned textbooks in methods courses, Jon Saphier's *The Skillful Teacher*, among the best-known American manuals on pedagogy, takes the argument for teacher-created curricula as a given. His references to formal curriculum are rare and slighting, and there is no mention of the need for a core of knowledge in his instructional model.[55]

Schools of education instruct future teachers on how to teach through "methods courses." Such courses are generic and often silent on a requirement to teach specific academic content. This approach follows the advice of the National Council for the Teachers of English (NCTE), whose recommendations for methods courses make no mention of instructional materials at all. Instead, we find exhortations to the effect that "coursework should provide candidates with opportunities to understand the historical, social, political, global, and economic influences that shape our work as English teachers" and that "methods coursework should prepare candidates to become engaged and effective teachers who can plan, implement, assess, and articulate rationales for pedagogical choices."[56]

The Council for the Accreditation of Educator Preparation (CAEP) mimics the NCTE. Once again, while there is a single reference to "curriculum integration when appropriate," there is no mention of using a published curriculum, of preparing teachers to distinguish between a weak and strong curriculum, or of developing their skills in assembling specific instructional materials.[57] Meanwhile, despite years of pressure from outside bodies, almost half the schools of education in the United States fail to teach the basics of reading science to future elementary school teachers, even though the science of reading has been available since the publication of "Report of the National Reading Panel: Teaching Children to Read" in 2000.[58]

When teacher candidates do emerge from their coursework and undertake their clinical preparation (their "practicum"), there is next to no quality control over their training. Rather, a faculty member from the school of education (usually an adjunct) and a mentor teacher from the school, neither of them with any relevant professional training, provide uncoordinated feedback to the student teacher.[59] One must only look at the profession of medicine to note the problem; based on massive evidence that variation in medical care was causing high numbers of unnecessary hospital deaths, medical training shifted to intensive clinical preparation and more rigorous training by 1900. Teacher preparation, however, has largely failed to follow suit.[60]

Unsurprisingly, the resulting record of schools of education is dismal. There is no strong research to support the claim that any teacher education program has consistently produced teachers who are highly effective, or even just significantly stronger than average. While the departments of education for states such as Louisiana and Delaware do offer some measures of the correlation between a school of education and the impact of its graduated teachers on their students' performance, policy initiatives derived from the data are tough to find.[61]

One study, out of Missouri, that set out to evaluate differences in effectiveness of preparation programs found only very small differences between programs—almost all of the variation came from intraprogram differences between the graduates of each particular school of education.[62] Further rigorous research has found that reported differences in the impact of schools of education in terms of the academic outcomes of children taught by graduates of those schools disappear once proper statistical controls are utilized.[63]

Tom Kane, a nationally renowned educational researcher, concludes that we have learned next to nothing about how best to train or develop teachers.[64] But this isn't quite fair. As the previous sections of this chapter suggest, we do know that the general worldview of our teacher preparation programs isn't conducive to graduating effective teachers. Schools of education are largely Dewey's children.[65] As Arthur Levine, the former president of Teachers College at Columbia University, suggests, "the education our teachers receive today is determined more by ideology and personal predilection than the needs of our children."[66]

In their coursework, schools of education teach future teachers the progressivist model and downplay the instruction of academic knowledge. That coursework usually occupies all but the final semester of studies, when students are placed into schools. There, the aspiring teacher is supervised by two adults—usually an adjunct professor from the education school and a school teacher (the "mentor"), neither of whom have any training for the task of insuring that the aspiring teacher masters effective teaching.

Unsurprisingly, research on that clinical preparation—that is, the apprenticeship learning experience that the student-teacher receives while in the school setting—has also failed to show any meaningful differences between schools of education. (What differences there are could have been easily predicted—for example, if you train in a school similar to the school you end up teaching in, you are likely to be a little more effective.[67])

One possible response to this criticism of teacher preparation programs is that it isn't their responsibility to teach teachers about academic content: Surely, knowledge of ELA or math or other disciplines should be provided through other college courses. For example, students entering medical school are expected to bring a solid academic knowledge of biology to their studies. In the case of teacher preparation, however, the quality control to ensure that would-be teachers bring adequate academic knowledge to their professional training is very low and getting lower. Even the modest GPA requirements to enter teacher preparation programs are often not respected.[68] The perennial need for teachers results in minimal demands on teacher preparation; states virtually compete to lower the barriers of entry into the profession.[69] But even if student teachers were coming to schools of education with adequate academic preparation, it would still be incumbent on those schools to ensure those future teachers to be guided by that academic content and teach it effectively.

ASSESSMENTS

"[High-performing school systems] typically have very tough examination systems . . . the goalposts are very clear."[70]

The progressive movement produced strong support for the use of IQ tests in schools in contrast to the use of subject-matter-based assessments. In its attack on fixed bodies of content knowledge, progressivism also helped to undermine the case for the rigorous testing of students' content knowledge, for it zealously championed the idea that no such content could be required in advance. (Recall that for Dewey and his progressivist colleagues, students construct knowledge based on their passions, not on a predefined body of knowledge established by teachers or test makers.)

The legacy of progressivism on our contemporary assessment regime is complex. We see it in the continued use of the SAT aptitude test, but equally and more importantly, in the fact that our subject matter tests are far weaker than those in most peer countries:

1. Our state tests are not linked to a specific academic curriculum.
2. Tests rely heavily on questions that call for multiple responses and short ("constructed") responses.
3. In ELA—and even in many social studies—our assessments test skills ("find the main idea"), not knowledge of the subject matter.
4. There are usually few consequences for students performing well or poorly on these tests.

Research shows that when tests are used as part of a focus on teaching rigorous content, they send important signals. Tim Oates, who led the redesign of England's national curriculum and assessment, is blunt about the importance of assessments, arguing that there is zero evidence from anywhere in the world that abandoning content assessments, or not adopting them, creates higher academic outcomes.[71]

In advancing this argument, Oates makes two assumptions. First, that a country's tests will assess a national curriculum, and second, that these tests are well designed, with what he calls "good questions" that prompt students to explore ideas in depth.[72] In the United States, the first assumption doesn't apply, and the second one isn't met: American state assessments are largely skills-based tests with no curriculum connections and poor questions. The remainder of this section digs into this country's assessment regime to show why we have arrived at this unfortunate practice.

First, the sheer number of tests the United States administers is surprising. The Council of the Great City Schools estimated in 2015 that a child going through the American K-12 public-school system takes, on average, 112 standardized tests.[73] But the numbers alone are not the key. Rather, it is that these tests are of many kinds and send many different signals:

- The SAT/ACT: aptitude tests.
- MAP and iReady: assessments of skills in math and ELA. The MAP test is norm-referenced (students are measured against each other's performance), while iReady is criterion-referenced (students are graded relative to a fixed performance standard). Together, these tests are taken

by almost 50 percent of America's students during their K-12 years, but neither test is required by any state or higher-education institution.

- State tests: usually aligned to skills-based state standards. Federal law requires math and ELA tests annually from grades 3–8 and once in high school, as well as periodic science tests. Passing such tests is not required for high-school graduation in most states.
- AP tests: subject-matter tests that enable students to skip freshman year, or at least some freshman courses, if they earn an approved score.
- Curriculum-based diagnostic tests used to place students into different groups and/or to differentiate instruction. For example, the increasingly popular Zearn math curriculum includes these tests prior to each unit.

The result of this proliferation of tests is that teachers are often awash in data that gives them different, sometimes conflicting, information.[74]

Second, many of these tests are designed in ways that create a reasonable spread of results, not to establish if the students have acquired important content knowledge. Some sense of psychometrics, the "science" of test design, is key to grasping why this is the case. Sam Wineberg, a professor of education at Stanford, shows that large-scale tests rely on a mathematical technique known as the "biserial correlation" such that each test item is linked mathematically to students' total scores. Individual items that do not conform to the overall test pattern are eliminated from the final version.[75]

How does this work in practice? Imagine a question about *Crisis* magazine, which W. E. B. Du Bois edited, that is answered correctly at higher rates by black students than by whites, but that overall, white students outscore black students on the test as a whole. The resulting correlation for the *Crisis* magazine question would be zero or negative, and the question would almost certainly be wrongly thrown out—wrongly because it is clearly worth asking.

Technically, this way of including or throwing out questions is necessary only in normed-based assessments (such as the MAP or SAT), where it is necessary to create a wide distribution of student results. Such tests rank each student against all other test takers irrespective of the overall performance of those test takers. By contrast, state assessments and the NAEP test are "criterion referenced" or "standards-based." This means that, hypothetically, every student should be able to reach the passing standard or better simply depending on the percentage of the questions answered correctly. In these kinds of tests, designers *should* be able to ask them the questions that matter—such as a question about *Crisis* magazine in a social studies test.

But the practices of biserial correlations are so ingrained in psychometric (test design) culture that for all intents and purposes, the construction of even criterion-referenced tests follow Wineberg's outline. This was confirmed by Steven Koffler, an administrator with the NAEP program that designed the

1987 history test, who reported that traditional item analysis and biserial correlations were used to create that supposedly standards-based test.[76]

Wineberg draws out the important consequence of creating tests in which questions are chosen to fit a performance curve. Using social studies assessments as his example, he points out that beyond handicapping students who may have historical knowledge their more generally high-scoring peers do not, it is simply not possible for all students to do well.[77]

Wineberg's technical criticism of test designs points to a more general problem. Our so called "high-stakes" tests have implications for schools and in some states for a small number of teachers. A school that performs especially poorly must be targeted by the state for intervention by its district. US assessments are thus designed to serve as a source of performance management for adults, which engenders an overemphasis on reliability because people's jobs depend on the results of the tests. Psychometricians have to come up with a design that grounds accountability systems as well as tests academic learning. As Wineberg suggests, the resulting tests favor the first purpose and undermine the second.

To add to the testing design issues, the question of what constitutes passing the test varies from year to year with the same test. Each year, state education commissioners can find themselves in the position of deciding the cut-off score that will separate passing from failing the test. While the theory is that a student taking the test this year would pass or fail exactly as she would have the previous year (assuming she had identical knowledge and skills), in practice, there is considerable leeway. In New York State, the commissioner's discretion enabled him to dictate that the pass rate on a state math test in 2010 be raised or lowered by some eight percentile points, which involved the passing or failing of thousands of students on that test.

There are further problems with US tests. ELA assessments do not test what students have read. As noted above, since teachers are largely creating their own playlists of materials, no standard curriculum can be assumed, much less tested. Instead, a typical state test will present a set of blocks of text that the student is asked to read and then decipher. Those chunks of text can be drawn anywhere from an original piece of literature to texts invented by assessment designers. Even in the former case, the chances the student has seen the text before are made remote to ensure that no student is unfairly advantaged. Instead, students are tested on the so-called skills of "finding the main idea" in a text the student has never before encountered. (There will be a full discussion of this issue in the next chapter.)

But what this means is that there is no incentive for any American ELA teacher to dig deeply into any particular text. Sliding over the surface of many texts doesn't serve students well, since they are less likely to add the knowledge gleaned from those texts to long-term memory. It is difficult to persuade teachers to slow down and unpack a complex work knowing that her or his students will never be tested on that work.

One should not assume this is only an ELA-assessment issue. Many state assessments in social studies likewise undermine the incentive to teach content, Take, as an example, the 2021 eleventh-grade social studies assessment designed by one of the largest US testing companies, Pearson, for the state of Delaware.[78] Apart from the fact that some of the questions are both juvenile and confusing at the same time (see figure 3.2 for an example), the most striking fact about the assessment is that no prior historical knowledge is actually assumed: The information needed to answer the question is in the question stem. In short, the test is far more a reading test than a history test.

The next problem—still more destructive of learning—is that in most cases, tests don't matter to the students taking them. Most countries tie their public examinations to important consequences: In Germany, performance on the Abitur—taken at the end of secondary education—enables university placement. The same is true with baccalaureate exams in France and the A-Level (advanced level qualifications) assessment in England. In the United States, where graduation from high school rarely depends on passing

Social Studies

1. This headline is about an action by a citizens' group.

Which step is **most important** for the citizens' group to achieve its goal?

A. Seeking suggestions for rally locations from participants

B. Communicating rules for public demonstrations to participants

C. Asking participants to wear the same color of clothing at the rally

D. Expecting participants to carry signs printed with a common slogan

Figure 3.2. Testing Social Studies "Knowledge." *Delaware System of Student Assessments, "2021 Grade 11 Social Studies Training Test," https://de.testnav.com/client/index.html#.*

an exam, even entry into state schools rests largely on course grades. The idea that teachers and schools be held responsible for the results of tests in which most students have nothing at stake is unique to the United States.

Finally, the traditional role of tests is now under critique. By definition, tests discriminate, which is simply to say that students with different levels of skill and knowledge score differently. But today, test designers have begun to question if this needs to be so. Already, American reading tests don't use vocabulary that certain students are less likely to have encountered than others. Thus, the word "yacht" is not permissible, because inner-city underprivileged students might never have encountered it. By omitting such words, the tests reduce performance differences but also signal to America's ELA teachers that underprivileged students need not strive to enlarge their vocabularies.[79]

More recently, test designers have imagined more major changes to assessments—but not in the direction of strong academic learning. On March 4, 2021, the governing board of the NAEP held a symposium on how students' varying background knowledge should be addressed in the forthcoming 2025 NAEP English Language Arts assessment.

A proposal from the board to change the framework of the reading section contained a radically new conception of testing. The new test places reading skills into a model that positions the reader and the text in a sociocultural context. The proposal contributors pointed out that while readers exercise their reading skills on diverse texts and for different purposes, those readers themselves are also diversified, each one "positioned" by sociocultural background, thus bringing a different but equally "authentic" set of reading skills to the test.

Given the assumption that students from different backgrounds bring *legitimately* different readiness to understand the passages on the exam, the new NAEP framework would try to equalize—as far as possible—the capacity of each student to understand the texts in the assessment so that the differences of what we usually call reading skills don't predetermine students' test results. The outcome? NAEP will "optimize the performance of the widest possible population of students in the NAEP Reading Assessment."[80]

This is Orwellian language. The proposed NAEP design tries to minimize the impact of formal education and undermine incentives for students to become fluent readers of a wide range of texts. The test design treats each student's culturally determined reading ability as equally valid, providing extra assistance to test-takers who need that help to understand the reading passages in the assessment.

Rather than allowing poor performance to serve as a signal that large knowledge gaps should be fixed through better education, however, the test would instead greatly reduce the impact of background knowledge on the reported test performance.[81] But, as the next chapter will show, deeper and broader background knowledge is what enables students to become good readers. A test of reading that removes the impact of background knowledge from what is tested would send exactly the wrong message to our nation's ELA teachers.

In the face of concentrated push-back, that draft proposal was eventually withdrawn, replaced by a second version that—while it removed the language about optimizing the performance of all students—still points to supplying greater support to equalize the playing field. The point of including the example is to serve as a warning: If the nation's gold standard assessment of educational attainment can flirt with approaches that render that test meaningless, the future of assessment is in fundamental doubt.

SIGNS OF HOPE?

The preceding discussion of curricula, teacher training, and assessments describes the great majority of current practices in the United States, but there are counterexamples, and they are important to note since they show that progress is possible.

The Rebirth of the Curriculum

In the last decade, we have seen the first stirrings of a reaction to the pervasive practice of teacher-curated instructional materials. First came the Common Core State Standards (CCSS) in ELA and Math in 2010, an effort endorsed by forty-one states to define what students should be able to do in those two subjects. While no state still calls their standards by that name, very few of those who adopted the CCSS have changed them substantively. More recently, efforts to integrate these skills-based standards into new, content-rich, academically rigorous curriculum are expanding.

For example, as part of its successful application for federal education funds under the "Race to the Top" competition, New York State was able to launch content-rich, free, online ELA and math curricula that was known as EngageNY.[82] Within a few years after EngageNY was launched, the RAND Corporation reported more than one hundred million downloads of it, with 30 percent of math teachers and more than 25 percent of English/language arts teachers nationally accessing the materials.[83] More recently still, an ever-greater number of ELA curricula have been published that are less skills-based and more akin to the McGuffey Readers—curriculum centered on the reading of high-quality texts.

Recent support for the importance of strong published curricular materials comes from the education research community. Compelling findings suggest that when teachers use such materials with fidelity, learning rises.[84] Since 2017, CCSSO (the Council for Chief State School Officers) has supported a group of twelve states through their High-Quality Instructional Materials and Professional Development (IMPD) Network.[85]

These states are committed to moving their respective public-school districts to use what are now called HQIM—high quality, content-rich instructional materials. From personal experience with advising in this initiative, it is clear there is still a long way to go. However, in Louisiana, Tennessee, and Mississippi, there has been some real progress, with the percentage of districts using HQIM rising steadily.[86]

Attention to Teacher Training

As in the case of curriculum, there is some modest push-back to the generally low-level expectations and practices of most teacher preparation programs. Organizations such as Deans for Impact and the National Center for Teacher Quality (NCTQ) have urged schools of education—with some success—to adopt the science of reading and other research-based practices in teacher training. NCTQ has pressed programs not to water-down entrance standards.[87]

When it comes to the crucial clinical elements of teacher preparation, there is evidence of a move from single semester to full-year clinical experiences, with both Louisiana and Maryland committed to shifting teacher preparation programs to a full-year requirement.

The most advanced work in raising the caliber of clinically based preparation has been done in Massachusetts. The state's requirements for clinical training include a set of observational assessments that stress "well-structured lessons with challenging tasks and measurable outcomes; appropriate student engagement strategies, pacing, sequence, resources, and grouping; purposeful questioning such that students are able to learn the knowledge and skills defined in state standards/local curricula."[88] It is not clear whether anyone fails these assessments, but they are at least a start. It remains to be seen if other states will upgrade their own requirements in the years to come.

Finally, there is some preliminary attention to training future teachers to understand, value, and use high quality curriculum. The CCSSO's IMPD fourteen-state consortium referenced above has recently included policy advocacy for including what I have termed "curriculum literacy" in teacher training. The idea is that instead of teaching future teachers to regard self-created curriculum as the preferred and only authentic pedagogical strategy, schools of education would instruct future teachers on the value of adopting and using high-quality published curriculum.[89] Once again, it is too early to determine if this fledgling effort will achieve national traction.

Assessments

As in the case of curriculum and teacher preparation, there is some recent, albeit more modest, progress. First, there is now US-based research that confirms the efficacy of integrating assessments with curriculum. Evidence from Chicago's use of the Diploma Program of the International Baccalaureate, in which a strong curriculum comes with its own rigorous assessment, shows very positive long-term educational outcomes for disadvantaged students.[90]

On a larger scale, and thanks to a provision in the federal ESSA (Every Student Succeeds Act) legislation, a few states have been able to rethink the designs of their tests. One such state, Louisiana, has supported the creation and early implementation of two ELA-curriculum integrated tests.[91] John White, the former superintendent of instruction for Louisiana, is about to release initial data suggesting that teachers and students find the new format compelling.

Teachers who are now able to instruct students on the texts and knowledge that will then appear in the ELA state assessments. This is creating an incentive to teach those texts in depth. Paired with the fact that students are now tested at the end of each unit of study instead of just once at the end of the year, these new assessments are proving popular with teachers and students alike.[92]

Most importantly, White has found that teachers have changed their pedagogy to focus more deeply on the knowledge that they know students will need to succeed on the new assessments. Recently, a consortium of test-design teams (drawn from the Johns Hopkins Institute of Education Policy, CenterPoint, New Meridian, NorthWest Evaluation Association (NWEA) and the National Center for Assessment (NCIEA)) has been brought together by Education First (an education policy and research think tank) to build on the Louisiana example.

The challenge is to design content-based state assessments that will cover multiple curricula in ELA and math from the ground up. These efforts have the potential to shift assessment design more generally to a model that supports strong curricular content and rewards knowledge-focused pedagogy.

SCHOOLS

Good schools are hard to create and nurture, for they require relationships of trust, challenge, and respect, qualities that take time to develop. These values become embedded in institutions as part of the common ground that unites the members of the schools.[93]

Contemporary American curricula, pedagogy, and assessments each bear the imprint of progressivism, and each one impacts student educational experiences and learning outcomes. One can be so focused on these specific elements, however, as to forget a key educational element: the school itself, its norms, values, and practices. One reason research tends not to focus on the school as a subject of analysis is the common assumption that a large proportion of differences in educational outcomes is due to students' socioeconomic backgrounds—regardless of the school students attend. There is certainly strong research supporting that assumption.[94] If schools are filled with underprivileged children, we simply assume poor academic outcomes.

But this is not by any means the full story. A careful look at the data suggests that this generalization misses a crucial point: It is true that when overall school performances are compared, students' economic background is strongly correlated with differences of performance between schools (i.e., schools with higher percentages of wealthier students do much better), but those correlations are based on averaging the academic outcomes of students in each school. When we look inside individual schools, "It turns out that between-school variation accounts for 20 percent of the variation in student performance in the United States, but within-school variation accounts for about 80 percent."

The data from the United States are especially striking since out of the sixty-nine nations that took the PISA tests, just eight have as much within-school variation as the United States.[95] Figure 3.3 presents supporting data from the international PISA tests given by the OECD. Referencing this data, Andreas Schleicher noted that while many American education analysts focus on the difference between schools, that difference is dwarfed by within-school performance variation.[96]

Macrostatistics of this kind must be interpreted carefully. Many countries funnel students based on their academic outcomes into distinct school types despite all of them being what Americans would call "public schools." As a result, fewer intraschool performance differences might be expected in each school. One obvious example is Germany, where fifth-grade students are sorted into four very distinct school types.

The United States also sorts students but does so by grouping them by academic results and then tracking them within a single school.[97] Nevertheless, American schools in general are made up of students of similar socioeconomic backgrounds. Due to the tight linkages between wealth, race, zip code, and school attendance, the actual variation of performance in American public schools should be considerably smaller in comparison to the rest of the world than the data suggest.[98]

Variation in reading performance between and within schools, and variation explained by the school's socio-economic intake as a percentage of the variance in student performance in PISA (2009)

⬚ Total between-school variance

▨ Between-school variance explained by the PISA index of economic, social and cultural status of students and schools

▨ Total within-school variance

▪ Within-school variance explained by the PISA index of economic, social and cultural status of students and schools

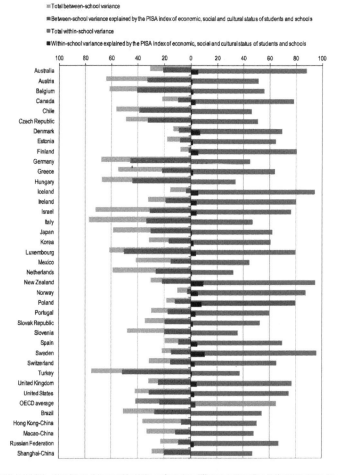

How to read this chart: This chart shows the extent to which performance differences in reading between students are explained by the school that they attend (between school variance) or by other factors (within school variance). The variance in performance is shown with and without taking into account the socio-economic background of students and schools. In Finland, for example, most of the variance in performance observed is within schools rather than between them, which indicates that schools have similar achievement levels and do not select students by academic ability. Differences in the socio-economic background of schools account for a small proportion of the already-small performance differences between schools, which suggest that there is little segregation along socio-economic lines. Non OECD member economies are included for comparison.

Figure 3.3. Reading Performance: National Variations in Inter- and Intraschool Effectiveness. *PISA 2009 Results: Overcoming Social Background: Equity in Learning Opportunities and Outcomes (Volume 11), OECD, Paris.*

Nor is the outsized variation in in-school achievement adequately explained by the high level of socioeconomic segregation in American schools. Recent research using extensive Florida data indicates that regardless of whether a school is made up of affluent or poor students, the large gaps in the performance of students within a given school are virtually the same. The same is true of racial achievement/opportunity gaps: "the portion of the Black–White achievement gap attributed to within-school differences in achievement was larger than the portion attributed to between-school differences."[99]

There is disagreement as to the potential impact of increasing the level of socioeconomic integration in schools. Some argue it is in unlikely to reduce the test score gap,[100] but on balance, the arguments favor doing so—children do learn from each other's experiences, and mixing children of very different economic backgrounds deepens that learning. There is no doubt that under-privileged children of color benefit from attending schools that are economically and racially integrated.[101]

There are a variety of explanations for why American intraschool outcomes show such large differences. One strong candidate is school culture: The more practices and beliefs in a school are integrated and pervasive across most aspects of teaching, discipline, and socialization, the greater the positive impact on student learning is likely to be.[102]

The most famous evidence supporting this thesis has been James Coleman's longitudinal report "High School and Beyond."[103] The study found that sophomores and seniors at Catholic schools outperformed their public-school peers by roughly a full grade level after controlling for family background. It also found that achievement gaps along lines of parental education, race, and ethnicity were smaller in Catholic schools than in public schools. Coleman concluded with some irony that "Catholic schools more nearly approximate the 'common school' ideal of American education than do public schools."[104]

Coleman's findings have since been challenged, both in a sophisticated reanalysis of the data Coleman used, and in an extensive review of NAEP results.[105] One careful meta-analysis concludes that "most studies [of the impact of school culture] do not provide a basis for deducing a directional influence and causal relations."[106] Correlational evidence suggests that there is no straight line between strongly defined school cultures and stronger academic results: The Netherlands publicly funds thirty-six different kinds of school, giving families a highly varied set of educational choices between schools that embody distinct cultures. All the students take the same national test, but the schools that prepare them for that test varyimmensely.

As Ashley Berner, an education professor at Johns Hopkins has argued, there are multiple grounds—political, cultural, and social—on which to find the pluralistic structure of Dutch schooling compelling, but Dutch academic results as measured by the PISA assessment are highly disparate—strong in math and weak in reading.[107]

Perhaps the best argument for the connection between overall school culture and academic outcomes is the performance of low-income African

American students in schools run by a few charter management organizations in some of our largest cities. In a 2015 report, Stanford University researchers found that students enrolled in urban charter schools outperformed similar students in traditional public schools by 0.055 of a standard deviation in math and 0.039 in reading. (That's the equivalent of forty and twenty-eight more days of school a year, respectively.[108]) Further research supports the Stanford findings: Compared to the typical inner-city regular public school, the majority of urban public charter schools do show better results.

Is this outcome due to aspects of school culture? Researchers who dug into this question found that the three factors that best explain the comparatively strong charter school learning gains were teacher feedback, intensive tutoring, and high suspension rates. They also found that the most commonly attributed explanation of strong charter school performance—high expectations—didn't make a measurable difference.

In other words, two of the three most salient factors explaining the positive impact of urban charter schools on student outcomes have to do with teaching. Suspension rates—a facet of school culture and not of pedagogy—were the least important of the three factors, failing to reach statistical significance.[109] The researchers conclude that by far the most important impact was provided by intensive tutoring.[110]

Given these various findings, what can we say about school culture? As previously noted, Tony Bryk stressed the importance of a safe, supportive environment and good communications with parents—two elements that have much to do with strong principals. There is evidence that these factors contribute to an open school climate that, in turn, positively impacts later civic outcomes.[111] But overall, there is little doubt that most of the school effect on students' academic achievement is the degree to which it impacts the daily pedagogic behavior of teachers: their expectations, methods, and choice of instructional materials.

When a school puts a shared commitment to instructional excellence at the heart of its cultural identity, everyone benefits: A 2012 study by the New Teacher Project found that teachers confirmed that it was their shared values and their sense of being fully supported by their principal that mattered for student performance.[112] The study further found that that schools that focused on a cohesive *instructional* culture retained more of their top teachers and had far higher proficiency rates in both reading and math than schools that did not.

In the end, what happens inside a school certainly matters, but it matters mostly because it impacts teacher practice. The key problem is that in so many American schools there is usually no consistency of effective instruction across the instructional staff. As a result, children must depend on luck in finding themselves in a classroom with effective teachers in any given year. The only effective path forward is to equip schools with principals who value the use of high-quality curriculum and to prepare teachers to share that commitment.

CONCLUSION

An effective education system minimally includes the following components:

- Teachers well prepared to value and thus to teach a rigorous curriculum
- Curricula that are matched with assessments that test the content of that curriculum
- Assessments that matter to students

In short, an effective education system integrates teacher practices, instructional materials, and assessments. This is the coherence triangle without which educational progress at scale is difficult to achieve. These components may not seem groundbreaking, but they have been nearly impossible in the American K-12 system. Given the American structure of education governance, progress toward a coherent educational system is—at least for now—unlikely to come from Washington, DC. Instead, individual states must lead the way, as we have seen in Massachusetts and, more recently, in Louisiana, Tennessee, and Mississippi. Across many other states, however, progress toward coherence has been slow or nonexistent.

The message to the United States is clear. If poorly prepared teachers—often focused on nonacademic outcomes—make up and teach their own curriculum, there can be little hope of raising national levels of learning outcomes. If assessments are dissociated from curriculum materials and don't matter to the children who take them, we cannot expect students to study academic content with much vigor. If principals have neither the training nor the authority to reduce the pedagogical performance differences between strong and weak teachers, there will be no consistency of learning levels in any given school. All three conditions are today a reality in the great majority of America's public schools.

Chapter 4

Basic Skills

The "Main Idea" in K-12 Education

Perhaps the most challenging dilemma for teachers today is that routine cognitive skills, the skills that are easiest to teach and easiest to test, are also the skills that are easiest to digitize, automate, and outsource.[1]

A coherent education system—one in which teacher preparation, curriculum, assessments, and school culture align—is the foundation of best practices in education students at home and abroad. However, the United States has created a fragmented system in which tests are unrelated to content, teachers curate their own materials with no adequate preparation to do so, and schools are filled with teachers of very different efficacies. Inside that system, teachers must resist the seductive claims of multiple distractors: Teachers have to maintain a belief in the importance of academic instruction and competing educational goals, including ameliorating racial disparities in learning outcomes and focusing on career and technical education.

Together, these multiple factors would be more than sufficient to describe a system in serious trouble, but there are further forces that impact what happens in America's classrooms, forces that act directly on what teachers are likely to teach. Most especially in our middle and high schools, those forces press teachers toward a lowest-common denominator, namely, the teaching of basic skills across all grade levels—especially in ELA.

What are these forces? The chapter starts by discussing the SAT (and, by extension, the ACT), which often serves to weaken the teaching of academic content. The focus then turns to academic instruction itself: What do we ask American ELA teachers to teach? Answering that question leads to a consideration of the skills of reading as they are now taught and tested in the United States. The argument will be that those skills embody an impoverished understanding of education that benefits no one—neither the teachers who are required to narrow their focus to often mindless instruction, nor the students who are understandably bored by their schooling.

THE SAT AND ACT

Until very recently, the American pathway from the K-12 system to higher education passed almost inevitably through the SAT (or, more recently, the ACT). The test in its modern incarnation was expressly created to provide poorer students who lacked access to strong academic teaching a more equitable route to college.[2] The SAT was thus originally designed to mimic IQ scores so as not to depend on the level of a student's mastery of subject matter learning but on that student's native "aptitude."

The College Board has since attempted to reinvent the test (the A in SAT was changed from "aptitude" to "assessment"; later, the name "SAT" was redefined to mean just that, the three letters S-A-T). Regardless of the relabeling, as research from Meredith Fry confirms, the SAT remains highly correlated to IQ and even more closely correlated to G—the measure of general intelligence.[3] Understandably, this correlation isn't much advertised, nor is the similar high correlation (.77) between the ACT and G.[4] The key fact is that the SAT and ACT remain primarily aptitude tests. As Fry points out after once again going through the extensive research record, to deny that they do not measure aptitude is simply false.

But because the modern SAT test remains so heavily an intelligence test, classroom study and even intensive tutoring for the SAT, on average, make a modest difference in test results. Students can become more familiar with the test format and brush-up on some vocabulary and relevant math skills, but a review of the research on prep work for the SAT shows consistently that prep work has only a small impact on scores.[5]

Further, the SAT and the ACT do a poor job of predicting overall college performance. In 2003, Jesse Rothstein, a professor at Princeton, argued that traditional measures of SAT predictive powers had been seriously overestimated.[6] More recently, researchers confirm the very low correlations of SAT and ACT scores with college grades.

In figure 4.1, both tests are compared to the predictive power of an older Massachusetts test (the MCAS) and with the later PARCC assessment, a test developed to align to the Common Core State Standards. For readers who expect to see a strong relationship between the SAT and college performance, these data will come as a shock. It shows a very low correlation between these two tests and college grades—even lower than the two included state-level assessments.[7]

The conclusions for a system of education are rather stark: If a key gateway to higher education is based on an aptitude assessment in which the lottery of wealth[8] and intelligence is the strongest predictor of results, then education in academic knowledge has essentially been a side-product to the

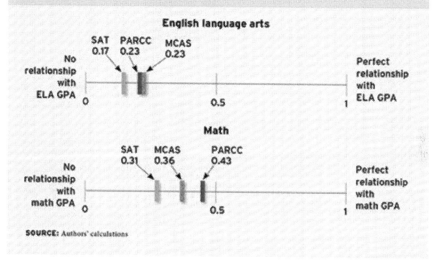

Figure 4.1. High School Tests: Correlations with College Performance. *https://www.educationnext.org/testing-college-readiness-massachusetts-parcc-mcas-standardized-tests/.*

most sought-after goal of K-12 education, namely access to higher education. Teachers and students might conclude that content knowledge building becomes an inessential part of schooling. It doesn't matter if we measure students by their parents' income, by students' general intelligence, their SAT/ACT scores, or the prestige of their higher education diplomas—all of these measures are strongly correlated, and all produce credentials that are strongly correlated with economic success. By contrast, none of these measures directly encourage the study of academic content in the classroom.

As indicated earlier, as gateways tests for college entrance, the SAT and ACT are currently in serious trouble, with hundreds of colleges and universities making them optional as admission criteria.[9] On the assumption that building academic knowledge is a core educational value, this could be a positive development. If students know that their academic course work has become more important, then surely American education will be put on a stronger track.

TEACHING THE BASIC SKILLS

Reality is not so simple, however. When we examine what American students learn in their classrooms, it isn't clear how much educational value will be added by their doing more of the same. Unpacking current instructional practices in ELA will illustrate why this is the case, and the focus on ELA in the following pages is justified because the ability to read is one of the best academic predictors of overall academic performance and life-time prospects.[10] Reading is also not simply an ELA skill; it carries over into the study of social studies and, perhaps surprisingly, to science and mathematics. Nevertheless, given the importance of reading in American K-12 education, the chapter will close with a brief consideration of where American K-12 education stands in math education and suggest an important similarity with ELA.[11]

As we review the teaching of ELA, it is helpful to distinguish between elementary and secondary education. From 1998 through the first decade or so of this century, America made some modest progress in teaching literacy and numeracy skills to young children.[12] This modest progress then stopped, but very recently, there have been some small but encouraging signs of progress. Some twenty years after the National Reading Panel urged the country to move in this direction, the adoption of "science of reading" practices (a focus on phonics, phonemic awareness, vocabulary, and fluency that together make up comprehension skills) is finally rising.

More schools of education are teaching it to future teachers. Mississippi, traditionally a state with weak levels of reading proficiency, has shown progress just a few years after retooling its reading instruction. In the NAEP's fourth-grade reading results, Mississippi rose from a ranking of forty-ninth in 2013 to twenty-ninth in 2019.[13]

THE "SKILLS OF READING"

The Common Core State Standards (CCSS) rightly place the mastery of phonetics, decoding, and other aspects of reading comprehension at the heart of the early grade-level instruction. Research overwhelmingly confirms that this is how students should be taught to read. But when it comes to the next step—reading to learn—something very distinct occurs. Building on the notion of decoding skills that make reading possible, David Coleman, the key architect of the ELA CCSS together with his colleagues, created a new set of reading skills for the nation's children that builds seamlessly on decoding. These new CCSS skills are designed to enable students to detect the crucial elements in any text and learn, in Coleman's words, to "read like a detective." [14]

Two of the most used words in the CCSS reading standards are "analyze" (as in "analyze a particular point of view") and "determine" (as in "determine a theme or central idea of the text").[15] The language used is deliberately empirical and sounds vaguely scientific. Moreover, that language keeps repeating itself. What is striking about the CCSS standards in reading is that they barely change in later grades. Students in fifth grade must "determine the meaning of words and phrases as they are used in a text, including figurative language such as metaphors and similes." Five years later, they must be able to "determine the meaning of words and phrases as they are used in the text, including figurative and connotative meanings."[16]

High-school seniors should be able to "determine two or more themes or central ideas of a text and analyze their development over the course of the text, including how they interact and build on one another to produce a complex account; provide an objective summary of the text." Seven years earlier, they were expected to "determine a theme of a story, drama, or poem from details in the text, including how characters in a story or drama respond to challenges or how the speaker in a poem reflects upon a topic; summarize the text."

Over the years of schooling, these skills don't change in any substantive way. The mastery of these skills is honed by requiring children to exercise them repetitively on more complex texts. But complexity here is not equated with subject matter, as in the difference between *Charlotte's Web* and Tolstoy's *War and Peace*. In practice, the determination of complexity is usually established by referencing the Lexile rating of a text. A Lexile rating is a measure of the difficulty of vocabulary. The Lexile measure is completely agnostic about both the content and the quality of any given texts. It tries to predict how difficult a work is to comprehend by measuring just two variables—word frequency and sentence length.[17]

Alongside the Lexile measurement itself, curriculum designers and teachers can consult a raft of other metrics that measure text difficulty, including Fleisch-Kincaid, Degrees of Reading Power, and Pearson Reading Maturity Metric. But they all offer slightly different versions of essentially the same thing as the Lexile levels. The practical consequence of all this is that the CCSS exert little to no pressure on schools to teach high-quality texts.

The idea that readers should act as detectives sifting through textual clues to determine the main idea(s) is an engaging notion, but this should not obscure the fundamental conceit. It is arresting that America's children are to be taught that books or articles should be treated as a crime scene to be solved. Even allowing Coleman a graceful exit from his detective vocabulary, what remains is an inescapably forensic conception of reading—one in which interpretation is rendered as a skill of uncovering based on the assumption of a stable truth to be laid bare, stripped, presumably, of any lingering ambiguity or uncertainty. What does it mean to "solve" a novel? Coleman's model assumes that behind any text there is a singular and transparent meaning to be found.

Coleman rejects the arguments of many decades of literary theorists who have suggested that words do not come with their meanings visibly and unproblematically attached. He downplays the views of historicists who argued that in many cases, we cannot understand texts unless we read them through the social, intellectual, and economic circumstances in which the text was written. He shrugs off the arguments of deconstructionists who argue that the written word is essentially ambiguous, of feminists who see gender as a powerful, even decisive factor in the way meaning has been constructed, and of "postcolonial" critics who find racial and Western value systems at play in multiple works of fiction as well as nonfiction.

Instead, we are assured, words mean just what they say. (In theoretical terms, Coleman is evoking an approach to interpreting literature known as "the New Criticism"—a view that what counts most is exactly what—and only what—is written on the page and looks to nothing outside the text. But the CCSS embodies a drastically reductive version of that interpretive model.)[18]

One could plausibly respond that teachers teaching books to teenagers should not be burdened with anything as complicated as competing theories of interpretation. But Coleman's use of the "detective" simile takes us to the opposite extreme, oversimplifying the act of reading when it comes to middle and high-school students.

The publishers' guidelines to the CCSS tells us that "student knowledge drawn from the text is demonstrated when the student uses evidence from the text to support a claim about the text. Hence evidence and knowledge link directly to the text."[19] In other words, no external information is needed; one can apparently decipher *The Divine Comedy* without knowing anything about the idioms (symbolic, theological, historical, allegorical) of Dante's work.

Second, the CCSS's forensic approach to reading assumes that the reader either successfully "solves" the riddles of a text or fails to do so. This is a view of reading skills ideally suited to the multiple-choice style of assessment. Hamlet was slow to avenge his father's death because of reason A, B, C, or D; circle the correct response. It enables test makers to decide in advance what a text means and then assess if the student can come up with the same finding.

The hope seems to be that a good reader can be equated with a scientist or mathematician. In fact, as the discussion later in this chapter suggests, the skill sets appropriate to more expertise in mathematics are complex, involving conceptual understanding, procedural fluency, strategic competence, and adaptive reasoning.[20] It is simplistic to see math as mechanistic. The great mathematician Harold Hardy wrote, "A mathematician, like a painter or poet, is a maker of patterns. The mathematician's patterns, like the painter's or poet's, must be *beautiful*. Beauty is the first test: there is no permanent place in the world for ugly mathematics."[21]

But the United States does not test children on the aesthetics of mathematics. Perhaps it is fair to say that at the level of K-12 math learning, the growing ability to tackle more complex mathematical problems, using more sophisticated mathematical tools, can be called the mastery of a set of forensic skills.

THE ACQUISITION OF "KNOWLEDGE"

To be clear, the key requirement that students master the skills of textual detection doesn't comprise the total of the reading standards. To avoid political controversy, the CCSS do not require the reading of anything specific beyond the American foundational documents and texts, and something from Shakespeare.

But the CCSS standards do at one point make clear that students need to exercise their reading skills on a variety of content. The standards state that only by reading texts in history, social studies, science, and other disciplines can students build the knowledge that not only introduces them to other academic fields but also exposes them more generally to the background knowledge that will enable them to be better readers across all content areas. Thus, while the CCSS don't offer any content for designing any specific ELA curriculum, they do point to the importance of rich content knowledge.[22]

The singular reminder that fluency in reading is not only about honing a forensic skill but also about accumulating knowledge is directly indebted to the life teachings of E. D. Hirsch, best known for his writings about cultural literacy. Hirsch's principal argument has been that reading fluency depends on a student's acquisition of a common body of knowledge. An expanding knowledge committed to memory, Hirsch maintains, acts as a reservoir of meanings that enables students successfully to understand passages with new vocabulary and information.[23] In short, if a student knows about the game of baseball, she or he will likely be far more successful at comprehending a text about baseball even if some of the vocabulary is new.[24]

In Hirsch's view, while mastery of decoding is essential when learning to read, it isn't enough to create fluent readers. Mastering basic reading skills is necessary, but without the acquisition of knowledge about the world, students will never be adequately equipped to read more than elementary texts without massive difficulties. Books and essays written for more advanced readers presuppose a level of background knowledge. Without that knowledge, students encountering a text about a subject they know nothing or little about will have to stop, go back, and study the relevant subject matter.

Hirsch could hardly be more direct: Students' "knowledge deficit is the major reason their reading comprehension scores remain low."[25] The research support for this claim is overwhelming supportive: Students in more affluent systems demonstrate more success in skill-based ELA assessments not because they are better at recognizing "main ideas" but because they are far more likely to know more about the subject matter discussed in any given text. [26]

Why exactly is building background knowledge so important? To simplify a complex matter, students become more effective readers as they build knowledge by successfully storing it in long-term memory. When they need to make sense of an otherwise incomprehensible text, they retrieve a relevant element of that background knowledge from that storehouse into their working memory.[27] Take as an example the following sentence: "Number eleven made a right mess of that googly—he probably thought it was a leg-spinner."

For most American readers, this makes no sense. But if one has childhood memories of playing school cricket in England, there will be recollection as to what a googly is, and that memory will be summoned to enable comprehension of the sentence. Even if one cannot remember any of the details (that a googly is delivered by the back of the hand and thus is disguised as a leg-spinner, which is why the number eleven batsman, usually the weakest on the team, probably messed it up), a British reader will be far closer to understanding the entire passage than the typical American reader.[28]

More recently, Hirsch has added new urgency to his call that we teach students core content about their world—its history, geography, literature, arts, and science. Hirsch (amplifying on the views of Amy Guttman, cited in this book's opening pages) argues that the accumulation of this knowledge is about more than reading fluently—it is also about the survival of American democracy. Only through the acquisition of a substantive body of knowledge about the historical and political values of the United States can children grow up able to participate in the discourse of democratic life. Most importantly, Hirsch argues, American citizens need to understand and value the foundational principles of American constitutionalism lest civic life collapse into fractious discord.[29]

Coleman is right to insist on the importance of teaching decoding skills in early education. Hirsch is correct that building a storehouse of knowledge is indispensable—both for reading fluency and for effective, participatory citizenship.[30] Yet just as Coleman erred in putting forensic skills at the core of reading mastery for all students, Hirsch's persuasive overarching claim about the importance of background knowledge is also flawed.

Consider two statements from an article Hirsch wrote in 1986: "To be culturally literate one does not need to know any specific text" and "It's acceptable to take one's entire knowledge of *Romeo and Juliet* from Cliff Notes. That is because cultural literacy is a canon of information, not of texts."[31] Hirsch argues that the fundamental case for education is *access*—access to the vocabulary of the American polity. What counts most in measuring educational success is the student's ability to draw on a broad vocabulary and, where necessary, to identify the source (say, the Declaration of Independence or a Shakespeare play) of that vocabulary.

Thus, in the case of *Romeo and Juliet*, it would be a handicap for any American student to lack basic knowledge of the plot of the play. There are no economic, social, or intellectual benefits, however, that accrue to having studied the words that Shakespeare wrote, the scenes he created, the characters he drew. Cultural literacy is the essential tool for making one's way in the world; it is what one needs to know to get ahead.

Hirsch, who frequently complains that he was wrongly pegged as a conservative, emphasizes that his arguments are essentially liberal and utilitarian; only by ensuring that underprivileged students gain the cultural vocabulary of the professional classes can education redeem their otherwise dismal social and economic life prospects. To be culturally literate, Hirsch insists, means having in one's memory the basic information needed to do well in the modern world.[32] That basic information is made up of the common storehouse of knowledge that all competent readers possess, and in Hirsch's view changes only slowly through time.[33]

When Hirsch writes that "the Enlightenment view of the value of knowledge is the only view we can afford," his reader is expected to accept the otherwise jarring juxtaposition of a vision of humanist learning with monetary language.[34] He is convinced that learning is an economically advantageous act of gathering and memorizing socially valued information. Success is achieved when adults can provide the right answer or recall relevant information rapidly.[35]

There is no shortage of criticism from educational theorists of Hirsch's reification of the vocabulary of the professional classes as *the* goal of education. For some, Hirsch's deliberate bracketing of the politics of knowledge formation—his valorization of the vocabulary of the successful—is politically intolerable.[36] Henry Giroux, a long-standing left-wing critic of current educational practices and values in the United States goes further, claiming that Hirsch endorses a model of literacy that is itself a key pillar of the most destructive elements of contemporary education.

For Giroux, Hirsch's call for students to learn about current public parlance is to render them conformists and apologists for the status quo, trained to reproduce the very social hierarchy that education should undermine.[37]

Hirsch's baseline assumption that there is a body of public knowledge that changes only very slowly and must be known by anyone aiming at economic stability is not shared by those who champion the authenticity—and assumed radicalizing potential—of children learning to champion historically marginalized perspectives and cultural knowledges.

In the end, the existing arguments about Hirsch's views comes down to this: Should one learn the vocabulary of the current social and economic "winners" to be better able to join them (and perhaps reform their ways) as Hirsch argues, or should students learn from the start that this vocabulary is embedded with racial and economic codes designed to discriminate and maintain the unjust status quo? Hirsch's side of the argument was well put decades ago by Hannah Arendt: "Exactly for the sake of what is new and revolutionary in every child, education must be conservative."[38] In other words, to change the world, one must first master its current language—the way in which it understands itself.

This is an important debate, reignited recently in the often-acrimonious arguments about the degree to which racism is embedded in American education. On balance, Hirsch and Arendt are persuasive—fighting for change without the linguistic tools or background knowledge of those protecting the status quo is generally not a winning recipe for achieving successful social reform.

But there is a second set of criticisms to be made of Hirsch's arguments, this time focused on his model of reading, specifically his claims about knowledge acquisition defined as the accumulation of information. The criticism to be made here is that this model produces impoverished ELA (and, in many cases, social studies) instruction.

To see why this is, one needs to unpack Hirsch's view of what it means to understand a text. Years before he began his studies of K-12 education, Hirsch was a professor of literature with strong convictions about hermeneutics, the act of textual interpretation. In his 1967 book *Validity in Interpretation*, Hirsch laid out an "objectivist" view in which the core idea was that the meaning of a text is what the author intended—and the reader's prime task is to grasp that meaning: "A text's meaning is what it is and not a hundred other things."[39]

Hirsch's argument was not necessarily intended to suggest a final or irrefutable truth. He writes elsewhere in the book, for example, that "on purely practical grounds . . . it is preferable to agree that the meaning of a text is the author's meaning."[40] But the "practical ground," for Hirsch, is what counts.

There is a direct link between Hirsch's early writings and his attribution years later of a fixed meaning to the words in a text. In his much later work, *What Your Sixth Grader Needs to Know*, Hirsch writes that the meaning of a word is just a brute fact, established by linguistic conventions. That brute fact, he maintains, is not something to be understood but to be memorized.[41] It is reasonable to assume that Hirsch would have applauded the lesson on *Macbeth* described earlier in the preface. The students in that high school in Newark certainly knew the plot and characters, and were fully capable of articulating and sharing that knowledge of the play with one another.

While Hirsch opposes Coleman's emphasis on forensic skills in favor of his focus on knowledge building, there is an important alignment between the two. Coleman equates the skills of reading with those of the detective, which is justified only if one believes that the text has a fixed and determinate meaning that can be uncovered and learned. For Hirsch, learning those fixed meanings—important facts—is the purpose of students' reading.

Moreover, Hirsch's demands on teachers of reading aren't more complex than Coleman's. The act of "knowing," in Hirsch's sense, is an act of recognition that certain facts go together (for example, that a particular battle is part of a particular war). It is the horizontal equivalent, if you will, of Coleman's vertical forensic dig for the main idea. Coleman assures us that we can uncover *the* meaning of a word or words in a text; Hirsch asks us to memorize those meanings and group them with others to generate the background knowledge one needs to become a stronger reader.

It is surely no accident that when Hirsch turned from reading theory to reading practice, he focused on the early childhood years, when accumulating factual knowledge is most important. Across his many books, he has nothing to say about high school (the Core Knowledge Language Arts curriculum stops at eighth grade). The issue is akin to Coleman's CCSS: Like the reading skills the standards lay out, Hirsch's understanding of reading offers no pathway to more complex acts of interpretation.

But children can and should develop a more sophisticated experience of reading, and at an early age. What does a more sophisticated experience consist of? One way to capture the distinction between models of simplistic and mature reading is to recover some ancient wisdom. In book ten of his *Republic* (596d-e), Plato's character Socrates discusses journeymen, the menials of Greek society who are forced to undertake the most mindless activities. Socrates describes an especially remarkable journeyman—an individual who can make anything, any object, any plant, even the sky and the gods. But Socrates then explains that this apparently extraordinary feat is available to anyone with a mirror—thus, the ultimate journeyman is no more than what Plato called "the imitator" of what others produce.[42]

The Coleman/Hirsch reader is not dissimilar: She is taught to imitate, to reproduce the main idea, the argument, the plot, the meaning of a word.

The key point is that, for Plato or Aristotle, this act of reproduction is nothing more than the lowest-level skill. At the core of reproduction is mindlessness. The worker who repeats the task of pulling a lever in the same way thousands of times to create the same object may do it incorrectly a few times, but muscle memory takes over, the activity becomes habitual. No conscious activity is required. By contrast, cognitively demanding skills are what craftsmen (τέκτων in Greek) can demonstrate. The skill of the τέκτων is τέχνη—transliterated as *technê*—is of a different order than mere reproduction. *Technê* can never become an automated skill. According to Aristotle,

> We consider that the master craftsmen in every profession are more estimable and know more and are wiser than the manual artisans, because they know the reasons of the things which are done; but we think that the artisans, like certain inanimate objects, do things, but without knowing what they are doing (as, for instance, fire burns); only whereas inanimate objects perform all their actions in virtue of a certain natural quality, artisans perform theirs through habit. Thus the master craftsmen are superior in wisdom, not because they can do things, but because they possess a theory and know the causes.[43]

What distinction is Aristotle driving at? In his book, *The Craftsman*, Richard Sennett uses that word to distinguish those who are focused on doing their work well as an end in itself, not simply to satisfy another end.[44] To do good work, as Sennett and Aristotle emphasize, the craftsman must make a judgment about what should constitute the endpoint, or *telos*, of the work. This entails understanding the medium (wood, stone, etc.) in which the work is achieved and knowing how that medium will react to one's interaction with it.

Sennett refers to the famous architect Renzo Piano in explaining this idea. Piano recalls that he goes from sketching, to drawing, to model making, to building, and then back to redoing his sketches, a circular process of cognition and experimental construction in which both elements always inform each other.[45]

The philosopher Martin Heidegger uses a similar example. A skilled cabinet maker, Heidegger argues, never slavishly follows a preset design. Instead, he studies the piece of wood, considers its properties, and forms an initial idea of the object to be carved. Then he refines that idea based on what the wood will enable, and then proceeds to the carving based on how a particular shape would bring out the best in that material. Without this dynamic relatedness, Heidegger suggests, there would be only busy work.[46]

How is this relevant to Hirsch's model of reading? In essence, Hirsch eliminates the creative interaction between reader and text. In *Validity and Interpretation*, Hirsh creates a rigid separation between the "meaning" or "interpretation" of the text (which he takes to be goal of reading) and the attribution by the reader of any particular "significance" to that text. Interpretation here means understanding the fixed and clear meaning of a text. This, however, is a strange use of vocabulary. We normally use the word "interpretation" to suggest an active and open-ended process—akin to what Heidegger describes in cabinet making.

But for Hirsch, that process would embodies acts of hopelessly subjective, open-ended criticism. Thus, generating "significance" is for Hirsch a negative when it comes to education. The teacher's task is to enable students to discover facts about the contents of the text, whereas "significance" names a vast number of possible references that the reader brings to the text. Hirsch complains that once a reader's perspective is the determinate factor in decoding a text, there will be as many meanings as there are readers.[47]

In Hirsch's model of reading, there is no *technê*. It enshrines a journeyman's reading "skill" as the way to learn, an act of transcription that treats the mind as a mirror of texts. The text says X and the act of reading is to reflect exactly that X into the reader's memory.

The *technê* of reading would be something more cognitively demanding. As the German philosopher of hermeneutics Hans Georg Gadamer suggests, an adequate act of reading neither regards the text as something with a fixed objective singular meaning nor eliminates the reader herself as a creative part of the reading process. Rather, the good reader is open to the possibility that the text offers multiple readings and aware that she brings her own prejudices and prejudgments to each act of reading. To be open to possible meanings, and to be aware of one's own preconceptions as to what the text ought to say is to exercise the technê of mature reading.[48]

That *technê* requires a dynamic working-out of the reader's encounter with the text. It is something far more exacting and enriching that must occur if a student is to *engage* with a novel, a poem, or a play. Reading is a creative act—a purposeful endeavor in which the medium of the text, the background knowledge of the student, the prejudices, the historical context and intent of the reading are each activated, and the result is, indeed, the source of multiple possible meanings.

In a careful treatment of reading that is neither "postmodern" (the text is never knowable) nor naïve in Hirsch's sense (the text says just *this*), literary critic Rita Felski writes that a reader's encounters with texts are immensely varied, complex, and unpredictable.[49] We cannot, she insists, pigeon-hole how a reading of a text must go; it might evoke an aesthetic response, or provoke ethical self-scrutiny, or incite us to political reflection or much else. Each may be a legitimate response.[50] This open-ended process runs directly counter to Hirsch's views, but it is also the particular and remarkable gift of an education in the humanities.

What is at stake here is what it means to read. Gadamer rightly insists that trying to infer exactly what the author means and for what audience at the moment of writing is an impoverished, reductionist model of reading. Once a text is written, it enters history. The act of reading a text is always conditioned by the historical context of both text and reader. Gadamer rejects the view that the temporal separation between a current reading and the time the text was written creates a negative gap, or "yawning abyss." On the contrary, the new perspectives we bring to a text give it an enduring presence and ensure that the meaning of a text is never singular or finished.[51]

The Coleman-Hirsch model of reading offers a clear but simplistic guide to readers as they read to learn. The idea that meaning is fixed and transparent is an illusion. But even if it were not, their model is confusing. Take a text of nonfiction. The Coleman-Hirsch reader decides that the text means X. But then what? Is X true? If so, how and to what extent can that truth be established? In the case of fiction, the model is still more incomplete. Having established that the text "says X," our work even as Coleman-Hirsch readers cannot just stop. Is what the text says at X consistent with, in productive or in creative tension with, previous passages?

And then the questions get more complex and interesting: Is what the text says at X illuminating of aspects of the human condition, of our hopes, fears, imaginings, and mortality? Nothing in the Coleman-Hirsch model encourages teachers to work with students at that level of reading—and yet this is where the value of learning in the humanities must surely find its most powerful educative justification.

These levels of interpretive layers aren't provided in the Coleman/Hirsch model because they can't be. Nothing else is to be achieved in "decoding" a text other than isolating an "objective" truth about what the text "says." But as Gadamer argues, even if we were to go through a second exercise of asking about the truth value of what we think the text says, this isn't close to a full or accurate picture of what happens in reading. As attentive readers, we encounter possible meanings of the text as interruptions of our prejudices about the world. We are then asked to wrestle with that encounter: What resulting ideas are posed to us? How do we react to them? Which of them resonate for us?

What kills thoughtful reading most is the idea that the purpose of reading is to provide an answer about the meaning of a text—an answer that is already known by others and must simply be "found" by the student. So understood, the students are not developing a reading; they are treated as Plato's journeymen, trying to reproduce, as with a mirror, a fixed definition. This is not a technê; it is not mindful, and it is damaging. In 2012, Dr. Ellen Wood, associate vice provost of Stanford, remarked that "freshmen, accustomed to the definitiveness of high-school learning, are surprised to learn that most questions don't have just one answer."[52] There can there be no greater indictment of our nation's instruction in reading.

To make the foregoing discussion more concrete, it is worth showing how the Coleman/Hirsch approach works with a piece of nonfiction and then a work of fiction. The nonfiction example is Lincoln's Gettysburg Address.

In presenting the ELA CCSS, Coleman uses this text as his example and references an extensive sample lesson on the address since made publicly available.[53]

The core of Coleman's approach is a laser-like focus on the vocabulary of the text. Specifically, teachers and students are asked to focus on the word "dedicate"—and to understand that Lincoln uses it in three distinct ways—to describe the founding values of the United States, to describe a religious action, and to profess a personal commitment. The point of the close reading of this key term is to make it clear to students that Lincoln is linking the foundational principles of the country with the need to defend them.

Students are more briefly told that the word "conceived" near the start of the address is meant to convey the meanings of "founded," "bring forth something new," "start something," and "to give birth." But nothing more is said—either by Coleman in his presentation nor by the sample lesson—about the last of these terms. This is a striking omission. After all, Lincoln speaks near the close of the text with declaring "that this nation, under God, shall have a new birth of freedom."

The speech is made at the battlefield, in the company of tens of thousands of the dead. The Gettysburg Address opens and closes by tying together metaphors of birth and rebirth, and in so doing frames the literal death (then repeatedly and explicitly referenced) of the soldiers who fought that day. To value their death, to honor their final sacrifice, Lincoln says, we must give a second birth to the nation—a birth that will finally enable Americans the lives in freedom that the first birth failed to deliver. In other words, what was once born as an ideal must be reborn as a reality, enshrined in the nation's practices and laws.

The themes of birth, death, and rebirth form a complex motif in the speech, with echoes of Christian resurrection, explicit references to the Declaration of Independence, and the Civil War. The men on the battlefield of Gettysburg had died to create a country in which that idea would become real, alive, and would not die again. Asking that students wrestle with the motifs—metaphorical and literal, secular and religious—of mortality, temporality, ideology, politics, and rebirth within Lincoln's own recreation of the American creed is what an education in reading of a great nonfiction text can and should provide.

But they cannot do so from the text alone: Students should also be taught enough to be able to place the speech within the rhetorical genre of the "battlefield address," a genre already central in Homer's *Iliad*, as Lincoln well knew. The *technê* of reading this passage is demanding. It requires that students not simply become aware of definitions or a set of meanings but also wrestle with complexity and with historical and literary context, weighing the claims of a text against the foundational values it subsumes, and to be attuned to the cadences of language and the power of metaphor.

The second example comes from the closing lines of a frequently taught text in American schools, Scott Fitzgerald's *The Great Gatsby*.

> Gatsby believed in the green light, the orgastic future that year by year recedes before us. It eluded us then, but that's no matter—tomorrow we will run faster, stretch out our arms farther. . . . And one fine morning—So we beat on, boats against the current, borne back ceaselessly into the past.[54]

The Coleman/Hirsch challenge to students (and their teachers) is to determine *exactly* what Fitzgerald meant by these lines, but that's a fool's errand.

Starting at the simplest level, is there a definitive answer as to how to interpret "green"? The actual light at the end of "Daisy's dock"? Or perhaps (we cannot know for sure) Fitzgerald intends for us also to hear in the word green the pervasive echoes of money throughout the text (Daisy's voice "was full of money")? Or perhaps the reader is supposed to recollect the use of the word green just a few paragraphs before: "I became aware of the old island here that flowered once for Dutch sailors' eyes—a fresh, green breast of the new world." If we allow the two explicit and one metaphorical reference to green to be equally present, we further complicate the challenge of reading the text—and we have yet to wrestle with the erotic imagery of "breast" and "orgastic." Just what is the import of Fitzgerald's explicit sexualizing of the American dream?

Then we arrive at the metaphors of running and rowing, of the nature of the futility summoned before us. Most commentators attribute these lines to a judgment on the hubris of the American dream. But what dream, and for whom? In the immediately preceding passage, Fitzgerald writes of the "last and greatest of all human dreams; for a transitory enchanted moment man must have held his breath in the presence of this continent, compelled into an æsthetic contemplation he neither understood nor desired."

This dream of enchantment was replaced by the American dream—of materialism as the pathway to happiness. Gatsby dreamed that dream, hoping that wealth would put him into Daisy's social orbit. Tom Buchannan was given that wealth; for the one, it led to disillusionment and death, for the other, inhumanity. Is Fitzgerald suggesting that the American dream is necessarily a tragedy?

What of the love and belief against the odds that animates the character of Gatsby? Do readers find an echo of Gatsby's hopeless passion in themselves—love, perhaps, for a person who no longer is what she/he once was? Or is the reader being asked to contemplate the nobility—or is it the bathetic nature—of hopeless love? Is the striving, the rowing against the current, an act of courage, of necessity, of foolishness, or some measure of each? Or perhaps we are to read the passage ecologically, materialistically, and historically, recalling the lost innocence of those first explorers who gazed on the pristine new world.

Finally, the closing language of the novel arguably sings as much as it says—the alliterations carry the reader back into the fantasy that was Gatsby's "drawn in by a cadence of tone, by particular inflections and verbal rhythms, by an irresistible combination of word choice and syntax."[55] Is Fitzgerald trying, quite literally, to carry us away into some impressionistic world of innocence and beginnings?

These arresting lines cannot be "solved" nor fixed any more than the experience of thought can be reduced to a certain meaning. Teenagers can learn richly from reading *The Great Gatsby*, and it is the privileged techné of teachers to enable them to do so without a predetermined result. An education that leaves the student knowing "what happens" doesn't merit the word. A carefully read text interrogates us—our beliefs, values, experience, hopes, and fears.

Reading to learn is to enter a dialogue between text and self, an experience with unknowable outcomes. To conceive of education as knowledge mining, as Hirsch does, is to raise—if the effort was ever successful—a nation of idiot savants. As used to be said of the nineteenth-century graduates of the famous *Ecole Normale* in France, "they knew everything, but, unfortunately, nothing else."

The legacy of Coleman-Hirsch is to have reduced education to a training. The *agogê* was the term given to the ancient Spartan education program, which drilled male youths in the arts of war. The word means "leading"—in the case of Sparta, leading the young to acquire the skills of combat. *Agogê* was modeled on inculcating habits of survival, physical prowess, and a laconic use of language.[56]

We no longer educate boys to steal without getting caught, but the American education system, too, is a form of training. An early skills-based education is pressed as far into future grades as possible. American multiple choice and short response assessments create powerful signals that the purpose of education is to find the solution to a problem—to exercise the skill of solving the equation or finding the correct evidence in the text. Students mature, but their education system fails to mature with them. As educators cling to the idea of a skills-based education, the promise of further education is undermined.

Researchers have tried to explain why gains in academic performance in the early grades fade out. A recent summary concludes that "this age pattern remains unexplained."[57] As the reader will recall, the performance standards in the United States don't substantively change from fifth grade to twelfth.

Perhaps one reason for stalled educational progress among older children is that we treat seventeen-year-olds very much as we do students when they are seven.

David Coleman and E. D. Hirsch are wrestling explicitly with what can reasonably be done in a nation of sixty million children and four million teachers. Their choices are informed by that ambition and that context, a context that theorists and philosophers can too easily ignore. Coleman and his colleagues work on CCSS in ELA has helped to shift *initial* American reading instruction gradually but very importantly in the right direction.[58] E. D. Hirsch and the Core Knowledge curricula his team has developed have helped ensure that Coleman's overemphasis on forensic reading "skills" is mitigated by instructional materials that offer strong elementary background knowledge to children—a knowledge that the CCSSS had called for but not required.

As with Coleman's insistence on rigorous instruction in learning to read, so, too, Hirsch's focus on knowledge-rich content is a major contribution to America's elementary schooling. But ELA education in the United States has been damaged by the fact that there was no different model of reading for older students to replace an approach best suited to very young students.

MATH EDUCATION

The fundamental assumptions stated in the CCSS standards in math are very different from those in ELA. Most strikingly, they sound quite constructivist. The standards argue that students who are strong in math explain problems to themselves and then engage in an active analysis: Successful students should be able to make conjectures about possible forms and meanings of various solutions, changing their approach if they find that they aren't progressing. All this sounds much more closely akin to the development of a technê in mathematics that isn't found in the case of ELA.[59]

Moreover, the CCSS standards were designed to respond to the research findings that William Schmidt, the distinguished researcher of math education at Michigan State University, and his colleagues reported decades ago. Schmidt found that American students fail to grasp the basic concepts of mathematics and cannot use mathematics to solve real-world problems.[60] Specifically referring to Schmidt's criticisms, the CCSS assured educators and policymakers that the new standards would no longer encourage math teaching that was "a mile wide and an inch deep."[61]

In 2019, more than eight years after the introduction of the math CCSS in over forty states, twelfth-grade NAEP math results indicate that American high-school student scores are identical to those in 2005, while the scores of less affluent children were declining. Meanwhile, fourth-grade results in 2019 were statistically identical to where they were in 2009, despite the fact that fourth-grade children would have been taught the CCSS in most states all the way through their grade-level instruction.[62] In terms of American students' math performance relative to those in other countries, the PISA results in 2018 saw American fifteen-year-olds record their (to date) lowest scores ever compared to those in other tested countries.[63]

One interpretation of these lackluster results is that the imposition of standards—even reasonably strong ones (to give CCSS the benefit of the doubt) have largely failed to impact the ingrained practices of teachers and schools. That is, for example, Tom Loveless's principal argument in his analysis of the "failure of Common Core."[64] But there is a second more obvious problem with the CCSS in math. The language cited about students being motivated to think their way through mathematical relationships occurs mainly in introductions to the specific grade-level standards. But once the math standards are laid out, that language largely disappears.

Take algebra. Under the CCSS standard HSA.APR.B.2, students are required to "Know and apply the Remainder Theorem: For a polynomial $p(x)$ and a number a, the remainder on division by $x - a$ is $p(a)$, so $p(a) = 0$ if and only if $(x - a)$ is a factor of $p(x)$."[65] Under "reasoning with equations," teachers are given a list of equation types and told to teach students to "solve" them.[66] At times, the math CCSS tell teachers that students should "recognize" or "understand" a mathematical operation as opposed to solving it, but there is no difference in the language that then follows. In each case, what is clearly called for is knowing (in E. D. Hirsch's sense) what the mathematical rules require.

Even when students are asked to do something like "explain" their reasoning, the language is synonymous with, "Show that you have followed the rules"; "Explain each step in solving a simple equation as following from the equality of numbers asserted at the previous step."[67] Most of the time, the CCSS directly tells the teacher what students must be able to do, with no gesture to creating time or pedagogical strategies for students to think their way to the solutions. So, for example, we find: "Use the properties of exponents to transform expressions for exponential functions."

Magdalene Lampert, who until recently was a professor of education at the University of Michigan in Ann Arbor and one of the nation's foremost experts in math pedagogy, notes that the Common Core frequently requires that students learn alternative mathematical procedures (many of them quite complex) to arrive at the same answer. But that doesn't, in Lampert's view, help them make sense of the math involved, or understand anything about the underlying mathematical concept in question.

Effective teachers can show why and how alternative approaches might illuminate that concept, but in the hands of teachers who cannot do so, Lampert concludes, the alternative algorithms in the CCSS are confusing. Better to have teachers present a single standard algorithm.[68]

Deborah Ball, who, alongside Lampert, is one of the most recognized figures in math education in the United States, likewise focuses on the fact that the math standards, unless they bring a wholesale change in pedagogy, aren't going to make a difference. In a presentation on the CCSS, Ball stressed that to make real progress in math, the country would need to build an entirely new way of teaching and assessing mathematics. For example, the CCSS calls for students to learn how to add mixed fractions, but unless teachers understand how to probe students for their understanding of, and thinking about, such operations, simply dictating the algorithms won't get them very far.[69]

By itself, no amount of thinking on the part of students can bring them to see the power of that expression. The core of Lockhart's lament echoes Deborah Ball's: We don't design math education to enable children to think their way toward possible mathematical hypotheses or possible solutions. Rather, we tell them how to find the answer and then ask them to practice doing so again and again. It's not that mathematical techniques or algorithms aren't important. It's that they need to be highlighted *after* students think about mathematical questions, not before they do so.[70]

Lockhart suspects we lay out mathematical standards and teach the way we do because teaching any other way is just too hard. To do mathematics, he argues, is to undertake acts of "discovery and conjecture." To make this possible, teachers need to create classroom environments in which students are carefully taught to try out a number of possible mathematical pathways. Then students need to reflect on the math that they have engaged with and understand what worked and why, or why not. Finally, they are taught to translate successful pathways into mathematical functions or formulae that will enable them to tackle similar challenges more efficiently.

The resulting pedagogical challenge is already demanding, but it is made worse when we insist on a long list of mathematical procedures that must be used to prove that children have reached proficiency.

It would be facile to claim that math education in the United States suffers from the same challenges as in ELA: The domains are naturally distinct, the pedagogical challenges different. But in an important respect, there is a clear connection. In both domains, we have simplified and lowered our expectations. This is a question not of the complexity of texts nor of mathematical algorithms. Clearly, it requires more vocabulary and background knowledge to read more sophisticated texts, just as using the quadratic equation is a more complex operation that adding whole numbers.

The point, rather, is that we have minimized the cognitive demands, most especially of middle and high-school students. In the case of ELA, we keep telling them to do the same thing: Find the main idea and remember the plot of the text, or the information in the work of nonfiction. In the case of mathematics, while we have added the requirement that students translate real-world narratives into mathematical notation, we still focus on having students memorize algorithms and apply them. We have largely avoided asking students to think mathematically. UCLA's James Stigler, who has been studying math education for more than forty years, put it simply: To enter the language of mathematics, students have to "think and struggle."[71]

America's K-12 education system asks middle and high students to do little of either. The reluctance to require students to wrestle with ambiguity, to work through multiple levels of possible interpretation, to have them think for themselves toward considered judgments that do not come with packaged, predetermined answers is systematically reinforced by both standards and assessments. It is high time to change direction.

Chapter 5

Learning to Think

"Schools have given up providing an education in human excellence—the very idea would be triggering!"[1]

"Look you, the stars shine still."[2]

The previous four chapters of this book have made inescapable the haunting thought that somehow, in too many places, especially in those inhabited by the poorest in America, our schools are falling short—despite our diligent efforts. We are failing to educate our children for the life that lies ahead of them. Unable to make good on the promise of education, we have built a system that too often leaves them stranded.

Imagining, still less creating, public schools in ways that match our ideals for well-being (our Constitution, uniquely, speaks of happiness) seems as elusive as it has ever been. The K-12 education system barely teaches students even basic levels of numeracy and literacy. Beyond that, schools are riven with distractions and competing goals, many of which undermine strong academic instruction. In the core subject of the English language arts, for example, we teach the same skills to students who are seventeen as we do to those who are seven.

Working in this fragmented system are poorly prepared teachers, most of whom design their own curriculum from a myriad of sources. These teachers try to impart a list of skills, often with little sense of the core values of the academic disciplines. The results are deeply troubling. We haven't reduced the iron grip of inequitable background conditions on students' learning outcomes, nor have we scaled up the heroic efforts of some extraordinary teachers and schools. Frustration is, understandably, causing some critics to shoot the messenger—to blame our tests, or decry our failure to embrace some preferred silver bullet. From middle school onward, we have lost our way, and the many students impacted by that loss respond with boredom and low academic effort.

Given our long reflection and endless efforts to improve American education, these findings are depressing. Our children deserve much more: rigorous teaching that enables them to build on their initial intuitions and inquisitiveness, the experience of hard work leading to energizing insight and understanding, the discovery of unimagined worlds and the mastery of new forms of thought through which to explore them. For each child, "the stars shine still," if we, their teachers, can but dispel what obscures the view.

Daniel Webster's arresting image is an invitation to think further, to look elsewhere, to probe more deeply. For all of us, it is a prompt and a catalyst to shift our vision of what education should look like. It compels us to embrace a broader horizon and to look beyond the fragmentation and reductionism that bedevil contemporary American schooling and the current discourse around it.

A broader horizon must encompass that primordial American hope that our lives might enable the pursuit of happiness. But what does that word comport? Twenty-four centuries ago, Aristotle coined the term "eudaimonia," human flourishing, to describe the concept of happiness. Eudaimonia is the greatest of human ends—the shared and universal telos of human existence. A well-lived life is one in which the aim of happiness, of human flourishing, is our north star, guiding our choices, our values, our hopes, and dreams. What makes the pathway to eudaimonia possible? Answering that question takes us back to fundamentals. As human beings, we cannot progress on that pathway without the most uniquely human of all our capacities—the capacity to think.

Other animals reproduce, hunt, build homes, communicate, remember, and experience emotions, as do we, but human beings alone can evaluate in language our own actions and those of others, appreciate beauty, and acquire facility in the different fields of knowledge—be they literary, mathematical, symbolic, scientific, or those expressed in musical or other artistic or physical forms. Ultimately, the education of our children revolves around this core question: "What does it mean to have achieved a well-lived life?"

Only human beings can think reflectively about their choices, their actions, and the trajectories of their lives. Without a well-developed capacity for such thoughtfulness, a life of eudaemonia isn't possible. A life lived at the mercy of instinct, of unfiltered emotion, is the life of a human puppet directed by chance and circumstance. (In his work *The Laws,* Plato famously compares such humans to puppets whose strings are pulled by the gods—our puppet masters.)

The most fundamental purpose of education is thus to nurture our capacity to think. Education is the means by which our most human capabilities are transformed from innate potential to a life in which we can interrogate experience so as to learn and integrate it into future action. The research that informs this book has raised perennial questions about "what's helpful" or "what's ineffective" in one or another educational strategy, but our root pedagogical failure, and the most pernicious, is that we are not educating our children to be thoughtful about the purposes of life and how best to pursue them.

Two observations by modern Aristotelians echo these claims. Together, they point to the triangular relationship between thought, education, and the human condition. One of them, Richard Kraut, is an historian of Aristotelian philosophy:

> The good of a human being must have something to do with being human; and what sets humanity off from other species, giving us the potential to live a better life, is our capacity to guide ourselves by using reason. If we use reason well, we live well as human beings; or, to be more precise, using reason well over the course of a full life is what happiness consists in.[3]

The second is Michael Oakeshott, a philosopher and political theorist committed to "uncovering a practical knowledge embedded in human practices."[4]

> The price of the intelligent activity which constitutes being human is learning. When the human condition is said to be burdensome what is being pointed out is not the mere necessity of having to think, to speak and to act (instead of merely being like a stone, or growing like a tree) but the impossibility of thinking or feeling without having slowly and often painfully learned to think something.[5]

While a right to a good education can be defended for many reasons, including economic and civic, our most essential responsibility as educators involves the guiding, the careful shepherding, of the children's learning to think.

THINKING

What is thinking, or thoughtfulness, itself? Thought is made possible in moments of a conscious, cognitive interruption that intrudes on the flow of unreflective experience. Thinking, if it then occurs, takes the form of a silent dialogue I have with myself. As political theorist Hannah Arendt explains, thinking isn't something that occurs automatically. It is a commitment of a particular kind. She writes: "the disposition to live together explicitly with oneself, to have intercourse with oneself, that is, to be engaged in that silent dialogue between me and myself which, since Socrates and Plato [is what] we usually call thinking."[6]

Education provides crucial material for that silent dialogue and essential practice in reflecting on that material. As children mature, both the material and the reflection should mature with them, growing in complexity, embracing ambiguity, and asking for greater cognitive acuity. At every stage of growth, the outcome of educated thought can remain private, but, of course, it may be externalized into shared writing, acts of creativity, public dialogue, and the full panoply of social activities.

But what makes up the content of educated thought? What is that "something" that Michael Oakeshott evokes in the passage quoted above? The argument of this chapter will be that there are three crucial elements in the education of thought: ethics, aesthetics, and wisdom. Our schools need to nurture ethical reflection, aesthetic sensibility, and academic learning. All three are crucial in forging a fulfilling life. The following analysis will take each of these elements in turn and describe why each one belongs to the core of schooling. The account of these three dimensions of learning will close with the suggestion that they intersect in fundamental ways, forming the coherent core of education—and education in how to think.

The following pages will discuss these three elements, both in theory and in ways intended to make them accessible for educational use in our heterogeneous society. The elements are meant to be inclusive, acceptable to those whose politics or beliefs would otherwise divide them. Their interpretation is also meant to be applicable to the real world of the classroom.

My central contention is that schools should nurture all three elements so children can become thoughtful adults.

To summarize: The contention of this chapter is that an education in ethics, aesthetics, and rigorous academics together create the vocabulary and content of that internal dialogue—of thought itself—such that the recipient is placed on a path to a well-considered life. Perhaps there are those for whom this claim sounds overly theoretical, but a question to those who would bracket the education of thought as trivial: What alternative vision of human life would be more appropriate to the education of a child?

ETHICAL BEHAVIOR AND JUDGMENT

When we react with condemnation or praise to the actions of another, we are often simply verbalizing raw emotion. As Alasdair McIntyre points out in *After Virtue*, contemporary appeals to ethics take the form of emotivism: that upsets me, you offended me, I feel that's wrong. The primary vehicle of expression is protest, the primary emotion indignation.[7] As is the case with other animals, we can react to events spontaneously and thus thoughtlessly, out of instinct, emotion, passion, or habituation. An education that nurtures ethical behavior and judgment breaks that pattern. Before we get to unpacking what the term ethics could mean in the K-12 context, it is worth pinpointing what it actually does mean in contemporary practice.

Educators have long believed in the need to constrain the tendency toward emotivism. In recent decades of American education, there have been various attempts to teach ethical behavior as a distinct part of the curriculum. The most famous such approach, emerging in the 1960s, was called "values clarification"—an effort to teach value-neutral ethics focused on getting children to clarify their confusions in one of eight categories of behaviors.[8]

That movement was followed in the 1980s and beyond by what was loosely known as "character education." Here the notion was to teach specific ethical behavior. For example, in 1991, the California Department of Education announced that effective schools were those that nurtured the traits of caring, fairness, and trustworthiness.[9]

As sociologist James Hunter chronicles, these and thousands of similar attempts were designed to teach students to behave virtuously. Built on the idea of nurturing psychological well-being through a series of readings and behavioral techniques, however, they failed. Hunter's research indicates "little or no association, causal or otherwise, between psychological well-being and moral conduct, and [that] psychologically oriented moral education programs have little or no positive effect upon moral behavior, achievement, or anything else."[10]

What is clear from Hunter's research is that while ethical education has proven elusive, children's ethical development has hugely important consequences for their lives. Reporting on a 1989 study of 5,000 children, Hunter found that children's basic ethical beliefs have long lasting impacts, providing the moral compass they will continue to use as they mature.[11] Hunter's findings applied regardless of the children's economic background, race, ethnicity, gender age, or family structure.[12]

There needs to be a restart. In contrast to previous failed efforts at teaching explicit "rudimentary ethical systems," we need to reconsider ethical behavior from the ground up. Aristotle is especially helpful here because he directly links eudaimonia (human flourishing) and ethics.[13] He also argues that it is our ability to employ reason guided by virtue that is indispensable to a well-lived life. The role of child-rearing and formal education are both crucial. Well rendered, they will maximize our capacity to make reasoned choices that embody ethical values and our ability to take appropriate actions based on those choices.

Phronesis: Ethical Judgment in Practice

From theory to practice: How to make the choices that forge a life of *eudaimonia*? There are two crucial elements. First, in making choices, rational and virtuous human beings can see themselves within a narrative of which they are a key author. They have learned to weigh the consequences of their choices in terms of how the outcomes will affect the trajectory of their life story and the values that story embodies. As Oakeshott explains, human beings can only fully answer the question of what they should do if they can answer the prior question of what narrative they find themselves in.[14]

Certainly, many elements of a life's narrative are predetermined by circumstances over which no human being has control. At the same time, the future always holds unpredictable events that will play their part in shaping a life. But through many decisions, people will, by choosing paths to take or let go, impact the shape, possibilities, and values of their life—and they can look back at the narrative they have built to date. No matter if we react by untutored instinct or by educated reflection, Aristotle argued, all of us are bound to make such choices, and recreate our lives as we do so, for worse or for better.

Second, Aristotle argues, in making choices that will shape the future narrative of their lives, well-educated humans will seek opportunities to exercise particular actions—those that are courageous, generous, and honorable. For example, they we will seek to cultivate deep friendships in part because such relationships may enable acts that are generous, even courageous. Genuine friendships will embrace sacrifices of time, wealth and/or professional opportunities if one sees a friend in need.

Aristotle calls the act of choosing or reasoning about one's actions *phronesis*, usually translated as the intellectual virtue of exercising "practical wisdom." When we exercise it, we combine the perspective discussed above—that of considering and creating the pathway or narrative of life and undertaking the virtuous course of action. *Phronesis* is a skill we acquire in living and practicing it: We learn to make sense of complex choices as we face different opportunities to exercise different virtues (and perhaps to suffer in different ways). This is a skill that takes much practice and maturity—relying *not* on the opinions of others but learning to think for ourselves about the overall purposes and choices of our lives.[15]

While it makes intuitive sense that we should thoughtfully try to "fit" our life choices into the wider horizon of our life, incorporating our aims and values in the process, why will we or should we accept that doing so requires us to be honorable or generous or exhibit other virtues? Aristotle's answer takes us one step further back to our childhood education: children who have become habituated to enjoying virtuous actions will forever be candidates for the strong exercise of *phronesis*. They will *want* to forge paths of living in which they can enjoy what a virtuously lived life can offer. In other words, they will have learned, insensibly, to desire the good.

How does this argument work? Aristotle is clear that we can't expect adults to be attracted to virtuous behavior and deeply considered life-pathways out of the blue. A grown-up driven purely (or mostly) by instinct or passion, for example, could hear a lecture about wise decision-making and still pay no heed to its message, even though perhaps understanding the advice cognitively. Just as one cannot reason with a deeply inebriated person, he cannot do so himself. That fact is no indictment of reasoning.

The inebriated are far from rare. The Aristotelian ethical theorist Alasdair MacIntyre calls them "modern selves"—people who move from one arbitrary stance to the next, with no rational criteria for evaluating their own actions or those of others. Their judgments will change depending only on the perspective they happen to occupy; tomorrow, that perspective could alter completely.[16]

How do we avoid becoming such a person—permanently inebriated, as it were? There really is no help for adults; it is too late. The inebriated can no longer learn the steps. The time to act is when we are young. For sober adults, Aristotle has a key message: Upbringing and education, rightly understood, keep children sober and thus ready to exercise *phronesis*.

Aristotle argues that we cannot just ask, implore, or require children to be ethical (thus the failures of American character education). Only through guided practice and curated exemplars of ethical choices and actions can children can be successfully habituated to making such choices and performing such actions for themselves. Practice, and the desire to emulate what is rightly admired, draw children into activities and experiences that they will one day understand to be worthwhile, and they are worthwhile because they are apposite to living a fulfilling life.

Aristotle's key point is this: If adults are to develop those criteria successfully, they must already have come to *enjoy* doing what is just, courageous, generous, and the like *as children*. In short, they will have developed that moral compass as children: "A good upbringing makes the noble a part, perhaps the chief part, of the pleasant for us."[17] Well-educated children will, as adults, judge virtuous activities not as burdensome constraints but as noble and enjoyable in themselves because that was their lived experience as children. When mature enough to engage in *phronesis*, adults will interrogate a given choice for its full potential—and ask thoughtfully and soberly what makes a given pathway more worthwhile than an alternative.

How Children Learn: Aristotle's "Hexis"

What exactly is virtuous or ethical behavior, and how do children learn to enjoy it? Let's take these in turn. Aristotle describes ethical virtue as a "*hexis*," a tendency or disposition of character, induced by our habits, to have appropriate emotions at the appropriate time.[18] How do virtue and emotion correlate? (Elucidating this question seems all the more important given MacIntyre's reminder that unmediated emotions are antagonistic to good judgment and reason.) Aristotle describes a child with appropriate hexis as one that is habituated to choosing actions that lie between two unethical extremes.

For example, in the face of a threat, that child will not instinctively exhibit flight or fight but rather seek to understand what the situation calls for. That child will have been habituated to value courage as an emotional response, but temper that emotion with judgment about what form of courage is appropriate, in this case, when to stand and face that threat and when to retreat.

There is no prior or innate knowledge about ethical choices. Rather, a child learns over time that the complete loss of self-control is likely to have dire consequences. She or he comes to realize over time that recklessness lacks the appropriate *hexis*. Thus, as the Aristotle scholar J. O. Urmson writes, "One's character can err in two opposed ways; one may exhibit an emotion too often or too rarely; about too many or too few things; toward too many or too few people . . . when it is uncalled for and not even when it is called for."[19]

Children learn virtuous *hexis* first through lived experience, under the guidance of their elders, who can help them make sense of that experience. In this way, children learn the connection between their actions and their consequences. Secondly, they learn it through more formal education, which through stories enables children vicariously to inhabit multiple worlds beyond their own horizons.

Phronesis relies on our ethically motivated capacity to place choices within the narrative of our life. *Hexis* prepares us for *phronesis* by habituating us to prefer the ethical pathway. The acquisition of *hexis*, in turn, relies on a capacity to draw from stories about others as an opportunity not only for the expansion of knowledge but of example and potentially of emulation. When education engages children emotionally and cognitively in the experiences of others, they become able to expand their internal universe such they can rehearse in their own imaginations the choices made in fiction and nonfiction alike. As MacIntyre emphasizes, children's encounters with stories are a crucial path to valuing virtues.[20]

This educative experience is ideally gradual and appropriate to the maturity of a child. In his seminal work on education, *Emile*, Jean-Jacques Rousseau argues against giving young children *Aesop's Fables* because he is convinced that their message is ambiguous and likely to be misunderstood.[21]

The Core Knowledge ELA curriculum disagrees: It sets *Aesop's Fables* as required reading for first-graders, along with Peter Rabbit.[22] Yet our choice of reading material for children is far from trivial. For example, is Peter Rabbit simply a tale about the virtue of obedience to parents, or something more about what happens when one tries to be something that one isn't? At what level of maturity are children open to this second lesson? Peter Rabbit also contains Homeric echoes (the adventuring hero returns home transformed) and asks fascinating questions about anthropomorphism.

No matter if it is the tale of Peter Rabbit, *Aesop's Fables*, or other classic tales accessible to children, the pedagogical opportunities for thinking about moral complexities are rich and inexhaustible. The curriculum we devise—the tales we read to children and those they begin to read for themselves—are not simply devices to enable them to master the mechanics of reading but key reference points for an education in ethics.

Through their capacity to imagine, children place themselves in hitherto unencountered circumstances. They associate with the characters in the stories they read and take their experiences to heart. The resulting lessons are ethically crucial: Children vicariously, in that imaginative space, rehearse the consequences borne by fictional or historical characters—learning, for instance, about the results of decisions made with too little thought.

The power of stories lies in their their power to create emotive response. Through empathy or rejection, and using her or his imagination, a child feels summoned to other possible worlds. The story is *Mufaro's Beautiful Daughters* or *The Chronicles of Narnia*—it's the invitation that is vital. As James Hunter suggests, stories summon students to imagine greater purposes—purposes that may involve acts of altruism such as sacrifice and devotion above and beyond their self-interest. Repositioned in new worlds of possibility, children's moral imaginations expand, and their energies are redirected.[23]

A curriculum must be responsive to the ethical dimension of storytelling. The curriculum will embody a staging in which ethics and the narrative first make their claims on the young. The role of the teacher is often crucial—an explanation, a nudge, a suggestion, a challenge to rethink, a request to notice what has escaped the reader, a lesson structure that prompts close reading.

A child's first conscious experience of a narrative is in the stories she or he is told: The child needs to grow into stories and with stories. Why? Because while a child's life consists of a series of spontaneous experiences—of pain, pleasure, frustration, exhaustion—it is through entry into the lives of others that children first come to the immediacy of time elongated, of the relationship between characters and their choices, of the ways in which a moment may echo into futurity. The flashlight beneath the sheets keeps open the story whose denouement has become so gripping as to waylay sleep.

Agreeing to the claim that stories for young children are a crucial source of ethical education, we can wrongly assume that the ethical content of reading fades away as children mature. On the contrary, as children grow, the stories they read must grow with them, offering more complex ethical dilemmas and food for more complex thought.

Recall the example of Macbeth as taught in the high school in Newark. The play offers dense material for ethical reflection. Macbeth is told by witches that he will become King of Scotland: Accepting their prophecy, he and his wife then conspire to murder Duncan, the reigning monarch. The act drives Lady Macbeth into madness and Macbeth to further grotesque deeds, and eventually to his death. But why did Macbeth not react differently to the prophecy? Why did he assume that it required of him the most unethical acts? The answer goes to his character, and to the way he conceived of his choices, to the deficiencies of his *phronesis*.

Or recall the ending of *The Great Gatsby*. "The dream that had seemed so close" is dead. Daisy refuses Gatsby once and for all. Even so, Gatsby chooses to lie to protect her. It's a lie that costs him his life. Is it a lie of courage? If so, of what kind? Is it born of self-delusion or nobility, or both? Does it represent an ethical choice given the life, the values, the emotions, and the imaginings ascribed to Gatsby? What can we draw from our reading of the novel in terms of our own thinking about the claims of love, illusion, and sacrifice? The texts older children will read create exponentially more complex ethical narratives, with themes of mortality, tragedy, eros, and clashing values.

Drawn to the virtues of fictional and nonfictional characters encountered in stories they read (or see), and accustomed to benefiting from their careful choice of the mean in ethically charged context, children will not yet understand *why* their moral or ethical choice is necessarily the right one. The progression from experiencing what is positive in the moral choice, hearing at times from parents/teachers that *this* is an instance of that choice, and finally coming to that judgment themselves is a gradual one.

It is thus not simply that education habituates us through practice into virtuous actions. It is rather, as the renowned classics scholar Myles Burnyeat points out, that "practice has cognitive powers, in that it is the way we learn what is noble or just."[24] Burnyeat continues:

> You need to be guided in your conduct so that by doing the things you are told are noble and just you will discover that what you have been told is *true*. What you may begin by taking on trust you can come to know if yourself. This is not yet to know it is true, but it is to have learned that it is true in the sense of having made the judgment your own.[25]

Learning to value the appropriate *hexis,* and thus acting ethically (with what the ancient Greeks called *aretê,* or virtue), is thus a progression that moves from experience to the habit of ethical behavior to the ability to make choices and behave in such ways that enable human flourishing. As we come to know and value what it is to behave honorably and courageously, to value friendships and nurture our capacity for projecting the pathways of our lives, we seek to live accordingly and we seek the means to do so through choosing those paths thoughtfully based on experience and education. Ethical education prepares us for the exercise of *phronesis*: "Virtue makes us aim at the right mark, and practical wisdom makes us take the right means . . . [so] it is impossible to be practically wise without being good."[26]

As we master *phronesis* in ourselves, so we prepare for active participation in the public sphere. What was nurtured as a private virtue can now be expanded to inform judgments shared with others. The internal dialogue that constitutes our own thoughtfulness is now externalized. The capacity to place decision-making within the narrative of a single or a domestic life is now made available to the community. The history, the present, and the future of that community now become the site for the exercise of *phronesis*.

But how will we know we are exercising *phronesis* well? Here Aristotle and his modern followers may disappoint. There is no "principal or test" to which we can appeal.[27] The central Aristotelian idea is that behaving ethically is not a matter of asking what rule to follow in each situation, nor is judgment a matter of excluding emotions (both elements of the teaching of Kantian liberals and Utilitarians alike). To act well isn't a case of deciding if the right procedure is to "look before you leap" rather than, say, "he who hesitates is lost." Instead, it is a matter of being educated to choose the right course of action for the right reasons based on being habituated to ethical behavior and thus being able *to act* on the result of reflection.

Instead of teaching ethical rules, we can gradually expose children to what the effective use of *phronesis* consists in. It will involve a conscious effort to slow down—to rehearse various pathways, to ask tough questions of oneself, to enable the imagination to draw on multiple possibilities, to deepen one's situational awareness: in short, to be thoughtful.[28]

In her reading of the demands of *phronesis*, Martha Nussbaum, one of America's most influential humanists, stresses that there is no "shortcut" in this thinking process. Intuitions and emotions, projections, memories of fiction, biography, history, and simply the messy lessons of lived experience are all invaluable sources of thought at the moment of choice.[29] Our capacity to draw concrete lessons from the complex interlacing that makes up the "cognitive material" of stories is the evidence of our ethical maturity.

The point is this: It is *because* of the absence of rules for deciding that careful ethical education is so crucial; it will have provided an ever more complex picture of ethical values and how they operate in human affairs.

From a very different starting point, John Dewey offers a compelling and accurate summary of Aristotelian *phronesis*:

The present, not the future is ours. No shrewdness, no store of information will make it ours. But by constant watchfulness concerning the tendency of acts, by noting disparities between former judgments and actual outcomes, and tracing that part of the disparity that was due to deficiency and excess indisposition, we come to know the meaning of the present acts, and to guide them in the light of that meaning. the moral is to develop conscientiousness, ability to judge the significance of what we are doing . . . by fostering those impulses and habits which experiences shown to make a sensitive, generous, imaginative, impartial in perceiving the tendency of our inchoate dawning activities.[30]

WHY ARISTOTLE?

A few final words about this approach to education and ethics. No single theory can satisfy everyone, but a proposed model should possess intellectual coherence, potential persuasiveness across ideological divides, and usability.

What Aristotle claims is that the goal of education should be to bring up children so that they can exercise their rational capacities to the fullest extent and achieve the best life possible. Habituation to ethical behavior and its benefits, thoughtfulness about life's goals in the context of a life story, and attention to what Aristotle defines as one's social, material, and intellectual endowments is arguably a more compelling path to *eudaimonia* than any nonreligious alternative.[31]

There are, of course, many other models, including rules for behavior which are drawn from religious belief. Due to their particularism, however, they fail to provide a secure pathway for our fundamentally heterogeneous public-school system. As suggested above, the most obvious nonreligious alternatives to an Aristotelian model of ethics are found in forms of contemporary liberalism that draw on the deontological ethics of Immanuel Kant ("Act only according to that maxim whereby you can, at the same time, will that it should become a universal law")[32] or some version of Utilitarianism ("Actions are right in proportion as they tend to promote happiness, wrong as they tend to produce the reverse of happiness").[33]

The clear difficulty with either approach is that we cannot agree what would be the best theory or the best rule.[34] For example, when a very prominent modern Kantian, John Rawls, grounded his own deontological ethics on the idea that we "agree to share one another's fate," his Harvard University colleague Robert Nozick simply disagreed.[35] The Aristotelian view—albeit understood broadly as sketched above—appeals to experience, encompassing known outcomes of childhood and the full complexity of the human condition. For the adult who has been well-educated in the Aristotelian sense, no hypothetical thought experiment is required.[36]

This chapter began by considering the place of thought in a human life and Hannah Arendt's point that thought occurs in the silent dialogue one has with oneself. It is important that Arendt also adds an ethical dimension:

> Socrates' deepest fear is that "I, being one, should be out of tune with myself and contradict myself (482b-c).."."... The meaning is clear: even though I am one, I am not simply one, I have a self and I am related to this self as my own self. This self is by no means an illusion; it makes itself heard by talking to - I talk to myself. . . . If I do wrong I am condemned to live together with a wrongdoer in an unbearable intimacy; I can never get rid of him.[37]

Arendt emphasizes that thinking ethically is not some luxury or minor by-product of our education. It is constitutive of who we are. Human thought has moral outcomes: Out of the activity of internal dialogue, we constitute ourselves as the person we are. An education that fails to provide the material that furthers a life of thoughtful choices grounded in the capacity to exercise them leaves us as straws in the wind. We risk becoming captive to instinct and passion, the unmediated molding of circumstance and social judgment.

Contemporary social mores press adults to tolerate and even respect the expression of one another's unmediated emotions and/or unreflective pronouncements. In other words, rather than seeking reasons for a set of utterances and evaluating those reasons, one is asked to grant them standing merely on the basis that they come from a human being. Surely, a problem emerges in the disproportion between our readiness to attribute weight to such pronouncements,and our readiness to accept them at face value, requiring no further rationale to grant them respect?

In Aristotle's understanding, an education in ethics is dedicated to nurturing children's reflections so that they can make ethically informed choices. From creating ethical knowledge through formal education and parental guidance, to habituation into ethical behavior, to the development of *phronesis*, children become adults capable of forging life narratives with merited claims to our respect. That is why Aristotle calls *phronesis* an intellectual virtue.

AESTHETICS

"But today Necessity is master, and bends a degraded humanity beneath its tyrannous yoke. is the great idol of the age, to which all powers must do service and all talents swear allegiance. In these clumsy scales the spiritual service of Art has no wait; Deprived of all encouragement, she flees from the noisy mart of our century."[38]

Arguing that an education in aesthetic appreciation is crucial is out of season in education policy circles. The reasoning goes the other way: arts education itself is an after-thought in many schools, a "nice thing" if the time and resources are available. Geometry, with its Euclidian proofs, is "serious"; the arts are not. Similarly, calculus with its privileging of abstraction and manipulation of symbols remains a centerpiece in our educational hierarchy, while developing a capacity to appreciate painting or music does not. Just why it should be this way isn't clear.[39] Perhaps when arts education is imagined, what comes to mind is young children having fun with colors, or older children learning a definition of "impressionism."

A much richer sense of the arts—inclusive of learning about graphics, design, and multimedia in addition to music making, acting, and arts appreciation—would offer far more possibilities for self-development and real-world economic returns than an ability to memorize some Euclidian proofs or to pass a calculus exam. While the return on geometry skills may be high in terms of college entrance expectations, colleges and universities are increasingly open to considering video of artwork, dance performances. and other work in the arts.

The arts and culture industry in pre-COVID times represented almost a trillion dollars of GDP a year.[40] A proven facility for creative design is at the heart of what some of the world's leading technology companies are seeking in their recruiting strategies.[41]

Justifying arts education in economic terms is important, because linking education to future career opportunities rightly or wrongly provides an important rationale for curricula choices, but the core argument here will be different, namely, that an education in aesthetics is justified in so far as it is shown to be necessary for the adequate development and the future life quality of all of America's children.

The nation owes more to its children than a learning that is contained within narrow paths of gathering facts and mastering basic skills. A life lived without an attunement to the beautiful will be as if the very colors of life's experiences are washed out. Children deserve opportunities to nourish their imagination, to spot the beautiful in the outside world or in a museum, instruction in playing an instrument, crafting a small sculpture, mastering a dance or perspective in a painting. To have to argue for an education in aesthetics is surprising given its value to human sensibility. It is also vital, since today it has so little standing in so many of our schools.

KANT ON AESTHETICS

It is not obvious what constitutes an aesthetic response, still less why educating for aesthetic judgment is crucial. When in front of an object made up of a piece of cloth, layers of paint, and a frame, what causes us to react with indifference, momentary attention, or on rare occasions with an inner gasp of astonishment and delight? What causes a deep emotive response to the daffodils in William Wordsworth's poem, *"I Wandered Lonely as a Cloud"?*

There isn't a simple answer to such questions. The first step is to develop a theoretical model—in this case a theory of aesthetic judgment—and then to discuss the educational implications of preparing children to exercise that capacity.

In establishing the importance of aesthetic judgment in education, the work of Immanuel Kant is compelling. His analysis has striking similarities with Aristotle's view of *phronesis*: In making aesthetic judgments, as Kant sees it, we are once again (as we were when making ethical choices as Aristotle understood them) in a realm of free choice—we cannot appeal to scientific principle or proof that something is worthy of being called beautiful. We are on our own, with just our experiences of beauty to rely on.

This is because when we make aesthetic judgments such as "this painting is beautiful," nothing is a given: Our cognitive faculties don't predetermine the nature of our experience, and we are free to react or not react to the painting as we please. But that produces a major problem, Are aesthetic judgments imply a matter of private opinion?

Kant rejects this view. He claims that when we make an aesthetic judgment, we do something very different. We are responding to something deep in human nature, and that response is so strong that we find ourselves wanting to share it with other people. When one says "this is beautiful," the claim is not just made on behalf of the speaker but for humanity. The assertion is made in a universal, collective human voice.[42]

How does such a judgment arise? What happens when we encounter something—a piece of music, a painting, a moment in a film, a poem, which we find arresting or exhilarating? Two things, Kant suggests. First, we must react freely to the object, without any desire to acquire or manipulate or use that object. We are not, for example, reacting to something positively because we hope to sell it at a profit. Second, we are not dealing with something like ice cream, where pleasure is a matter of taste buds: I prefer chocolate, you prefer vanilla, and there is no point in arguing about it.

Aesthetic judgment is something quite different. As we encounter the object, our thoughts about it coalesce into a spontaneous and powerful urge to share our reaction with others. We are convinced that they, too, should be struck by the quality of what has created our own reaction: "Don't you see/ hear how beautiful it is?"

What occurs inside our mind when we are moved by the beauty of an object, when it evokes this powerful urge to celebrate, retain, and communicate our experience? Kant suggests that, in that moment, our faculties of imagination and understanding are totally unconstrained. If an object creates an experience of what Kant calls the "free harmony" of both faculties, we feel that unity as deep pleasure—a pleasure that is the experience of beauty. In Kant's words:

> Imagination and understanding are cognitive powers, but when they are not engaged for the purpose of cognition, their harmony or lack of it is felt as pleasure or displeasure in that which occasions it. The aesthetic judgement that comes about has its ground in the heightened but non-cognitive awareness of the fittingness of the object for my enjoyment.[43]

It would take us into dense philosophical thickets to unpack exactly what Kant means by imagination and cognition, respectively. Roughly, imagination is the name he gives our ability to take the input from our senses and give them order. Understanding generates the specific rules for such ordering. In moments of aesthetic pleasure, Kant argues, the understanding is no longer subject to the rules: both faculties are in free play. Essentially, he maintains that the pleasure that occasions an aesthetic judgment is felt in the fact that we aren't trying to figure out, say, the piece of art (exactly what colors are in it, for example) but are impelled to a moment of unconstrained experience—to take it in, bask in it, be still in front of it.

A vast and unending secondary literature suggests that in his discussion of how imagination and cognition come together in a moment of aesthetic apprehension and judgment, Kant's account is not without technical problems. He tries to describe something that is surely very familiar to all of us. A piece of music or art startles us out of complacency—we are drawn to it, powerfully. We may make some effort to describe it, but that effort gives way before the experience that the painting, for example, keeps pressing on us. We can be wowed, amazed, delighted, and horrified.

The British philosopher Peter de Bolla describes his aesthetic judgment in front of Barnett Newman's abstract painting, *Vir Heroicus Sublimis* as follows:

> "The image seems to compose me, to generate a sense of well-being . . . this composed tranquil space is the materiality of my affective response." Here, de Bolla recalls that the experience of standing before this large painting held him between an emotional response and a sense that the painting was offering him

new forms of cognition. The painting offers him the "feeling like one is knowing something"—a heightened sense of the self being well composed.

That aesthetic knowing-feeling that de Bolla places between "emotive sensation and cognition" is extremely powerful, even if it cannot be fully understood or defined. De Bolla's experience bears existential witness to what Kant described as the encounter with the beautiful.[44] De Bolla invites, or perhaps urges, readers to see the painting and share in the experience. He recounts something subjective (after all, it is *his* reaction to the canvas), but his claim for that experience is that it should be universal—available to each and all of us.

That claim may fail: As the German philosopher Hans Georg Gadamer reminds us, aesthetically motivated appeals cannot force our agreement, but that appeal is made in the strongest hope of agreement. We shouldn't muddle this with claims made in the name of what is fashionable, Gadamer maintains. Only deep, individual conviction can carry the weight of a genuine aesthetic judgment.[45] In short, if we are open to experiencing what de Bolla so powerfully experienced, we should and would agree with him.

The potentially universal status of an aesthetic judgment is the key. Kant argues that when one person appeals to another to share an aesthetic judgment, that appeal is to a common sense ("sensus communis"). That shared sense is to not to understood in its trivial meaning "just be sensible" but as a claim that if the second person experiences *this* music, she or he will likewise recognize its beauty. This is because, as human beings, each of us shares a common sensibility grounded on the possession of imagination and understanding.

It is striking that John Dewey, whose philosophical views are so deeply anti-Kantian, comes so close to Kant in describing the essence of an aesthetic experience. Dewey, like Kant, regards such an experience as critical, complex, and uplifting. What Kant speaks of as harmony of the understanding and the imagination, Dewey calls the "intuiting of the aesthetic experience to which "no name" can be given.[46] He, too, writes of the realization of the aesthetic moment as one in which there is a "final measure of balance or symmetry."[47] Just as Kant suggests we find ourselves keen to bring our experience to the attention of others, Dewey writes that we discover in aesthetic experience an "expansion of ourselves."[48]

It should be clear by this point that making aesthetic claims in the Kantian or Deweyan sense calls on mental capacities that are quite distinct from those used in finding—and reporting—"the main idea" in a text. First, as de Bolla shows, it's not at all easy to do. There is no obvious message to be found in a painting. The claim that the painting has aesthetic quality involves a more elusive but emotively powerful assertion. Describing the color, the zip-lines, the scale of the Newman painting won't do the trick. What is being conveyed is the sense of being "recomposed" as a viewer, being placed in a certain emotional-cognitive state by the experience of looking at the painting and trying to communicate the exhilaration that results.

Compared to the exercise of annunciating multiple perspectives based on reporting facts about the canvas—an exercise in which the personal intellectual engagement is relatively weak—the effort of evoking an aesthetic claim is searching and demanding. It involves translating a very intimate experience into a sharable language, what de Bolla calls a "mutual terrain." The experience of sharing can then be a powerful aesthetic experience that produces a deep sense of communality.[49]

These aren't just theorctical claims. In 2021, researchers from US and German universities examined the reactions of some 850 subjects from the United States, the United Kingdom, and India while looking at an image, or listening to music, or recalling a personal experience of beauty. The results strongly echo Kant's model: "Top-rated beauty experiences are strongly characterized by six dimensions: intense pleasure, an impression of universality, the wish to continue the experience, exceeding expectation, perceived harmony in variety, and meaningfulness."[50]

BACK TO SCHOOL

How should schools create opportunities to develop the aesthetic sensibilities of students? The answers cover a vast range. Making art, observing art, and reflecting on artistic experience are all about enabling encounters with a wide variety of art forms with the goal of evoking students' aesthetic experience.[51]

Across such an enormous panoply of possible encounters, one theme stands out, wellarticulated by perhaps the most impactful arts educator in the United States, Maxime Greene. She insists that the affect of children in the presence of art is key—an affect that includes thoughtfulness, attentiveness, and imaginativeness. She emphasizes that bringing children to artistic experiences is not to "explain" the work but to have children work at doing so themselves.[52] Even when the activity is circumscribed—as in, say, tracing and copying an existing piece of art—it is important to leave a wide degree of choice as to which art to trace, and to give children the responsibility of reflecting on the results.

As in the case of an Aristotelian education in ethics, the development of an aesthetic sensibility can start early, and not always by way of making art or reacting to it in a conventional sense. In some British schools, it begins with what used to be called "Observations." The idea was to take a simple experience such as a striking a match and then to express the experience in written form.

The key is to slow down and pay attention. In this example, it includes noticing the tactile sensation of scraping, the smells, the thoughts evoked by the drawing of a sailing ship on the box, the colors of the flame, the gradually disappearing and crinkling wooden match, and then just the curling whisps of smoke and, with the last match lit, an empty box. Observations were written down: "Now the box is useless. That beautiful tea clipper tossing on a rolling sea must go to complete waste. It is very sad but with a toss of my hand it is gone."[53]

The work of close observation—first of an experience and then in engaging with a work of art—embodies John Dewey's view of an aesthetic experience. He focuses on the need to learn how to gather the details present in an aesthetic experience, noting that there is a lot of work required lest we shortcut the whole. Dewey emphasizes the difference between aesthetic perception, a "controlled activity" in which we "take in" the object or event being encountered, and just being a passive recipient in an artistic encounter.[54]

No matter if the student is making art by way of listening or looking on the one hand, or acting, painting, dancing, singing, sculpting, carving or playing an instrument, on the other, the second element of aesthetic appreciation is self-awareness: Students are encouraged to reflect on their own experience in reacting to what they are seeing, hearing or creating.

As Kant suggests, the language of thought and emotions are not siloed here but simultaneously present. A child becomes conscious of the sound she is trying to produce on the violin, she struggles, knowing that she isn't there yet, and experiences her own knowing struggle as frustration. Or to take an example from the visual arts, imagine a student in front of a Rothko painting in a museum. The awareness that there is no immediately accessible "meaning" may be off-putting, and the tendency is to keep walking. Aware of this reaction, the teacher prompts the student to stop, to encounter, to keep looking, making the student hyper-aware of what is going on in the visual encounter.

Ultimately, in a full aesthetic experience, the entire experience is synthesized: Playing the piece on the violin with full muscle memory, the player becomes one with the piece, The Rothko painting and the viewer have generated what John Dewey called the consummatory moment, where the student in front of the canvas can no longer separate the painting from the experience of viewing it, feeling-knowing only that he is no longer where he was in his mind a few minutes before.

To offer students a rich set of such aesthetic experiences is a core value of education. Of immense value in themselves for the joy they can create, they also teach that the self is incomplete, that it can expand and grow in the presence of something that took trouble, time, attention, to encounter, to make it one's own. To simple pleasures, aesthetic education adds cognitive and emotional maturity. As William Butler Yeats teaches us:

> I walk through the long schoolroom questioning;
> A kind old nun in a white hood replies;
> The children learn to cipher and to sing,
> To study reading-books and history,
> To cut and sew, be neat in everything
> In the best modern way—the children's eyes
> In momentary wonder stare upon
> A sixty-year-old smiling public man.
> Labour is blossoming or dancing where
> The body is not bruised to pleasure soul,
> [....]
> O chestnut tree, great rooted blossomer,
> Are you the leaf, the blossom or the bole?
> O body swayed to music, O brightening glance,
> How can we know the dancer from the dance?
> (Excerpts from "Among School Children, William Butler Yeats.[55])

WISDOM: THE EDUCATION OF THOUGHT

"The learning of many things does not teach understanding."[56]

"Wherever we went, boredom was pervasive."[57]

As the previous chapters have suggested, the acquisition of basic academic proficiencies in the multiple domains through which much of human knowledge becomes accessible is a core responsibility for any education. The United States has yet to make good on that responsibility. Previous chapters in this book have addressed the ways in which our educational system—with its conflicted and fragmentary aims and disparate educational tools—has brought us to a place from which reaching even this modest goal has become next to impossible.

Failure to teach basic literacy, numeracy, and knowledge to young children must be remedied at the appropriate stage of learning in elementary school. The solutions—the integration of teacher preparation, strong instructional materials, integrated assessments, and schools focused on academic instruction, have been detailed in previous pages. But middle- and high-school education cannot succeed if they just extend an education in underdemanding skills and surface knowledge.

Perhaps the most pressing problem in American K-12 education is that the teaching of academic knowledge in our middle schools, and still more so in our high schools, leaves students bored, undermotivated, and often unable to move beyond the most basic levels of understanding.

The answer is not to inflate grades further, or abolish testing, or continue the dumbing-down of instructional materials. There is no substitute for effective, advanced instruction in native language, both oral and written, in foreign languages, in numerical symbols and their operations, in computer code or statistical language, in the disciplines of the arts, and in the specialized languages and algorithms of the sciences.

Teachers may reasonably hope that as students mature, they will want to criticize the ways in which these languages work, how they empower some and leave others marginalized, how they obscure underlying modes of authority, or provide questionable legitimacy to the current political, social and/or cultural paradigms. But a capacity for criticism depends most fundamentally on the acquisition of specialized academic content and concepts. Before use or criticism must come the acquisition of these academic languages themselves.

Acquiring facility in the academic disciplines can, of course, be justified in purely economic terms. Employment opportunities strongly reward those who have mastered one or more branches of learning, be that the surgeon, the software engineer, the successful artist, composer, or writer.[58] But acquiring facility in the academic languages is above all an end in itself: Without that facility, we leave learning to the vicissitudes of a child's home environment and subsequently to chance. Consistent with our argument that education must address what makes human beings unique, ensuring the effective learning of the disciplines is the only way to give students direct access to the languages of human knowledge.

Simply calling for more advanced academic instruction is futile. The pathway forward must be to pull students out of their current boredom and render compelling the opportunity for challenging studies. It is time to address the heart of the matter—the teaching of disciplinary knowledge beyond the elementary level and in ways that engages students' energies and potentially powerful satisfaction in the act of grasping new vistas of knowledge.

How can we work toward such a major shift? As an important start, to better utilize the often wasted later years of schooling, it is essential that students be able to discover fields of study that might interest them and motivate their efforts. To enable this to happen, education policymakers must first break the American obsession with ranking fields of study. In the United States, we have created a class system of academic and artistic subjects. ELA and math are given first-class treatment—not just for the first few years of schooling but all the way through high school, with far more class time devoted to them than any other subject. Schools have no choice but to focus heavily on ELA and math: Federally required examinations in both subjects are mandated from third grade on.

In the second class is science, with required testing three times during the K-12 years, supported most recently by an effort to establish cross-state standards (the NexGen science standards).[59] Alone, too, in third class, is social studies; a few states require testing in this subject matter, but most don't.[60] Then there are foreign languages and the arts, economics, computer studies—offered in many schools (but far from all) without tests at all, which become fourth-class subjects. Finally, everything else—philosophy, sociology, graphic design—is found in a small minority of schools.

The second feature of America's high-school education system has been noted earlier: There is a disconnect between state-mandated testing and entry into higher education. Why should students take subject-matter state tests seriously when they are rarely required for graduation?

The American hierarchy of academic subject matters and disconnect between high-school subject-matter testing and college entrance isn't the norm abroad, as a brief comparison with other high-school academic structures shows. In Germany, the Abitur exam at the end of high school involves tests in five subjects (including literature, the arts, and foreign languages).[61] Passing the Abitur is required for entry into German universities.

The structure of the French exam, the General Baccalaureate, is wider in scope than the Abitur. First, there is a required core curriculum that spans multiple subjects: French literature, philosophy ("humanités scientifiques"), English, another foreign language, civics, history/geography, physical education, and science/technology ("numérique").[62] In addition, we have several electives, including computer science, classics, advanced math, geopolitics, individual science subjects, and more. Any of these chosen subjects count equally in the final result. Once again, entrance into university is dependent on success on this exam.

In England, the choices are greater still. At fifteen or sixteen years old, all students take three subject exams—math, English, and science, and then pick, on average, six or seven more from a list of more than forty subjects.[63] At the end of high school, students going to college take the so called "A" (advanced)-level assessments offered by five state-authorized examination "boards."

The choice of which subject to study for the A level is up to the student, who chooses between a large number (at least fifty) of subjects (including Hindi, moving image art, sports science, and environmental technology), depending on what their school offers, or their willingness to study the subject online.[64] Students' choices will be based on matching their interests to the requirements of university course work or career path.

It makes sense to try to ensure that all children are basically literate and numerate, but why force all children to study, say, trigonometry when the interests and talents of the vast majority may well lie elsewhere? Why did we decide that the world of knowledge accessible to a child sixteen years old is hierarchical, with subjects such as economics or computer science or graphic design or Chinese or philosophy not worthy of an assessment that a university or employer could consider? Putting emphasis on so few fields almost guarantees that in the absence of truly inspired teaching, children who aren't drawn to that subject matter will be bored and disengaged (just as the US survey data confirm).[65]

Supporting the teaching of a far wider range of subjects at the high-school level by enabling the outcomes to be recognized by college-recognized assessments would be an important step forward in energizing the learning of young adults, but it won't solve the core problem of pedagogy—the teaching of disciplinary knowledge beyond a basic level. What do we know about how that can be done well? Perhaps the most thorough treatment of teaching in today's American high schools—and the most searching examination of what keeps students active, engaged, and learning—comes from *In Search of Deeper Learning* by Jal Mehta and Sarah Fine. The authors searched classrooms across the country for examples of teaching that occasions "deep cognitive engagement" from students.

What stands out most from this extensive study is that, in the end, what causes deeper learning is the passionate teaching that doesn't eschew disciplinary rigor. Metha and Fine, for example, paraphrase approvingly Jerome Bruner's view that a teacher's "real mastery is the ability to see the structure of how knowledge is organized in a field."[66] They emphatically reiterate that effective teaching prioritizes "depth over breadth" and emphasizes clear conceptual understanding of core ideas and instructs students in the epistemology of academic disciplines.[67]

The teachers Mehta and Fine chose as exemplary stand out for their capacity to privilege a learning experience that puts consistent, sometimes exacting, demands on students. The field study undertaken by Mehta and Fine ultimately tells us that only a rigorous practice of academic teaching provokes students to commit to learning and to achieving proficiency in their studies.[68]

What exceptional teachers provide above all in their classrooms is the teaching of what is compelling in an academic discipline—unpacking its mysteries, demonstrating its unique ways of empowering the learner. The result is a rewarding exercise for both parties involved. Defined by exigencies, this approach may seem to bracket off consideration of the "whole child," but in fact, in prioritizing exacting learning, it succeeds where it matters most It helps students learn well, for life, and gives them authentic reasons for self-esteem.

The key point is that Fine and Mehta didn't find quite what they expected. While they clearly brought to their task a sympathy for a progressivist approach—that is, child-centered and project-based learning—they found that the strongest teachers adopted a wide range of pedagogical styles. What these teachers shared, by contrast, was a love of their subjects. It mattered deeply to them that their students worked to master the internal logic, the forms of argument as well as the way meaning is constructed, in the academic disciplines they were studying. The combination of infectious passion and exacting standards for good work, all based on the teacher's own deep understanding of her or his discipline, was the key to success.[69]

To summarize: what Mehta and Fine actually rediscover is that an education in "deep learning" places major demands on the teacher, no matter if the language to be taught is in mathematical symbols, computer coding, musical notation, or the blank verse of Elizabethan drama. In every case, there are different conceptual frameworks that legitimate certain forms of use or procedures.

There are no shortcuts to mastering these principles. As the internationally recognized curriculum scholar Graham McPhail points out, anything beyond a surface familiarity with an academic discipline requires that students grasp what he calls the "epistemic structure" of that discipline, along with key concepts, competencies, and the interrelationship between them.[70]

The research in this area is compelling. If we want them to learn effectively, students cannot just be given bits and pieces—a math skill here, an algorithm there, a concept at some future date. Organizing and teaching the core concepts in an academic discipline is needed to facilitate retention in memory, to develop habits of mental processing, and to support analytic reasoning. But students also need conceptual frameworks: specific information delivered in the form of disparate pieces and items and dispensed as mere gobbets will decay into noise unless students have concepts and principles to organize and interpret content.[71]

Students also need to care about what they are studying. We cannot simply expect that adolescents take an interest in academic subjects, still less enough interest to work intensely to learn them effectively. The materials and teaching style must engage the student's interest. Engaged learning is made of what Nietzsche, in the ninety-fourth aphorism in *Beyond Good and Evil*, once called the seriousness of a child at play. The intensity, the energy, the desire to achieve success come from an emotional energy that is fed by genuine fascination.

Unsurprisingly, the quality of teaching that can provide academic structure and inspires that energy in students is rare. It takes practice, wisdom, and lots of the relevant content knowledge. Reviewing what Mehta and Fine write about the finest teachers they encountered is revealing: All but one had at least ten years of teaching experience, and in several cases, they were highly educated. Each of the star science teachers had PhDs. Even where the teachers' formal education was more modest, each of them had benefited from unique and often fortuitous learning experiences (one had been a Buddhist priest) that created formative experiences subsequently essential to their teaching.[72]

A REALITY CHECK

To restructure American education to deliver instruction that is ethically inspired, aesthetically rich, and academically compelling is a daunting, multigenerational task. It will not be accomplished by tinkering with a state's education standards or making piecemeal changes in teacher preparation.

That task will require a major shift in how America conceives of the role of its teachers. Too often, the nation restricts them to being the purveyors of information and basic skills. By contrast, teachers can and should be enabled to educate in a far more encompassing fashion. Tomorrow's teachers should invite students into the normative examination of literature, social studies, and science, preparing future citizens to examine ethical issues not only in their private lives but for the community.

Teachers in the future should introduce students to new fields of study, attuned to the aesthetic dimensions of human cognition across a much broader set of curricula choices. Master teachers will lead their colleagues in the exacting teaching of academic content, enabling students to grasp the conceptual foundations of each discipline.

For a profession already very short on new teacher candidates, to attract and prepare teachers of this caliber at scale would take a sea-change in the career pipeline, working structure, and compensation of the teaching profession.

Above all, it would require a cultural transformation in how pedagogy is conceived—not simply by education leaders at the national and state level but by our universities, where teachers are prepared and where many of our expectations for what constitutes learning in schools are created. As colleges and universities expect, so K-12 tries to deliver. If college entrance required students to demonstrate the capacities described in this chapter, America's schools would begin the task of teaching them. Such a shift in college expectations would require college presidents, chancellors, and boards of trustees to focus on the core values of a humanist education in ways that are currently absent.

In the K-12 system, a parallel transformation is needed. It would center on creating differentiated professional roles. What is required is the opportunity for teachers to specialize in the very different professional roles of mentor, curriculum expert, and master teacher.

Mentors will be focused on supporting novice teachers, giving immediate feedback, and providing emotional support. Curriculum experts will ensure that instructional materials are not only rigorous and multidimensional, providing opportunities for teachers to make vivid the ethical and aesthetic aspects of learning. These experts will also focus on building accelerated pathways for less-well-prepared students to catch up with their peers. Finally, master teachers will have overall responsibility for an instructional team that will include novice teachers, subject-matter teachers, and specialists in the teaching of children with special needs and English-language learners.

At the heart of effective instruction are the instructional materials themselves. Teacher preparation programs will have to stop suggesting that strong curricula are straightjackets. To the contrary, such materials can provide the vital foundation, the launching pad of effective instruction. Figure 5 illustrates a unit from *Journeys*, a strong high-school ELA curriculum unit being used in many public schools across Louisiana.

This lesson takes students deeply into the material of a Shakespeare play. It makes considerable cognitive demands, asking students to focus on specific linguistic motifs while also thinking about the relationship of this scene to the denouement of the play. There are weaknesses here, too, still too many low-level cognitive demands on students, such as the requirement that they summarize content. And there are unrealized opportunities: The

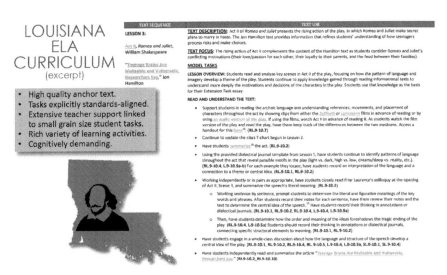

Figure 5.1. *Romeo and Juliet,* **Curriculum Excerpt.** *https://www.louisianabelieves.com/docs/default-source/teacher-toolbox-resources/ela-grade-9---romeo-and-juliet-1-0-unit.pdf?sfvrsn=604d8b1f_2.*

compelling inclusion of multiple perspectives on the play by combining the text with different film versions should prompt explicit investigations of aesthetic response. The ethical dimension of the material is more hinted at than surfaced.

But this curriculum excerpt does suggest the essential point: A strong curriculum teaches teachers as much as it teaches students. Such curricula draw attention to specific content in ways that teachers may not have imagined and suggest classroom practices that lead to exacting study, raising probing questions for students. This is true of strong curricula in all academic subjects, not only in ELA.[73]

Multiplying the subjects that will count for higher education; elevating the teacher profession so that we attract more middle- and high-school teachers knowledgeable in their subjects and well prepared to share their love of subject matter with students; and accelerating the use of high-quality curricula will together move the K-12 system closer to the essential task of teaching older students more advanced understanding of academic content.

WISDOM: THE TAPESTRY OF THOUGHT

In the absence of a ready-made ethical compass, there is a powerful human tendency to rely on instinct and emotion in lieu of reason. Meanwhile, beauty in its myriad forms can go unnoticed. Though perhaps intuitively felt by the child, beauty will only begin to shimmer when it is made present through carefully framed experience. Finally, without a compelling invitation into the exacting thought and creative power of knowledge, cognitive laziness can become habitual.

This chapter has treated these three crucial elements of an education as separate and distinct, But in practice, the lines blur, and each can make invaluable contributions to learning in the other domains. In an effective education, these three threads are not just taught—they are endlessly interwoven.

Martin Heidegger emphasizes the interaction between aesthetics and cognition, writing that our encounters with objects that are beautiful are not simply a matter of feeling but are among the most "thought-provoking" of all encounters.[74] More recently, Stanford University professor Elliot Eisner made the claim that arts education is cognitively invaluable. Eisner points out that much of what we can know lies outside of language. Developing the ability to think in images and symbols engages intelligence and understanding in nonlinguistic but powerful forms. Meanwhile, as we saw from de Bolla's account of looking at a Barnet Newman canvas, thinking pervades the entire aesthetic experience.[75]

The English language arts, or "literature," as a domain, also have their place in this picture. As discussed earlier, stories are ethically charged, offering children powerful insights into ethical choices and their consequences, but they have other dimensions as well. Rita Felski asserts that literature "heightens our ethical sensibilities" and intensifies "the power of our attachments." She also points out—as the close of *The Great Gatsby* makes vividly clear—that texts possess aesthetic qualities. They can enchant the reader, creating an emotional-cognitive response that is every bit as aesthetically powerful as that of listening to music or looking at art.[76]

Aesthetic experiences, in turn, have an ethical dimension. As the cultural critic Roger Kimball reminds us, when we share aesthetic responses with one another, we are drawn to a common humanity, of our capacity to share freely the sense of beauty that elevates our feelings as human beings. Kimball recalls Kant's statement that beauty is a "symbol of morality" because in our aesthetic experiences, "the mind is made conscious of a certain ennoblement and elevation."[77]

Theater and performance arts should be added to the material in which aesthetics, ethics, and rigorous learning intersect. In 1970, Nelson Mandela, then imprisoned in South Africa's notorious Robben Island prison, took part in a performance of Sophocles's *Antigone*. He embraced Antigone's stance, writing that she "symbolised [sic] our struggle . . . she defied the law on the grounds that it was unjust."

But Mandela agreed to play the role of King Creon, enacting the perspective of autocratic power.[78] Reading, acting, and thinking about Sophocles's text, Mandela wouldn't have separated ethics from aesthetics from rigorous study—the three strands of educated thought become one in the experience of learning the play. The prisoners in Robben Island chose *Antigone* because the play could teach them so much—about the beauty of language, sacrifice and courage, family and power, love and belief.

Strong teaching can happen anywhere, even without any of the resources we take for granted. Confronted by the loss of all their textbooks (removed by the Russians), teachers in schools of Tbilisi, Georgia, taught from memory, just as had the ancient Greeks. They had to rely on telling stories, creating science and math problems, and reciting poetry and literature—some of it from the twelfth century—by heart, or from a single copy.[79] Teaching the literature of their country was an ethical and academic act and a means of political resistance, but it was also something beautiful to watch.[80]

Teaching can be a joy, just as it's vastly demanding and incalculably important. Serving as dean of the Hunter College School of Education at the City University of New York, a welcome responsibility was to address the degree recipients in front of their peers, professors, family, and friends. It seems appropriate to close this book with a brief excerpt:

You have chosen a great calling: The life prospects, the imaginings, the interior furnishings of your students' minds rest in some great measure with you. Of course, there will be grim days as well as joyous ones. You will need what Paul Eluard has called *"Le dur désir de durer"*—the difficult desire to endure. But each day, remind yourself that on this day your teaching may open a world to a young person. There is no greater privilege.[81]

CONCLUDING IN HOPE

What is waiting for this child in the classrooms down the corridor? Perhaps the walls are not bare; perhaps her teachers have thought extensively about the ethical import of the stories they will share with her and the worlds those stories open to her imagination. Perhaps as the years progress, the child will encounter teachers passionately committed to making their academic expertise an invitation to exciting and exacting study. Perhaps this child will be able to nurture her talents even if they lie outside mathematics, English, or science. Perhaps she will have the chance to excel in Chinese, or philosophy, environmental studies, graphic design, and to experience a flight-simulator or a robotics lab. Perhaps her teachers will raise compelling questions that matter for a lifetime and invite her to explore answers with energy and acuity.

If her schooling can open these doors, this child will have received, step by step, the most precious of education's many gifts: the joy of thought; a foretaste of wisdom.

Figure 5.2. Child in Hallway.

Notes

PROLEGOMENON

1. Gutmann, *Democratic Education*. Digital edition.
2. McConnell, "EDUCATION DISESTABLISHMENT."
3. McConnell.
4. McConnell.
5. McConnell.
6. Gutmann, *Democratic Education*.
7. Gutmann.
8. Galston, "PARENTS, GOVERNMENT, AND CHILDREN."
9. Berner, *Pluralism and American Public Education: No One Way to School*.
10. Wagner, "Two Polls Diverged On The Issue Of School Choice."
11. Carter, "The Democratic Unraveling Began With Schools"; Wagner, "Two Polls Diverged On The Issue Of School Choice."
12. Pondiscio, "Pondiscio."
13. PDK Poll, "49th Annual PDK Poll of the Public's Attitudes Toward the Public Schools."
14. Modan, "What Does Carson v. Makin Mean for Ed Leaders?"
15. Hart Research Associates, "Public School Parents on the Value of Public Education: Findings from a National Survey of Public School Parents Conducted for the AFT."
16. O'Brien, "What Do Parents Want From Schools?"
17. Morrison, "Creative, Flexible, Global."
18. Brown, "How Should States Approach Early Childhood Policy?"
19. Some examples of this argument are Shakeel, Wolf, and Anderson, "The Participant Effects of Private School Vouchers across the Globe: A Meta-Analytic and Systematic Review"; Wolf, *School Choice*; Erickson, Mills, and Wolf, "The Effects of the Louisiana Scholarship Program on Student Achievement and College Entrance."
20. Barnum, "Do School Vouchers Work?"
21. Polikoff, *Beyond Standards*, 110.
22. Coleman, "The Relations between School and Social Structure."

CHAPTER 1

1. Pangle and Pangle, *The Learning of Liberty*, 6.

2. Pelaez and Keehner, "School District Budgets Show Wide Disparity in Funding per Pupil - Featured."

3. Langer Research Associates of New York, "51st Anuual PDK Poll of the Public's Attitudes Toward the Public Schools," 5, 9.

4. Rebell, "Preparation for Capable Citizenship."

5. Eva, "How to Inspire Students to Become Better Citizens."

6. Krachman and Larocca, "The Scale of Our Investment in Social-Emotional Learning."

7. Langer Research Associates of New York, "51st Anuual PDK Poll of the Public's Attitudes Toward the Public Schools."

8. FairTest, "Graduation Test Update: States That Recently Eliminated or Scaled Back High School Exit Exams."

9. Green, "High Proportion of Maryland Students Continue to Meet Graduation Requirements."

10. St. George, "Maryland Investigates Claim of Inappropriate Help on Diploma-Related Projects."

11. Tyner and Munyan-Penney, "Gotta Give 'Em Credit." For examples, see *Los Angeles Times* Editorial Board, "Opinion"; Edelman, Mongelli, and Golding, "'Fail Me' School's Kids Can Take Year's Worth of Classes in 6 Weeks"; and Mattingly, "This Is Just Outrageous."

12. Chetty, Friedman, and Rockoff, "Measuring the Impacts of Teachers II."

13. Jackson et al., "School Effects on Socio-Emotional Development, School-Based Arrests, and Educational Attainment."

14. NCES, "Fast Facts: High School Graduation Rates."

15. Aldric, "Average ACT Score for 2021, 2020, 2019, 2018, and Earlier Years." The reason for using ACT and not SAT scores is that the SAT is harder to summarize because the test changed in 2017.

16. The Nation's Report Card, "Results From The 2019 NAEP High School Transcript Study."

17. The Nation's Report Card, "NAEP Reading: Reading Results, Grade 12."

18. Technically, this is true of the long-term NAEP, which continues to ask the same questions over many years. The second, or "Main NAEP," test is updated for content to reflect current educational norms. But in each test, the performance indicators are matched to an external standard of achievement and are not impacted by teachers' practices.

19. Rojstaczer, "National Trends in Grade Inflation, American Colleges and Universities."

20. Lindsay, "The 'Other' College Scandal."

21. Kraemer, "Statistic of the Month."

22. Berner, "Introducing Pluralism to Public Schooling."

23. Schwartz, "Digging Deeper Into the Stark Declines on NAEP: 5 Things to Know."

24. The Nation's Report Card, "NAEP Long-Term Trend Assessment Results: Reading and Mathematics."

25. Loewus, "Majority of Teachers Say Reforms Have Been 'Too Much.'"

26. "Brown, Oregon's Democratic governor . . . signed Senate Bill 744 . . . discarding the requirement that high-school graduates be able to demonstrate an ability to read, write, and do math at a high-school level. A spokesman for Brown explained that this would benefit 'Oregon's Black, Latino, Latina, Latinx, Indigenous, Asian, Pacific Islander, Tribal, and students of color.'" From Hess, "Oregon Democrats Resurrect the 'Soft Bigotry of Low Expectations.'"

27. Social Security Administration, "Research Summary."

28. *New York Times*, "Excerpts from Bush's Speech on Improving Education."

29. It also has other sometimes unintended consequences. A recent grade-*deflation* policy in the humanities at Wellesley had the net effect of increasing enrollment in STEM disciplines. From Butcher, McEwan, and Weerapana, "The Effects of an Anti-Grade-Inflation Policy at Wellesley College." Ironically, rampant grade inflation in the humanities has failed to reverse a collapse in student enrollment. Students believe (mostly correctly) that the job market knows the low value of their inflated humanities GPA. From Burke, "Humanities Majors Don't 'Catch Up' to Peers, Report Says."

30. Donahue, "Teacher: Am I Guilty of Grade Inflation? I'll Admit, My Approach to Grading Has Evolved."

31. Hofstadter, *Anti-Intellectualism in American Life*.

32. Hanushek and Woessmann, "Education and Economic Growth." For further independent confirmation of Hanushek's research, see Goczek, Witkowska, and Witkowski, "How Does Education Quality Affect Economic Growth?"

33. Hanushek and Woessman, "The High Cost of Low Educational Performance: The Long-Run Economic Impact of Improving PISA Outcomes."

34. Schleicher and Tang, "Editorial | Education Post-2015: Knowledge and Skills Transform Lives and Societies," 10.

35. *Hoover Education Summit*.

36. The College Board defines STEM math as AP courses in calculus AB, calculus BC, computer science principles, computer science A, and statistics. Smith et al., "AP® STEM Participation and Postsecondary STEM Outcomes: Focus on Underrepresented Minority, First-Generation, and Female Students."

37. Rotermund and Burke, "Elementary and Secondary STEM Education | Post-High School Transitions."

38. Hess and McShane, "Few Students Take AP STEM Exams."

39. Anderson, "Report Finds New AP Computer Science Course Is Diversifying the Field."

40. Anderson.

41. New York State Education Department, "NY STATE - NEW YORK STATE REPORT CARD [2017–18]."

42. Broady and Hershbein, "Major Decisions."

43. Smith, "Advancing Racial Equity in Career and Technical Education Enrollment."

44. Anderson Institute of Technology, "Program Links / Digital and Visual Art and Development."

45. Passarella, "The Necessary Components of an Effective Career and Technical Education (CTE) Program."

46. Passarella, 4.

47. Hoffman and Schwartz, "Gold Standard: The Swiss Vocational Education and Training System."

48. Hanushek, Woessmann, and Zhang, "General Education, Vocational Education, and Labor-Market Outcomes over the Life-Cycle."

49. Cedefop, "Benefits of Vocational Education and Training in Europe: For People, Organisations and Countries," 20.

50. For more information on the Swill model, see Hoffman and Schwartz, "Gold Standard: The Swiss Vocational Education and Training System," 5.

51. Carnevale, Cheah, and Wenzinger, "The College Payoff: More Education Doesn't Always Mean More Earnings."

52. Krugman, "Rip Van Skillsgap."

53. Brunner, Dougherty, and Ross, "The Promise of Career and Technical Education."

54. Leybold-Johnson, "Can You Study after an Apprenticeship?"

55. PDK Poll, "49th Anuual PDK Poll of the Public's Attitudes Toward the Public Schools."

56. Passarella, 32.

57. The author confirmed this in person through a review of courses and an on-site visit.

58. Maryland Commission on Innovation & Excellence in Education, "Blueprint for Maryland's Future: Final Report." The author participated on the commission that produced this report.

59. One example of the academic standards necessary is offered by the International Baccalaureate Career-related Programme (IBCP), which integrates demanding IB coursework from its regular Diploma Programme with industry approved CTE-based studies.

60. U.S. Bureau of Labor Statistics, "Most New Jobs."

61. U.S. Bureau of Labor Statistics, "Computer Programmers."

62. CareerOneStop, "Careers with Most Openings."

63. Levanon et al., "How Employers Combat Labor Shortages: Insights From Online Job Ads Data."

64. Cedefop, "EU Workforce: Overeducated yet Underskilled?"

65. Redden, "41% of Recent Grads Work in Jobs Not Requiring a Degree."

66. Noguera, *City Schools and the American Dream*, 42.

67. Jencks and Phillips, *The Black-White Test Score Gap*.

68. The Nation's Report Card, "NAEP Mathematics: Mathematics Results, Grade 12."

69. Hanushek, "What Matters for Student Achievement."

70. Reardon et al., "Is Separate Still Unequal?"

71. Rothstein and Wozny, "Permanent Income and the Black-White Test Score Gap."

72. TNTP, "The Opportunity Myth."

73. Garcia, "Schools Are Still Segregated, and Black Children Are Paying a Price"; The Century Foundation, "Closing America's Education Funding Gaps"; Ingersoll and May, "The Minority Teacher Shortage: Fact or Fable?"; Rothstein, "The Racial Achievement Gap, Segregated Schools, and Segregated Neighborhoods—A Constitutional Insult"; Anderson, "A Root Cause of the Teacher-Diversity Problem"; Fryer and Beren, "An Empirical Analysis of 'Acting White.'"

74. For a thoughtful discussion of these topics, see Ladson-Billings, "From the Achievement Gap to the Education Debt."

75. Valant, "The Banality of Racism in Education."

76. Dee, "Teachers, Race, and Student Achievement in a Randomized Experiment."

77. For example, there is a "Minority Teachers of Illinois (MTI)" Scholarship Program through the Illinois Student Assistance Commission. To date, we lack strong research on the relationship between Hispanic teachers and Hispanic student outcomes.

78. Belsha and Darville, "A New National Effort to Promote School Integration Is Underway. More than Two Dozen School Districts Want In."; Cowan et al., "Teacher Licensure Tests: Barrier or Predictive Tool?"; Goldhaber and Hansen, "Race, Gender, and Teacher Testing"; Chung and Zou, "Teacher Licensing, Teacher Supply, and Student Achievement"; and Taylor, "Regents Drop Teacher Literacy Test Seen as Discriminatory."

79. Warden, "Knowing Better, Doing Better."

80. Bakshi and Steiner, "Acceleration, Not Remediation."

81. Slavin and Steiner, "Tutoring as an Effective Strategy in Our Troubled Times."

82. Rothstein, *Class And Schools*.

83. Rothstein, "Grading the Education Reformers."

84. Green, "New Biden Administration Rules for Charter Schools Spur Bipartisan Backlash."

85. CREDO, "Urban Charter School Study: Report on 41 Regions."

86. Ferrare and Setari, "Converging on Choice."

87. For a nuanced analysis of these issues, see Pondiscio, *How The Other Half Learns*.

88. NAACP, "Calling for Moratorium on Charter School Expansion and Strengthening of Oversight in Governance and Practice | NAACP."

89. Miller, "Why Charter Schools Are Failing Black Students."

90. Sawchuk, "What Is Critical Race Theory, and Why Is It Under Attack?"; Schwartz, "Map."

91. Conwright, "American Education Is Founded on White Race Theory."

92. *New York Times*, "The 1619 Project."

93. Kendi, *How to Be an Antiracist*, 18.

94. DiAngelo, *White Fragility*, 149.

95. "'Anti-Racist' Education Is Neither."

96. Silverstein, "An Update to The 1619 Project."

97. Quote from Jeff Duncan-Andrade, associate professor of Latina/o Studies and Race and Resistance at San Francisco State University featured in a Teach for America manual shared with the author but not publicly available.

98. equityXdesign, "Racism and Inequity Are Products of Design. They Can Be Redesigned."

99. equityXdesign.

100. Pondiscio, "I Believe 'Antiracism' Is Misguided. Can I Still Teach Black Children?"

101. Peterson, "The Education Exchange"; "Discussing the Practice of Critical Race Theory in Schools."

102. Pondiscio, "How US Schools Became Obsessed with Race."

103. Hess, "5 Takeaways for Education From Virginia's Governor Race"; *Sun Sentinel* Editorial Board, "DeSantis Weaponizes the Anguish of Children | Editorial."

104. Prather, "The Classics Are an Instrument of Freedom for Black People."

105. Eric Liu, cited in Grier and Sheasley, "Public education, democracy, and the future of America."

106. CivXNow, "Civic education has massive cross-partisan appeal as a solution to what ails our democracy."

107. The Nation's Report Card, "NAEP Report Card: Civics."

108. Center for Civic Education.

109. Cited in Kandel, "The Impact of the War on American Education."

110. There is a strong case to be made for the role of extracurricular activities such as service-learning experiences in fostering habits of civic participation. The focus here is only on in-school civic learning.

111. Galston, "Political Knowledge, Political Engagement, and Civic Education."

112. Winthrop, "The need for civic education in 21st-century schools."

113. Schwartz, "Map: Where Critical Race Theory Is Under Attack."

114. Boxell, "Country Trends in Affective Polarization."

115. Rebell, "Preparation for capable citizenship: The schools' primary responsibility."

116. Finn, "Educating young Americans for citizenship is our schools' top job."

117. Educating For American Democracy, "20th Century African Heritage: Civil Rights in Rhode Island."

118. Educating for American Democracy.

CHAPTER 2

1. Accenture, "It's Learning. Just Not as We Know It."

2. See the following for a typical summary: M. P. Foundation, "Nurturing the Whole Child."

3. For a representative list, see Buckle, "A Comprehensive Guide to 21st Century Skills."

4. Critical Thinking Web, "[C01] What Is Critical Thinking?"

5. Dweck, *Mindset.*

6. Wikipedia, "Grit (Personality Trait)."

7. Innis, "Social Emotional Health; a Strong Indicator of Academic Success."

8. *Merriam-Webster Dictionary*, "Metacognition."

9. The Glossary of Education Reform, "21st Century Skills Definition."

10. Reboot Foundation, "Critical Thinking Survey Report."

11. Willingham, "Critical Thinking."

12. OECD, "PISA 2021 Creative Thinking Framework (Third Draft)."

13. Hitchcock, "Critical Thinking."

14. Foundation for Critical Thinking, "Defining Critical Thinking."

15. Foundation for Critical Thinking.

16. Dewar, "Teaching Critical Thinking."

17. Willingham, "Critical Thinking: Why Is It So Hard to Teach?"

18. Willingham, "Critical Thinking."

19. Hitchcock, "Critical Thinking."

20. This section draws on the author's previously published work. See Steiner, "Make Sense of the Research."

21. For a much-cited scholarly discussion of effect sizes in education, see Kraft, "Interpreting Effect Sizes of Education Interventions."

22. Harrison, "Are Interventions Promoting a Growth Mindset Effective in Raising Academic Achievement in School-Aged Pupils?"

23. What Works Clearinghouse, "WWC SUMMARY OF EVIDENCE FOR THIS INTERVENTION | Growth Mindset."

24. There is an active debate in the literature about how to characterize effect sizes. Most recently, the push has been to be more generous—that is, to classify effect sizes between 0.05 and 0.20 as medium rather than small—but only when the research is at the RCT level of rigor and linked to standardized academic achievement tests. [From Kraft, "Interpreting Effect Sizes of Education Interventions."]

25. Claro, Paunesku, and Dweck, "Growth Mindset Tempers the Effects of Poverty on Academic Achievement."

26. OECD, "PISA 2018: Sky's the Limit."

27. OECD.

28. OECD.

29. OECD.

30. OECD.

31. Sisk et al., "To What Extent and Under Which Circumstances Are Growth Mind-Sets Important to Academic Achievement?"

32. Sisk et al.

33. Dweck, "Carol Dweck Revisits the 'Growth Mindset.'"

34. DeWitt, "Why a 'Growth Mindset' Won't Work."

35. DeWitt.

36. Dweck, "What Having a 'Growth Mindset' Actually Means."

37. American University School of Education, "How to Foster a Growth Mindset in the Classroom."

38. Bashant, "Developing Grit in Our Students: Why Grit Is Such a Desirable Trait, and Practical Strategies for Teachers and Schools."

39. Maguire, "What Is Resilience?"

40. Duckworth and Seligman, "Self-Discipline Outdoes IQ in Predicting Academic Performance of Adolescents." The study later acknowledges that if standardized test results were used instead of GPA, then there was no statistically significant difference between self-discipline scores and IQ as predictors of test outcomes. It also argues that GPA is a better outcome measure.

41. Mischel, Ebbesen, and Raskoff Zeiss, "Cognitive and Attentional Mechanisms in Delay of Gratification."

42. Watts, Duncan, and Quan, "Revisiting the Marshmallow Test."

43. Barshay, "Research Scholars to Air Problems with Using 'Grit' at School."

44. Credé, Tynan, and Harms, "Much Ado about Grit."

45. Barshay, "Research Scholars to Air Problems with Using 'Grit' at School."

46. Duckworth, "Don't Grade Schools on Grit"; Hattie, "We Aren't Using Assessments Correctly."

47. Zernike, "Testing for Joy and Grit?"

48. Clarke et al., "Adolescent Mental Health: A Systematic Review on the Effectiveness of School-Based Interventions."

49. CASEL, "What Is the CASEL Framework?"

50. Durlak et al., "The Impact of Enhancing Students' Social and Emotional Learning."

51. Durlak et al.

52. Durlak et al.

53. Balfanz and Byrnes, "Connecting Social-Emotional Development, Academic Achievement, and On-Track Outcomes: A Multi-District Study of Grades 3 to 10 Students Supported by City Year Americorps Members."

54. Balfanz and Byrnes.

55. Bavarian et al., "Using Social-Emotional and Character Development to Improve Academic Outcomes."

56. McCormick et al., "Do Intervention Impacts on Academic Achievement Vary by School Climate?"

57. West et al., "Promise and Paradox."

58. West et al.

59. Balfanz and Byrnes, "Connecting Social-Emotional Development, Academic Achievement, and On-Track Outcomes: A Multi-District Study of Grades 3 to 10 Students Supported by City Year Americorps Members."

60. Balfanz and Byrnes.

61. Slavin, "Tutoring Could Change Everything."

62. Balfanz and Byrnes, "Connecting Social-Emotional Development, Academic Achievement, and On-Track Outcomes: A Multi-District Study of Grades 3 to 10 Students Supported by City Year Americorps Members."

63. Balfanz and Byrnes.

64. Balfanz and Byrnes.

65. Balfanz and Byrnes.

66. Balfanz to Steiner, "Untitled Email," March 29, 2022.

67. Balfanz and Byrnes, "Connecting Social-Emotional Development, Academic Achievement, and On-Track Outcomes: A Multi-District Study of Grades 3 to 10 Students Supported by City Year Americorps Members."

68. Jackson et al., "School Effects on Socio-Emotional Development, School-Based Arrests, and Educational Attainment"; Jackson, "The Full Measure of a Teacher."

69. Greene, "The Moral and Religious Roots of Social and Emotional Learning."

70. This is the implication of the Kirabo Jackson et al. piece: "School Effects on Socio-Emotional Development, School-Based Arrests, and Educational Attainment."

71. Pondiscio, "The Unexamined Rise of Therapeutic Education: How Social-Emotional Learning Extends K–12 Education's Reach into Students' Lives and Expands Teachers' Roles."

72. Santens, "Stop Teaching Students What to Think. Teach Them How to Think."

73. Saavedra and Opfer, "Nine Lessons on How to Teach 21st Century Skills and Knowledge."

74. Center for Global Education, "Teaching and Learning 21st Century Skills."

75. The Glossary of Education Reform, "21st Century Skills Definition."

76. Schraw and Dennison, "Assessing Metacognitive Awareness."

77. Christodoulou, *Seven Myths About Education*, 52.

78. Fleming and Lau, "How to Measure Metacognition."

79. Chick, "Metacognition."

80. Terada, "How Metacognition Boosts Learning."

81. Terada.

82. The National Commission on Excellence in Education, "A Nation at Risk: The Imperative for Educational Reform."

83. OECD, "PISA 2021 Creative Thinking Framework (Third Draft)," 5.

84. OECD, 5.

85. OECD, 5.

86. OECD, 8.

87. OECD.

88. OECD, 26.

89. McPhail, "The Search for Deep Learning."

90. Christodoulou, *Seven Myths About Education*, 5.

91. Christodoulou, 79–80.

CHAPTER 3

1. Oates, "Could Do Better."

2. Barnum, "3 Not-Quite-True Claims about the Pandemic and Schools."

3. Will, "Fewer People Are Getting Teacher Degrees. Prep Programs Sound the Alarm."

4. Levin and Bradley, "Understanding and Addressing Principal Turnover."

5. Consortium on Chicago School Research, "The Essential Supports."

6. Consortium on Chicago School Research.

7. Chenoweth, *Schools That Succeed*, 45–46.

8. Kirp, *Improbable Scholars,* 9.

9. Kirp, 79.

10. Schmidt, Houang, and Cogan, "A Coherent Curriculum: The Case of Mathematics."

11. Crato, *Improving a Country's Education: PISA 2018 Results in 10 Countries,* 108.

12. Suto and Oates, "High-Stakes Testing after Basic Secondary Education: How and Why Is It Done in High-Performing Education Systems?"

13. Hirsch, *Why Knowledge Matters.*

14. Oates, "England: England and PISA - The Long View."

15. We should add that as indicated above, principals have a strong influence—second only to teachers—on what impacts student results (in-school). However, so much of what makes them important is their support of teachers teaching strong content. From Branch, Hanushek, and Rivkin, "School Leaders Matter: Measuring the Impact of Effective Principals." The research from Tony Bryk (cited previously) points to the principals' impact on creating "strong learning climates" and supportive of "teacher leadership around school-wide goals." From Allensworth and Hart, "How Do Principals Influence Student Achievement?"

16. NEA, "Great Teaching and Learning."

17. Schleicher, *Building a High-Quality Teaching Profession.*

18. Oates, "Could Do Better," 135.

19. Oates, 135.

20. Butler, "No Grammar Schools, Lots of Play."

21. Sahlgren, Press Regarding "Real Finnish Lessons: The true story of an education superpower."

22. *Hoover Education Summit.*

23. Kirp, *Improbable Scholars.*

24. Dewey, *Democracy and Education,* 23.

25. Dewey, "The Quest for Certainty," 12.

26. For an extensive discussion of these issues, see: Steiner, *Rethinking Democratic Education* (particularly chaps. 5 and 6).

27. Dewey, *Experience and Nature,* 38.

28. The PE Specialist, a creator on YouTube, has a video that acts as direct instruction on how to avoid direct instruction titled "Teaching Tips - Be a Guide on the Side not a Sage on the Stage." For a more typical, highly sympathetic contrasting of the bad old ways with the new constructivism, take Alison King's "Sage on the Stage to Guide on the Side" from the journal *College Teaching.*

29. Kober and Rentner, "History and Evolution of Public Education in the US."

30. McGuffey, *McGuffey's Sixth Eclectic Reader.*

31. Willis et al., *The American Curriculum.* 53–54.

32. The reports had an initial publishing run of thirty thousand copies, with multiple subsequent reprints.

33. Cited in Ravitch, *Left Back,* 31.

34. Cited in Ravitch, 181.

35. Cited in Willis et al., *The American Curriculum,* 173–75.

36. Summarized in Ravitch, *Left Back*, 46.

37. Cited in Ravitch, 94.

38. Ravitch, 266.

39. Ravitch, 137.

40. Hofstadter, *Anti-Intellectualism in American Life*, 1075–76. Ebook edition.

41. Ralph Waldo Emerson describes "the fusing process" that "transforms the English, the German, the Irish emigrant into an American. . . . The individuality of the immigrant, almost even his traits of race and religion, fuse down in the democratic alembic like chips of brass thrown into the melting pot." Cited in Thornton, "America's Problem of Assimilation."

42. Tyack, *Seeking Common Ground*, 125.

43. Tyack, 63.

44. Tosh et al., "Digital Instructional Materials: What Are Teachers Using and What Barriers Exist?"

45. Blazar et al., "Learning by the Book."

46. TNTP, "The Opportunity Myth."

47. For the results, see Bjorklund-Young and Plasman, "Reducing the Achievement Gap: An Empirical Analysis of Middle School Math Performance in Six States and Washington, D.C."
For a discussion of remediation and its alternatives, see Steiner and Weisberg, "Steiner & Weisberg."

48. Oxford, "Constructivism." See also David Steiner, "Skewed Perspective."

49. For a critical view of this belief system from inside a leading school of education, see Richardson, "Constructivist Pedagogy."

50. Cydis, "Authentic Instruction and Technology Literacy."

51. Open Culture Staff, "The Summerhill School, the Radical Educational Experiment That Let Students Learn What, When, and How They Want (1966)."

52. Fliegel, "Debbie Meier and the Dawn of Central Park East."

53. Ashman, "Understanding the PISA 2015 Findings about Science Teaching."

54. Crato, *Improving a Country's Education: PISA 2018 Results in 10 Countries*.

55. Saphier, Haley-Speca, and Gower, *The Skillful Teacher*.

56. The National Council of Teachers of English, "Beliefs about Methods Courses and Field Experiences in English Education."

57. NCTE and NCATE, "NCTE/NCATE Standards for Initial Preparation of Teachers of Secondary English Language Arts, Grades 7–12."

58. Will, "Teacher-Preparation Programs Make Gains in the 'Science of Reading,' Review Finds."

59. For a trenchant indictment of teacher preparation in the United States, see NIH, "National Reading Panel Publications." See also Levine, "Educating School Teachers."

60. Only one state, Louisiana, has instituted a plan aimed at extending teacher clinical preparation for a full year, as opposed to a single semester, and one other—Maryland—has a plan to do so. Alternative preparation programs offer student-teachers a few weeks of summer training prior to putting them into classrooms as teachers of record.

61. The data can suggest that certain programs do better than others in a given year. See Honawar, "Gains Seen in Retooled Teacher Ed." However, we lack any rigorous research that shows multiyear consistency of stronger outcomes that are linked to specific program designs. The only state that has, to date, made substantive changes in state policy regulating education preparation programs is Louisiana, which has strengthened its clinical preparation. See Louisiana Department of Education, "Believe and Prepare."

62. Koedel et al., "Teacher Preparation Programs and Teacher Quality: Are There Real Differences Across Programs."

63. Hippel and Bellows, "Rating Teacher-Preparation Programs."

64. Kane, "Connecting to Practice."

65. There are exceptions. For example, the Relay Graduate School of Education, which focuses on clinical practice based, in turn, on strategies shown to raise student learning outcomes in strong charter schools. (Disclosure: the author is a board member of Relay.) Relay Graduate School of Education, "Better Attendance, Fewer Suspensions, More Teachers of Color - Findings from Recent Research."

66. Levine, "Educating School Teachers," 19.

67. Hollins and Warner, "Evaluating the Clinical Component of Teacher Preparation Programs."

68. To give but one example, the prestigious Teaching Fellows program in NYC had a 3.0 GPA requirement, but the NYC Department of Education has pressured schools of education to accept students with GPAs as low as 2.2.

69. De Avila and Hobbs, "Teacher Shortage Prompts Some States to Lower the Bar."

70. Schleicher, *Hoover Education Summit*.

71. Suto and Oates, "High-Stakes Testing after Basic Secondary Education: How and Why Is It Done in High-Performing Education Systems?" 3.

72. Oates, "Assessment - Perhaps It's Just about Good Questions . . . "

73. Hart et al., "Student Testing in America's Great City Schools: An Inventory and Preliminary Analysis."

74. In their report "The Opportunity Myth," TNTP "looked at district-mandated interim assessments to understand what kind of feedback they were providing teachers about their students' performance against grade-level state standards. All of our districts required their teachers to administer at least quarterly interim assessments in both math and ELA—but none of these assessments met the bar for full alignment to the standards: of a sampling of thirty-eight interim assessments in math and ELA, just two were 'partially aligned' to appropriate benchmarks. The remaining thirty-six were 'not aligned,' largely because they did not ask students grade-appropriate questions." TNTP, "The Opportunity Myth."

75. What is biserial correlation? "Those who performed well on all questions should have performed well on the one being measured; those who did poorly on all should have done poorly on the one being measured. For each question, the closer to +1 the coefficient, the better the question fits with the other questions on the exam." From Connor, "Interpreting Biserial Correlation Scores."

76. Wineburg, "Crazy for History," 1409.

77. Wineburg, 1409.

78. Delaware System of Student Assessments, "2021 Grade 11 Social Studies Training Test Booklet."

79. Steiner, "The New Common Core Assessments."

80. National Assessment Governing Board, "Draft Reading Assessment Framework for the 2025 National Assessment of Educational Progress."

81. Steiner and Bauerlein, "A Feel-Good Report Card Won't Help Children."

82. Disclosure: I was New York State Education Commissioner and led the process of securing federal funding for EngageNY.

83. Kaufman et al., "Use of Open Educational Resources in an Era of Common Standards."

84. Polikoff, *Beyond Standards*, 8–12; Chiefs for Change, "Hiding in Plain Sight: Leveraging Curriculum to Improve Student Learning."

85. I have first-hand familiarity with the IMPD Network as I am frequently a guest speaker at CCSSO events.

86. The data from the project is not yet public. Robert Pondiscio published an overview of what has happened in Louisiana (in 2017) for *Education Next*.

87. See the websites for Deans for Impact and the National Council on Teacher Quality (NCTQ).

88. DOE-Mass, "Educator Preparation - CAP Guidelines."

89. For a more extensive discussion of this topic, see Steiner, Jensen, and Magee, "Curriculum Literacy in Schools of Education? The Hole at the Center of American Teacher Preparation."

90. Steiner and Berner, "Chicago's Use of the International Baccalaureate: An Education Success Story That Didn't Travel."

91. U.S. Department of Education, "Innovative Assessment Demonstration Authority"; Louisiana Believes, "Louisiana Innovative Assessment Program."

92. Disclosure: I have been an integral part of the creation of Louisiana's Pilot Assessment since the start of the project and continue to be heavily involved as it proceeds. Likewise, I am the chair of John White's dissertation committee.

93. Tyack, *Seeking Common Ground*.

94. Eshetu, "Parental Socio-Economic Status as a Determinant Factor of Academic Performance of Students in Regional Examination."

95. Tucker, "Differences in Performance WITHIN Schools."

96. *Hoover Education Summit.*

97. Brookings, "The Resurgence of Ability Grouping and Persistence of Tracking."

98. For the statistical details, see Garcia, "Schools Are Still Segregated, and Black Children Are Paying a Price." While magnet schools *are* designed to attract a diverse body of students, the total number of U.S. students at such schools is modest—below 5 percent.—For the numbers, see NCES, "Table 216.20, Number and Enrollment of Public Elementary and Secondary Schools, by School Level, Type, and Charter and Magnet Status: Selected Years, 1990–91 through 2014–15," 216.

99. NAEP and IES, "School Composition and the Black–White Achievement Gap," 2.

100. Figlio and Karbonik, "Some Schools Much Better than Others at Closing Achievement Gaps between Their Advantaged and Disadvantaged Students."

101. The Century Foundation, "The Benefits of Socioeconomically and Racially Integrated Schools and Classrooms."

102. Deal and Peterson (1990) defined school culture as "deep patterns of values, beliefs, and traditions that have been formed over the course of [the school's] history," Heckman (1993) stated that the school culture lies in "the commonly held beliefs of teachers, students, and principals." Both quotes cited in Stolp, "Leadership for School Culture."

103. Coleman, *High School and Beyond*.

104. West, "Schools of Choice: Expanding Opportunity for Urban Minority Students."

105. Willms, "Catholic-School Effects on Academic Achievement"; Braun, Jenkins, and Grigg, "National Assessment of Educational Progress: Comparing Private Schools and Public Schools Using Hierarchical Linear Modeling."

106. Berkowitz et al., "A Research Synthesis of the Associations Between Socioeconomic Background, Inequality, School Climate, and Academic Achievement."

107. Berner, *Pluralism and American Public Education: No One Way to School*; Schleicher, "PISA 2018 Insights and Interpretations."

108. CREDO, "Urban Charter School Study: 41 Regions Workbook."

109. Chabrier, Cohodes, and Oreopoulos, "What Can We Learn from Charter School Lotteries?"

110. Chabrier, Cohodes, and Oreopoulos.

111. "Evidence from around the world suggests that studying within 'distinctive educational communities in which pupils and teachers share a common ethos' vastly increases the odds of students acquiring academic and civic knowledge, skills, and sensibilities." From Berner, "How School Culture Drives Civic Knowledge and Shapes the Next Generation of Citizens."

112. TNTP, "Greenhouse Schools: Executive Summary."

CHAPTER 4

1. Schleicher, *Building a High-Quality Teaching Profession*.

2. For a full treatment of the history of the SAT test, see Lemann, *The Big Test*.

3. Frey, "What We Know, Are Still Getting Wrong, and Have Yet to Learn about the Relationships among the SAT, Intelligence and Achievement"; Frey and Detterman, "Scholastic Assessment or g?"

4. As the researcher Meredith Frey points out, the word intelligence doesn't appear on the ETS (Educational Testing Service) website (ETS administers the SAT for the College Board). Nor does it appear in any documentation about the specifications for the SAT, its validity, or any other available literature. See Frey, "What We Know, Are Still Getting Wrong, and Have Yet to Learn about the Relationships among the SAT, Intelligence and Achievement." For the ACT correlations, see Koenig, Frey, and Detterman, "ACT and General Cognitive Ability."

5. Hambrick and Chabris, "Yes, IQ Really Matters."

6. Rothstein, "College Performance Predictions and the SAT."

7. Nichols-Barrer et al., "Testing College Readiness."

8. Markovits, *The Meritocracy Trap*, 107.

9. Walsh, "Major Harvard Change Underscores the Decline of Standardized Testing."

10. Diakiw, "Reading and Life Success."

11. Akbasli, Sahin, and Yaykiran, "The Effect of Reading Comprehension on the Performance in Science and Mathematics."

12. The Nation's Report Card, "NAEP Mathematics: Mathematics Results, Grade 4"; The Nation's Report Card, "NAEP Reading: Reading Results, Grade 4."

13. Collins, "Mississippi Rising?"

14. Coleman, "Bringing the Common Core to Life."

15. Common Core State Standards Initiative, "English Language Arts Standards » Introduction," Common Core State Standards Initiative, 2015, http://www.corestandards.org/ELA-Literacy/introduction/how-to-read-the-standards/.

16. Even I cannot figure out why determining "connotative meaning" is supposed to be a more sophisticated skill than unpacking metaphors and similes.

17. Lexile, "What Does the Lexile Measure Mean?"

18. Steiner, "The Common Core."

19. Coleman and Pimentel, "Revised Publishers' Criteria for the Common Core State Standards in English Language Arts and Literacy, Grades 3–12."

20. National Research Council, *Adding It Up: Helping Children Learn Mathematics*.

21. Cited in Rieger, "The Beautiful Art of Mathematics†."

22. Common Core State Standards Initiative, "English Language Arts Standards » Anchor Standards » College and Career Readiness Anchor Standards for Reading."

23. Pondiscio, "Testing Alone Won't Make Good Readers."

24. Core Knowledge Foundation, "The Baseball Experiment."

25. Hirsch, *The Making of Americans*. Digital edition.

26. For a primer in the research on "background knowledge," see Smith et al., "The Role of Background Knowledge in Reading Comprehension"; Cabell and Hwang, "Building Content Knowledge to Boost Comprehension in the Primary Grades."; McCarthy and McNamara, "The Multidimensional Knowledge in Text Comprehension Framework."

27. Lyons, "Rethinking the Way We Learn: UVA Psychologist Debunks Myths about How the Brain Works," *Virginia Magazine*, Spring 2013, https://uvamagazine.org/articles/rethinking_the_way_we_learn.

28. I grew up in the United Kingdom, where this would be common—the "you" in question is him speaking from memory.

29. Hirsch, *The Making of Americans*.

30. A personal note from me: I should add that I was an early convert to Hirsch's arguments about knowledge building—serving on the Board of The Core Knowledge Foundation for many years. I am currently working at Johns Hopkins University to pressure publishers and school districts alike to take seriously the responsibility to

design ELA curriculum that build students' knowledge of literature, history, science, and the arts.

31. Hirsch et al., "Responses to Robert Scholes," 120.

32. Hirsch, *Cultural Literacy*, xiii.

33. Hirsch, 2.

34. Hirsch, 113.

35. Hirsch, *What Your Sixth Grader Needs to Know*, 164.

36. Buras, "Questioning Core Assumptions: A Critical Reading of and Response to E. D. Hirsch's The Schools We Need and Why We Don't Have Them."

37. Cited in Hitchens, "Why We Don't Know What We Don't Know: Just Ask E.D. Hirsch."

38. Arendt, *Between Past and Future*, 93.

39. Hirsch, *Validity in Interpretation*.

40. Hirsch, 25.

41. Hirsch, *What Your Sixth Grader Needs to Know*, 111.

42. Plato, "Perseus Under Philologic: Pl. Resp. 597e."

43. Aristotle, *Metaphysics*, sec. 981a.

44. Sennett, "The Troubled Craftsman," 20.

45. Cited in Sennett, 40. Too many CTE (career and technical education) programs in American schools have historically trained students in mindless, low-level skills. There is a deep difference between "woodwork" understood as learning repetitive skills and carpentry as discussed here.

46. Heidegger, *What Is Called Thinking?* 14.

47. Hirsch, *Validity in Interpretation*, 213.

48. Gadamer, *Truth and Method*, 238.

49. Felski, *Uses of Literature*, 8.

50. Felski, 15.

51. Gadamer, *Truth and Method*, 263–65.

52. Quoted in Chesley, "Freshmen Eager to Learn Purpose of Education through New Thinking Matters." (Stanford is arguably the world's most selective university. Minerva College claims that it takes a smaller percentage of applicants than Stanford, but the applicant pools are not comparable.)

53. For Coleman's presentation, see *The Gettysburg Address*. For the sample lesson, see EngageNY, "Common Core Unit: A Close Reading of Lincoln's Gettysburg Address."

54. Fitzgerald, *The Great Gatsby*.

55. Felski, *Uses of Literature*, 63. Felski is writing about the capacity of literature to enchant. She wasn't writing here about this particular text, but her phrase illuminates an aspect of Fitzgerald's language.

56. Mark, "Agoge, the Spartan Education Program."

57. Hanushek et al., "Closing the SES Achievement Gap: Trends in U.S. Student Performance."

58. Louisa Moats, a national expert on reading instruction, points out that the CCSS embodied political compromises that softened their focus on the findings of reading

science. See Moats, "Reconciling the Common Core State Standards with Reading Research."

59. Common Core State Standards Initiative, "Standards for Mathematical Practice."

60. Schmidt, McKnight, and Raizen, *A Splintered Vision*.

61. Common Core State Standards Initiative, "Mathematics Standards."

62. The Nation's Report Card, "NAEP Mathematics: Mathematics Results, Grade 4"; The Nation's Report Card, "NAEP Mathematics: Mathematics Results, Grade 12"; The Nation's Report Card, "NAEP Mathematics 2019 Highlights Grade 12."

63. OECD, "International Student Assessment (PISA) - Mathematics Performance (PISA)."

64. Loveless, *Between the State and the Schoolhouse*.

65. Common Core State Standards Initiative, "High School: Algebra » Arithmetic with Polynomials & Rational Expressions."

66. Common Core State Standards Initiative, "High School: Algebra » Reasoning with Equations & Inequalities."

67. Common Core State Standards Initiative.

68. Green, "Why Do Americans Stink at Math?"

69. Ball and Forzani, "Learning to Teach Something in Particular: A Common Core for the Training of Teachers."

70. Lockhart, "A Mathematician's Lament."

71. Wolpert, "Why so Many U.S. Students Aren't Learning Math."

CHAPTER 5

1. Wooldridge, "Kissinger Knows Why the Global Leadership Deficit Is Getting Worse."

2. Webster, *The Duchess of Malfi*. Act IV, Scene 1.

3. Kraut, "Aristotle's Ethics."

4. Munro, "Michael Oakeshott."

5. Oakeshott, *The Voice of Liberal Learning*, 5.

6. Arendt, *Responsibility and Judgment*, 44–45.

7. MacIntyre, *After Virtue*, chap. 6.

8. Raths, Harmin, and Simon, *Values and Teaching*, 7.

9. CA Department of Education, "Character Education - Youth Development."

10. Hunter, *The Death of Character*, 152.

11. Hunter, 163. Other studies have confirmed these findings. See, for example, "The 1996 Survey of American Public Culture," cited by Hunter on p. 282 of this same book.

12. Hunter, 169.

13. While I am using the most common translation of eudaimonia as "human flourishing," it is important to note that the Greek term is richer. It includes the acknowledgement of the actions of anonymous divine forces that we can imperfectly call "chance."

14. MacIntyre, *After Virtue*, 215–16.

15. Aristotle, *Aristotle on Practical Wisdom*, l. 1140a.

16. MacIntyre, *After Virtue*. Digital Edition.

17. Burnyeat, "5. Aristotle on Learning to Be Good," 87.

18. Aristotle, *Aristotle on Practical Wisdom*, ll. 1105b25-26.

19. Urmson, "9. Aristotle's Doctrine of the Mean," 161.

20. MacIntyre, *After Virtue*, 216.

21. For further discussion, see Lewis, "Rousseau and the Fable."

22. The Core Knowledge Foundation, "CKLA Grade 1."

23. Hunter, *The Death of Character*, 226. It is striking that Hunter, who dismisses "neo-classical" ethics in a few pages largely by eliding it with ultraconservative contemporary ideologues nevertheless ends up speaking in such Aristotelian and MacIntyrian terms. He argues that the force of such narratives depends on a sense of "transcendence" (227), but the noun does more work than a kind of hand-waving to his preference for religious as opposed to other powerful sources of altruism or ethical responsiveness.

24. Burnyeat, "5. Aristotle on Learning to Be Good," 73.

25. Burnyeat, 74.

26. Aristotle, *Aristotle on Practical Wisdom*, l. 1144a.

27. Ackrill, "2. Aristotle on Eudaimonia," 31.

28. Wiggins, "13. Deliberation and Practical Reason," 222–23.

29. Nussbaum, *Love's Knowledge*, 74.

30. Dewey, *The Middle Works of John Dewey, 1899–1924: Human Nature and Conduct, 1922*, 14:144. It is striking that as radically different a thinker as Martin Heidegger summons a portrait of thinking that echoes Dewey. Here is Simon Crichley's gloss: "I project towards the future, but what comes out of the future is my past, my personal and cultural baggage, what Heidegger calls my 'having-been-ness' (*Gewesenheit*). But this does not mean that I am somehow condemned to my past. On the contrary, I can make a decision to take over the fact of who I am in a free action. This is what Heidegger calls 'resoluteness.'" Critchley, "Heidegger's Being and Time, Part 8."

31. Wilkes, "18. The Good Man and the Good for Man in Aristotle's Ethics," 354.

32. Kant, *Grounding for the Metaphysics of Morals*, 30.

33. Mill, *Utilitarianism*, 77.

34. "Agreement on what the relevant rules are to be is always a prerequisite for agreement upon the nature and content of a particular virtue. But this prior agreement in rules is . . . something which our individualist culture is unable to secure." MacIntyre, *After Virtue*, 244.

35. Rawls, *A Theory of Justice*; Nozick, *Anarchy, State, and Utopia*.

36. It might be objected that Aristotle equates the highest good with philosophical contemplation—and, at times, he does. But as multiple commentaries make clear (see, for example, the essays cited above), he also offers a more inclusive view which points to the multiplicity of human aims.

37. Arendt, *Responsibility and Judgment*. Digital Edition.

38. Schiller, *On the Aesthetic Education of Man*, 26.

39. An education in the arts was central in Ancient Greece. For Plato, the best education included singing and dancing in choruses as well as considerable demands for memorization, discussed below.

40. BEA, "Arts and Cultural Production Satellite Account, U.S. and States."

41. See, for example, Cain, "Want to Work for the World's Tech Giants?"

42. Schaper, "Taste, Sublimity, and Genius: The Aesthetics of Nature and Art," 375–76.

43. Schaper, 374–75.

44. Bolla, *Art Matters*, 53, 55.

45. Gadamer, *Truth and Method*, 34, 36.

46. Dewey, *Art as Experience*, 193.

47. Dewey, 180.

48. Dewey, 195.

49. Bolla, *Art Matters*, 19.

50. Brielmann, Nuzzo, and Pelli, "Beauty, the Feeling."

51. For an introduction to the activities of arts education across the United States, see Rabkin and Redmond, *Putting the Arts in the Picture.*

52. Greene, "The Spaces of Aesthetic Education."

53. Steiner, "Fair Copy Book." Possession of the author.

54. Dewey, *Art as Experience*, 54, 53.

55. Yeats, "Among School Children."

56. "Heraclitus."

57. Mehta, "Jal Mehta."

58. "In every domain that has been explored, considerable knowledge has been found to be an essential prerequisite two expert skill. . . . The extent of the knowledge and expert must be able to call upon is demonstrably large." Herbert Simon, quoted in Christodoulou, *Seven Myths About Education*, 79–80.

59. Next Generation Science Standards, "THE THREE DIMENSIONS OF SCIENCE LEARNING."

60. NCES, "Table 2.16. Social Studies Statewide Assessment Name/Title and Grade Administered, by State: 2018."

61. German International School of Silicon Valley, "German International Abitur."

62. Mcnally, "The New French Baccalaureat Changes in 2021."

63. Cambridge University Press & Assessment, "Cambridge O Level Subjects."

64. Cambridge University Press & Assessment, "Cambridge International AS and A Level Subjects."

65. Stringer, "Bored in Class."

66. Mehta and Fine, *In Search of Deeper Learning*, 13.

67. Mehta and Fine, 348, 349.

68. Mehta and Fine, 351.

69. Mehta and Fine, 352–53.

70. McPhail, "The Search for Deep Learning."

71. McPhail.

72. While the great majority of students at the Perse school came from what was then referred to as "lower-middle-class," the English teacher who prompted searching thinking about Othello had a doctorate from Cambridge.

73. See the author's examples of strong and weak curriculum in mathematics in Steiner, Jensen, and Magee, "Curriculum Literacy in Schools of Education? The Hole at the Center of American Teacher Preparation."

74. Heidegger, *What Is Called Thinking?* 31.

75. See Eisner, *The Arts and the Creation of Mind*, particularly chap. 8, "What education can learn from the arts" (196–208).

76. Felski, *Uses of Literature*, 33.

77. Kimball, "Schiller's 'Aesthetic Education.'"

78. For the quotation, see Plato, "Finding Nelson Mandela's Creon in Mark Rothko's Antigone." For further discussion, see Wilson, "Antigone: Nelson Mandela Plays Creon."

79. The author was privileged to encounter such teachers in Georgia.

80. I was privileged to visit schools in Tbilisi.

81. Steiner, "Commencement Address to the Graduates of The Hunter College School of Education" (2005–2009).

Bibliography

Accenture. "It's Learning. Just Not as We Know It: How to Accelerate Skills Acquisition in the Age of Intelligent Technologies." G20: Young Entrepreneurs' Alliance, 2018. https://www.accenture.com/_acnmedia/thought-leadership-assets/pdf/accenture-education-and-technology-skills-research.pdf.

Ackrill, J. L. "2. Aristotle on Eudaimonia." In *Essays on Aristotle's Ethics*, edited by Amélie Oksenberg Rorty. Vol. 2. Major Thinkers Series. Berkeley: University of California Press, 1980. https://doi.org/10.1525/9780520340985.

Akbasli, Sait, Mehmet Sahin, and Zeliha Yaykiran. "The Effect of Reading Comprehension on the Performance in Science and Mathematics." *Journal of Education and Practice* 7, no. 16 (2016): 108–21.

Aldric, Anna. "Average ACT Score for 2021, 2020, 2019, 2018, and Earlier Years." *PrepScholar* (blog), October 17, 2020. https://blog.prepscholar.com/average-act-score-by-year.

Allensworth, Elaine M., and Holly Hart. "How Do Principals Influence Student Achievement?" University of Chicago Consortium on School Research, 2018. https://consortium.uchicago.edu/sites/default/files/2018–10/Leadership%20Snapshot-Mar2018-Consortium.pdf.

American University School of Education. "How to Foster a Growth Mindset in the Classroom." *American University School of Education* (blog), December 10, 2020. https://soeonline.american.edu/blog/growth-mindset-in-the-classroom/.

Anderson Institute of Technology. "Program Links / Digital and Visual Art and Development." Anderson Institute of Technology, 2022. https://www.anderson5.net/Page/http%3A%2F%2Fwww.anderson5.net%2Fsite%2Fdefault.aspx%3FPageID%3D37109.

Anderson, Melinda D. "A Root Cause of the Teacher-Diversity Problem." *The Atlantic*, January 23, 2018. https://www.theatlantic.com/education/archive/2018/01/a-root-cause-of-the-teacher-diversity-problem/551234/

Anderson, Nick. "Report Finds New AP Computer Science Course Is Diversifying the Field." *Washington Post*, December 14, 2020. https://www.washingtonpost.com/education/2020/12/13/advanced-placement-computer-science/.

Arendt, Hannah. *Between Past and Future*. New York: Penguin Classics, 2006.

Arendt, Hannah. *Responsibility and Judgment*. Reprint ed. New York: Schocken, 2005.

Aristotle. *Aristotle on Practical Wisdom: Nicomachean Ethics VI*. Translated by C. D. C. Reeve. Critical ed. edition. Cambridge, MA: Harvard University Press, 2013.

Aristotle. *Metaphysics*. Edited by W. D Ross. Oxford: Clarendon Press, 1924.

Ashman, Greg. "Understanding the PISA 2015 Findings about Science Teaching." *Filling the Pail* (blog), March 19, 2017. https://gregashman.wordpress.com/2017/03/19/understanding-the-pisa-2015-findings-about-science-teaching/.

Bakshi, Simaran, and David Steiner. "Acceleration, Not Remediation: Lessons from the Field." *The Thomas B. Fordham Institute Flypaper* (blog), June 26, 2020. https://fordhaminstitute.org/national/commentary/acceleration-not-remediation-lessons-field.

Balfanz, Robert, and Vaughan Byrnes. "Connecting Social-Emotional Development, Academic Achievement, and On-Track Outcomes: A Multi-District Study of Grades 3 to 10 Students Supported by City Year Americorps Members." Everyone Graduates Center at the Johns Hopkins University School of Education, May 2020. https://new.every1graduates.org/wp-content/uploads/2020/05/201200507_EGC_CityYearReport_BalfanzByrnesFINAL.pdf.

Balfanz, Robert. Letter to David Steiner. "Untitled Email," March 29, 2022.

Ball, Deborah Loewenberg, and Francesca M. Forzani. "Learning to Teach Something in Particular: A Common Core for the Training of Teachers." School of Education, University of Michigan, May 11, 2011. https://www.msri.org/workshops/596/schedules/13124/documents/871/assets/14327.

Barnum, Matt. "3 Not-Quite-True Claims about the Pandemic and Schools." *Chalkbeat* (blog), February 11, 2022. https://www.chalkbeat.org/2022/2/11/22928029/myths-schools-teacher-turnover.

Barnum, Matt. "Do School Vouchers Work? Here's What Research Really Says." *Chalkbeat* (blog), February 21, 2020. https://www.chalkbeat.org/2017/7/12/21108235/do-school-vouchers-work-as-the-debate-heats-up-here-s-what-research-really-says.

Barshay, Jill. "Research Scholars to Air Problems with Using 'grit' at School." *The Hechinger Report* (blog), March 11, 2019. http://hechingerreport.org/research-scholars-to-air-problems-with-using-grit-at-school/.

Bashant, Jennifer. "Developing Grit in Our Students: Why Grit Is Such a Desirable Trait, and Practical Strategies for Teachers and Schools." *Journal for Leadership and Instruction*, Fall 2014. https://files.eric.ed.gov/fulltext/EJ1081394.pdf.

Bavarian, Niloofar, Kendra M. Lewis, David L. DuBois, Alan Acock, Samuel Vuchinich, Naida Silverthorn, Frank J. Snyder, Joseph Day, Peter Ji, and Brian R. Flay. "Using Social-Emotional and Character Development to Improve Academic Outcomes: A Matched-Pair, Cluster-Randomized Controlled Trial in Low-Income, Urban Schools." *The Journal of School Health* 83, no. 11 (November 2013): 10.1111/josh.12093. https://doi.org/10.1111/josh.12093.

BEA. "Arts and Cultural Production Satellite Account, U.S. and States." U.S. Bureau of Economic Analysis (BEA), March 30, 2021. https://www.bea.gov/news/2021/arts-and-cultural-production-satellite-account-us-and-states.

Belsha, Kalyn, and Sarah Darville. "A New National Effort to Promote School Integration Is Underway. More than Two Dozen School Districts Want In."

Chalkbeat (blog), October 9, 2020. https://www.chalkbeat.org/2020/10/9/21509770 /new-national-effort-school-integration-bridges-collaborative-desegregation.

Berkowitz, Ruth, Hadass Moore, Ron Avi Astor, and Rami Benbenishty. "A Research Synthesis of the Associations Between Socioeconomic Background, Inequality, School Climate, and Academic Achievement." *Review of Educational Research* 87, no. 2 (April 2017): 425–69.

Berner, Ashley Rogers. "Introducing Pluralism to Public Schooling." *American Compass: Retooling American Education* (blog), June 1, 2022. https:// americancompass.org/essays/introducing-pluralism-to-public-schooling/.

Berner, Ashley. "How School Culture Drives Civic Knowledge and Shapes the Next Generation of Citizens." *The 74 Million* (blog), April 18, 2017. https://www .the74million.org/article/berner-how-school-culture-drives-civic-knowledge-and -shapes-the-next-generation-of-citizens/.

Berner, Ashley. *Pluralism and American Public Education: No One Way to School*. New York: Palgrave MacMillan, 2017. http://www.palgrave.com/us/book /9781137502230.

Bjorklund-Young, Alanna, and Jay S. Plasman. "Reducing the Achievement Gap: An Empirical Analysis of Middle School Math Performance in Six States and Washington, D.C." Policy Brief. Baltimore: Johns Hopkins Institute for Education Policy, April 2019. https://drive.google.com/file/d/18aMAWlQRhx -l70jx_eFRvOAlFuOYQnEk/view.

Blazar, David, Thomas Kane, Douglas Staiger, Dan Goldhaber, Rachel Hitch, Michal Kurlaender, Blake Heller, et al. "Learning by the Book." Cambridge, MA: Harvard University, March 2019. https://cepr.harvard.edu/files/cepr/files/cepr-curriculum -report_learning-by-the-book.pdf.

Bolla, Peter de. *Art Matters*. 1st ed. Cambridge, MA: Harvard University Press, 2001.

Boxell, Levi, Matthew Gentzkow, and Jesse Shapiro. "Country Trends in Affective Polarization." National Bureau of Economic Research *Working Papers*, November 2021. https://www.nber.org/papers/w26669.

Branch, Gregory F., Eric A. Hanushek, and Steven G. Rivkin. "School Leaders Matter: Measuring the Impact of Effective Principals." *Education Next*, Winter 2013.

Braun, Henry, Frank Jenkins, and Wendy Grigg. "National Assessment of Educational Progress: Comparing Private Schools and Public Schools Using Hierarchical Linear Modeling." Washington, D.C.: The National Center for Education Statistics (NCES), July 2006. https://nces.ed.gov/nationsreportcard/pdf/studies/2006461.pdf.

Brielmann, Aenne A., Angelica Nuzzo, and Denis G. Pelli. "Beauty, the Feeling." *Acta Psychologica* 219 (September 1, 2021): 103365. https://doi.org/10.1016/j .actpsy.2021.103365.

Broady, Kristen, and Brad Hershbein. "Major Decisions: What Graduates Earn over Their Lifetimes." *Brookings* (blog), October 8, 2020. https://www.brookings .edu/blog/up-front/2020/10/08/major-decisions-what-graduates-earn-over-their -lifetimes/.

Brookings Institution. "The Resurgence of Ability Grouping and Persistence of Tracking." Brown Center Report on American Education, Washington, D.C.,

March 18, 2013. https://www.brookings.edu/research/the-resurgence-of-ability
-grouping-and-persistence-of-tracking/.

Brown, Patrick T. "How Should States Approach Early Childhood Policy?" American
Enterprise Institute (AEI), April 2022. https://www.aei.org/wp-content/uploads
/2022/04/How-Should-States-Approach-Early-Childhood-Policy.pdf?x91208.

Brunner, Eric, Shaun Dougherty, and Stephen Ross. "The Promise of Career and
Technical Education." *Brookings* (blog), September 20, 2019. https://www
.brookings.edu/blog/brown-center-chalkboard/2019/09/20/the-promise-of-career
-and-technical-education/.

Buckle, Jenna. "A Comprehensive Guide to 21st Century Skills." *Panorama
Education* (blog), n/d. https://www.panoramaed.com/blog/comprehensive-guide
-21st-century-skills.

Buras, Kristen. "Questioning Core Assumptions: A Critical Reading of and Response
to E. D. Hirsch's The Schools We Need and Why We Don't Have Them." *Harvard
Educational Review* 69, no. 1 (Spring 1999). https://www1.udel.edu/educ/whitson
/897s05/files/Hirsch%20Essay%20Review.pdf.

Burke, Lilah. "Humanities Majors Don't 'Catch Up' to Peers, Report Says." Inside
Higher Ed, February 22, 2021. https://www.insidehighered.com/quicktakes/2021
/02/22/humanities-majors-don%E2%80%99t-%E2%80%98catch-%E2%80%99
-peers-report-says.

Burnyeat, M. F. "5. Aristotle on Learning to Be Good." In *Essays on Aristotle's Ethics*,
edited by Amélie Oksenberg Rorty, 2:69–92. Major Thinkers Series. Berkeley:
University of California Press, 1980. https://doi.org/10.1525/9780520340985–008.

Butcher, Kristin F., Patrick J. McEwan, and Akila Weerapana. "The Effects of an Anti-
Grade-Inflation Policy at Wellesley College." *Journal of Economic Perspectives*
28, no. 3 (September 2014): 189–204. https://doi.org/10.1257/jep.28.3.189.

Butler, Patrick. "No Grammar Schools, Lots of Play: The Secrets of Europe's Top
Education System." *The Guardian*, September 20, 2016, sec. Education. https:
//www.theguardian.com/education/2016/sep/20/grammar-schools-play-europe-top
-education-system-finland-daycare.

California Department of Education. "Character Education - Youth Development."
April 8, 2022. https://www.cde.ca.gov/ls/yd/ce/.

Cabell, Sonia Q., and HyeJin Hwang. "Building Content Knowledge to Boost
Comprehension in the Primary Grades." *Reading Research Quarterly* 55, no. S1
(2020): S99–107. https://doi.org/10.1002/rrq.338.

Cain, Aine. "Want to Work for the World's Tech Giants? You'll Need a Particular
Set of Skills." *World Economic Forum* (blog), February 28, 2017. https://www
.weforum.org/agenda/2017/02/the-7-skills-you-need-to-get-a-job-at-google-apple
-or-microsoft/.

Cambridge University Press & Assessment. "Cambridge O Level Subjects." Cambridge
Assessment International Education, 2022. https://www.cambridgeinternational
.org/programmes-and-qualifications/cambridge-upper-secondary/cambridge-o
-level/subjects/.

Cambridge University Press & Assessment. "Cambridge International AS and A
Level Subjects." Cambridge Assessment International Education, 2022. https:

//www.cambridgeinternational.org/programmes-and-qualifications/cambridge -advanced/cambridge-international-as-and-a-levels/subjects/.

CareerOneStop. "Careers with Most Openings." Sponsored by the U.S. Department of Labor, Employment and Training Administration, 2022. https://www.careeronestop .org/Toolkit/Careers/careers-most-openings.aspx.

Carnevale, Anthony P., Ban Cheah, and Emma Wenzinger. "The College Payoff: More Education Doesn't Always Mean More Earnings." Washington, D.C.: Georgetown University, Center on Education and the Workforce, 2021. https: //1gyhoq479ufd3yna29x7ubjn-wpengine.netdna-ssl.com/wp-content/uploads/cew -college_payoff_2021-fr.pdf.

Carter, Zachary D. "The Democratic Unraveling Began With Schools." *The Atlantic* (blog), November 3, 2021. https://www.theatlantic.com/ideas/archive/2021/11/ virginia-election-youngkin-education/620596/.

CASEL. "What Is the CASEL Framework?" Collaborative for Academic, Social, and Emotional Learning (CASEL), n.d. https://casel.org/fundamentals-of-sel/what-is -the-casel-framework/.

CEDEFOP. "Benefits of Vocational Education and Training in Europe: For People, Organisations and Countries." Luxembourg: European Centre for the Development of Vocational Training (CEDEFOP), 2013. https://files.eric.ed.gov/fulltext/ ED560841.pdf.

CEDEFOP. "EU Workforce: Overeducated yet Underskilled?" #ESJsurvey Insight. Thessaloniki, Greece: European Centre for the Development of Vocational Training (CEDEFOP), 2016. https://www.cedefop.europa.eu/files/esjinsight_no _7_underskilling_il_final.pdf.

Center for Civic Education. https://www.civiced.org/.

Center for Global Education. "Teaching and Learning 21st Century Skills." Asia Society, n/d. https://asiasociety.org/education/teaching-and-learning-21st-century -skills.

Chabrier, Julia, Sarah Cohodes, and Philip Oreopoulos. "What Can We Learn from Charter School Lotteries?" *Journal of Economic Perspectives* 30, no. 3 (September 2016): 57–84. https://doi.org/10.1257/jep.30.3.57.

Chan Zuckerberg Initiative. "Whole Child Approach to Education." *Chan Zuckerberg Initiative* (blog), 2022. https://chanzuckerberg.com/education/whole-child -approach-to-education/.

Chenoweth, Karin. *Schools That Succeed: How Educators Marshal the Power of Systems for Improvement.* Cambridge, MA: Harvard Education Press, 2017.

Chesley, Kate. "Freshmen Eager to Learn Purpose of Education through New Thinking Matters." *Stanford Report* (blog), August 2, 2012. http://news.stanford .edu/news/2012/august/thinking-matters-debut-080212.html.

Chetty, Raj, John N. Friedman, and Jonah E. Rockoff. "Measuring the Impacts of Teachers II: Teacher Value-Added and Student Outcomes in Adulthood." *American Economic Review* 104, no. 9 (September 2014): 2633–79. https://doi.org/10.1257 /aer.104.9.2633.

Chick, Nancy. "Metacognition." Vanderbilt University Center for Teaching, 2013. https://cft.vanderbilt.edu/guides-sub-pages/metacognition/.

Chiefs for Change. "Hiding in Plain Sight: Leveraging Curriculum to Improve Student Learning." August 2017. http://chiefsforchange.org/policy-paper/4830/.

Christodoulou, Daisy. *Seven Myths About Education.* 1st ed. London: Routledge, 2014.

Chung, Bobby W., and Jian Zou. "Teacher Licensing, Teacher Supply, and Student Achievement: Nationwide Implementation of EdTPA." EdWorkingPaper. *EdWorkingPapers.Com.* Annenberg Institute at Brown University, July 25, 2021. https://www.edworkingpapers.com/ai21–440.

CivXNow. "Civic education has massive cross-partisan appeal as a solution to what ails our democracy." In iCivixs, August 2021. https://civxnow.org/wp-content/uploads/2021/08/CivXNow-infographic-Luntz-polling-FINAL.pdf.

Clarke, Aleisha, Miriam Sorgenfrei, James Mulcahy, Pippa Davie, Claire Friedrich, and Tom McBride. "Adolescent Mental Health: A Systematic Review on the Effectiveness of School-Based Interventions." Westminster, London: Early Intervention Foundation, July 21, 2021. https://www.eif.org.uk/report/adolescent-mental-health-a-systematic-review-on-the-effectiveness-of-school-based-interventions.

Claro, Susana, David Paunesku, and Carol S. Dweck. "Growth Mindset Tempers the Effects of Poverty on Academic Achievement." *Proceedings of the National Academy of Sciences* 113, no. 31 (August 2, 2016): 8664–68. https://doi.org/10.1073/pnas.1608207113.

Coleman, David, and Susan Pimentel. "Revised Publishers' Criteria for the Common Core State Standards in English Language Arts and Literacy, Grades 3–12." Common Core State Standards Initiative, April 12, 2012. http://www.corestandards.org/assets/Publishers_Criteria_for_3–12.pdf.

Coleman, David. "Bringing the Common Core to Life." Presentation to the New York State Education Department, Albany, New York, February 2, 2011.

Coleman, James. "The Relations between School and Social Structure." In *The Social Organization of Schools. New Conceptualizations of the Learning Process*, edited by M. T. Hallinan. New York: Plenum, 1987, 177–204.

Coleman, James. *High School and Beyond.* New York: Basic Books, 1986.

Collins, Todd. "Mississippi Rising? A Partial Explanation for Its NAEP Improvement Is That It Holds Students Back." *The Thomas B. Fordham Institute Flypaper* (blog), December 4, 2019. https://fordhaminstitute.org/national/commentary/mississippi-rising-partial-explanation-its-naep-improvement-it-holds-students.

Common Core State Standards Initiative. "English Language Arts Standards » Anchor Standards » College and Career Readiness Anchor Standards for Reading." 2015. http://www.corestandards.org/ELA-Literacy/CCRA/R/.

Common Core State Standards Initiative. "English Language Arts Standards » Introduction." 2015. http://www.corestandards.org/ELA-Literacy/introduction/how-to-read-the-standards/.

Common Core State Standards Initiative. "High School: Algebra » Arithmetic with Polynomials & Rational Expressions." 2015. http://www.corestandards.org/Math/Content/HSA/APR/.

Common Core State Standards Initiative. "High School: Algebra » Reasoning with Equations & Inequalities." 2015. http://www.corestandards.org/Math/Content/HSA/REI/.

Common Core State Standards Initiative. "Mathematics Standards." 2015. http://www.corestandards.org/Math/.

Common Core State Standards Initiative. "Standards for Mathematical Practice." 2015. http://www.corestandards.org/Math/Practice/.

Connor, Peter. "Interpreting Biserial Correlation Scores." Colorado State University | The Institute for Teaching and Learning. Accessed June 3, 2022. https://tilt.colostate.edu/TipsAndGuides/Tip/43.

Consortium on Chicago School Research. "The Essential Supports." October 2018. https://consortium.uchicago.edu/sites/default/files/2018–10/9954essentialsupports_onepager_final-2.pdf.

Conwright, Anthony. "American Education Is Founded on White Race Theory." *The New Republic*, July 29, 2021. https://newrepublic.com/article/163093/critical-race-theory-history-white-american-education.

Core Knowledge Foundation. "The Baseball Experiment." *Core Knowledge Foundation Blog* (blog), November 15, 2017. https://www.coreknowledge.org/blog/baseball-experiment-two-wisconsin-researchers-discovered-comprehension-gap-knowledge-gap/.

Cowan, James, Dan Goldhaber, Zeyu Jin, and Roddy Theobald. "Teacher Licensure Tests: Barrier or Predictive Tool?" American Institutes for Research/CALDER, October 2020. https://files.eric.ed.gov/fulltext/ED609773.pdf.

Crato, Nuno, ed. *Improving a Country's Education: PISA 2018 Results in 10 Countries*. Switzerland: Springer Nature, 2021.

Credé, Marcus, Michael C. Tynan, and Peter D. Harms. "Much Ado about Grit: A Meta-Analytic Synthesis of the Grit Literature." *Journal of Personality and Social Psychology* 113, no. 3 (2017): 492–511. https://doi.org/10.1037/pspp0000102.

CREDO. "Urban Charter School Study: 41 Regions Workbook." Stanford, CA: Center for Research on Education Outcomes, March 2015. http://urbancharters.stanford.edu/download/Urban%20Study%2041%20Region%20Workbook.pdf.

Critchley, Simon. "Heidegger's Being and Time, Part 8: Temporality." *The Guardian*, July 27, 2009, sec. Opinion. https://www.theguardian.com/commentisfree/belief/2009/jul/27/heidegger-being-time-philosophy.

Critical Thinking Web. "[C01] What Is Critical Thinking?" n.d. https://philosophy.hku.hk/think/critical/ct.php.

Cydis, Susan. "Authentic Instruction and Technology Literacy." *Journal of Learning Design* 8, no. 1 (2015): 68–78.

De Avila, Joseph, and Tawnell D. Hobbs. "Teacher Shortage Prompts Some States to Lower the Bar." *Wall Street Journal*, September 6, 2017, sec. US. https://www.wsj.com/articles/teacher-shortage-prompts-some-states-to-lower-the-bar-1504699200.

Dee, Thomas S. "Teachers, Race, and Student Achievement in a Randomized Experiment." *The Review of Economics and Statistics* 86, no. 1 (February 1, 2004): 195–210. https://doi.org/10.1162/003465304323023750.

Delaware System of Student Assessments. "2021 Grade 11 Social Studies Training Test Booklet." Delaware Department of Education in partnership with Pearson, 2019. http://delaware.pearsonaccessnext.com/resources/practice-tests/BRF/ SocialStudies-UEB/DE1127820_Gr11SS_TB.pdf.

Dewar, Gwen. "Teaching Critical Thinking: An Evidence-Based Guide." PARENTING SCIENCE, January 2, 2012. https://parentingscience.com/teaching -critical-thinking/.

Dewey, John. *Art as Experience*. 1st ed. New York: TarcherPerigee, 2005.

Dewey, John. *Democracy And Education*. 1997 ed. New York: Free Press, 1916.

Dewey, John. *Experience and Nature*. New York: Dover Publications, 1958.

Dewey, John. *The Middle Works of John Dewey, 1899–1924: Human Nature and Conduct, 1922*. Edited by Jo Ann Boydston. 1st ed. Vol. 14. *Collected Works of John Dewey*. Carbondale: Southern Illinois University Press, 1983.

Dewey, John. "The Quest for Certainty." In *The Later Works of John Dewey, 1925–1953*, edited by Jo Ann Boydston. 1st ed. Vol. 4. *Collected Works of John Dewey*. Carbondale: Southern Illinois University Press, 1981.

DeWitt, Peter. "Why a 'Growth Mindset' Won't Work." *Education Week*, July 17, 2015, sec. Student Well-Being. https://www.edweek.org/leadership/opinion-why-a -growth-mindset-wont-work/2015/07.

Diakiw, Jerry. "Reading And Life Success." *HuffPost: The Blog* (blog), May 4, 2017. https://www.huffingtonpost.ca/jerry-diakiw/reading-and-life-success_b_16404148 .html.

DiAngelo, Dr Robin. *White Fragility: Why It's So Hard for White People to Talk About Racism*. Reprint ed. Boston: Beacon Press, 2018.

"Discussing the Practice of Critical Race Theory in Schools: Ian Rowe on Chicago's Morning Answer." *Chicago's Morning Answer*. American Enterprise Institute (AEI), August 18, 2021. https://www.aei.org/press/discussing-the-practice-of -critical-race-theory-in-schools-ian-rowe-on-chicagos-morning-answer/.

DOE-Mass. "Educator Preparation - CAP Guidelines." Massachusetts Department of Elementary and Secondary Education, July 28, 2021. https://www.doe.mass.edu/ edprep/cap/guidelines.html.

Donahue, Tim. "Teacher: Am I Guilty of Grade Inflation? I'll Admit, My Approach to Grading Has Evolved." *USA TODAY*, August 21, 2021. https://www.usatoday .com/story/opinion/voices/2021/08/24/class-grade-inflation-high-school-teacher /8185250002/.

Duckworth, Angela L., and Martin E. P. Seligman. "Self-Discipline Outdoes IQ in Predicting Academic Performance of Adolescents." *Psychological Science* 16, no. 12 (December 1, 2005): 939–44. https://doi.org/10.1111/j.1467–9280.2005.01641 .x.

Duckworth, Angela. "Don't Grade Schools on Grit." *New York Times*, March 26, 2016. https://www.nytimes.com/2016/03/27/opinion/sunday/dont-grade-schools -on-grit.html.

Durlak, Joseph A., Roger P. Weissberg, Allison B. Dymnicki, Rebecca D. Taylor, and Kriston B. Schellinger. "The Impact of Enhancing Students' Social and Emotional Learning: A Meta-Analysis of School-Based Universal Interventions." *Child*

Development 82, no. 1 (2011): 405–32. https://doi.org/10.1111/j.1467–8624.2010 .01564.x.

Dweck, Carol. "Carol Dweck Revisits the 'Growth Mindset.'" *Education Week*, September 23, 2015, sec. Student Well-Being. https://www.edweek.org/leadership/ opinion-carol-dweck-revisits-the-growth-mindset/2015/09.

Dweck, Carol. *Mindset: The New Psychology of Success*. Updated ed. New York: Ballantine Books, 2007.

Dweck, Carol. "What Having a 'Growth Mindset' Actually Means." *Harvard Business Review*, January 13, 2016. https://hbr.org/2016/01/what-having-a-growth -mindset-actually-means.

Edelman, Susan, Lorena Mongelli, and Bruce Golding. "'Fail Me' School's Kids Can Take Years' Worth of Classes in 6 Weeks." *New York Post* (blog), August 5, 2015. https://nypost.com/2015/08/05/fail-me-schools-kids-can-take-years-worth -of-classes-in-6-weeks/.

Educating for American Democracy. "20th Century African Heritage: Civil Rights in Rhode Island." The Rhode Island Historical Society. https://www .educatingforamericandemocracy.org/educator-resources/?sword=&design -challenge%5b%5d=55#popup-ead-post-8238.

Educating for American Democracy.:9/11 and the Constitution." Center for Civic Education. https://www.educatingforamericandemocracy.org/educator-resources/ ?sword=&design-challenge%5b%5d=55#popup-ead-post-4819.

Eisner, Elliot W. *The Arts and the Creation of Mind*. New ed. New Haven, CT: Yale University Press, 2004.

EngageNY. "Common Core Unit: A Close Reading of Lincoln's Gettysburg Address." n.d. https://condor.depaul.edu/tps/resources/level1/exemplar.pdf.

equityXdesign. "Racism and Inequity Are Products of Design. They Can Be Redesigned." *Medium* (blog), January 30, 2019. https://medium.com/@ equityXdesign/racism-and-inequity-are-products-of-design-they-can-be -redesigned-12188363cc6a.

Erickson, Heidi H., Jonathan N. Mills, and Patrick J. Wolf. "The Effects of the Louisiana Scholarship Program on Student Achievement and College Entrance." *Journal of Research on Educational Effectiveness* 14, no. 4 (October 2, 2021): 861–99. https://doi.org/10.1080/19345747.2021.1938311.

Eshetu, Amogne Asfaw. "Parental Socio-Economic Status as a Determinant Factor of Academic Performance of Students in Regional Examination: A Case of Dessie Town, Ethiopia." *African Educational Research Journal* 3, no. 4 (November 2015): 221–29.

Eva, Amy M. "How to Inspire Students to Become Better Citizens." *Greater Good Magazine* (blog), November 6, 2018. https://greatergood.berkeley.edu/article/item/ how_to_inspire_students_to_become_better_citizens.

FairTest. "Graduation Test Update: States That Recently Eliminated or Scaled Back High School Exit Exams." FairTest: The National Center for Fair and Open Testing, May 2019. https://www.fairtest.org/graduation-test-update-states-recently -eliminated.

Felski, Rita. *Uses of Literature*. 1st ed. Malden, MA: Wiley-Blackwell, 2008.

Ferrare, Joseph J., and R. Renee Setari. "Converging on Choice: The Interstate Flow of Foundation Dollars to Charter School Organizations." *Educational Researcher* 47, no. 1 (January 1, 2018): 34–45. https://doi.org/10.3102/0013189X17736524.

Figlio, David, and Krzyszlof Karbonik. "Some Schools Much Better than Others at Closing Achievement Gaps between Their Advantaged and Disadvantaged Students." *Brookings* (blog), July 20, 2017. https://www.brookings.edu/research/some-schools-much-better-than-others-at-closing-achievement-gaps-between-their-advantaged-and-disadvantaged-students/.

Finn, Chester E. "Educating young Americans for citizenship is our schools' top job." Thomas Fordham Institute. September 1, 2002. https://fordhaminstitute.org/national/commentary/educating-young-americans-citizenship-our-schools-top-job.

Fitzgerald, F. Scott. *The Great Gatsby*. Electronic resource. Edited by Michael Farris Smith. Chicago: Oldcastle Books, 2021. http://ebookcentral.proquest.com/lib/jhu/detail.action?docID=6372581.

Fleming, Stephen M., and Hakwan C. Lau. "How to Measure Metacognition." *Frontiers in Human Neuroscience* 8 (2014). https://www.frontiersin.org/article/10.3389/fnhum.2014.00443.

Fliegel, Seymour. "Debbie Meier and the Dawn of Central Park East." *City Journal*, 1994. https://www.city-journal.org/html/debbie-meier-and-dawn-central-park-east-12572.html.

Foundation for Critical Thinking. "Defining Critical Thinking." 2019. https://www.criticalthinking.org/pages/defining-critical-thinking/766.

Frey, Meredith C. "What We Know, Are Still Getting Wrong, and Have Yet to Learn about the Relationships among the SAT, Intelligence and Achievement." *Journal of Intelligence* 7, no. 4 (December 2, 2019): 26. https://doi.org/10.3390/jintelligence7040026.

Frey, Meredith C., and Douglas K. Detterman. "Scholastic Assessment or g? The Relationship between the Scholastic Assessment Test and General Cognitive Ability." *Psychological Science* 15, no. 6 (June 2004): 373–78. https://doi.org/10.1111/j.0956–7976.2004.00687.x.

Fryer, Roland G, and Robert M Beren. "An Empirical Analysis of 'Acting White.'" Cambridge, MA: Harvard University; National Bureau of Economic Research, July 2009. https://scholar.harvard.edu/files/fryer/files/an_empirical_analysis_of_acting_white.pdf.

Gadamer, Hans-Georg. *Truth and Method*. Translated by Joel Weinsheimer and Donald Marshall. 2nd, rev. ed. New York: Crossroad, 1989.

Galston, William A. "Parents, Government, and Children: Authority Over Education in the Liberal Democratic State." *Nomos*, Child, Family, and State, 44 (2003): 211–33.

Galston, William. "Political Knowledge, Political Engagement, and Civic Education." *Annual Review of Political Science*, 4. (2001).

Garcia, Emma. "Schools Are Still Segregated, and Black Children Are Paying a Price." *Economic Policy Institute* (blog), February 12, 2020. https://www.epi.org/publication/schools-are-still-segregated-and-black-children-are-paying-a-price/.

German International School of Silicon Valley. "German International Abitur." n.d. https://www.gissv.org/gissv-home-english/learning/german-international-abitur.

Goczek, Łukasz, Ewa Witkowska, and Bartosz Witkowski. "How Does Education Quality Affect Economic Growth?" *Sustainability* 13, no. 11 (January 2021): 6437. https://doi.org/10.3390/su13116437.

Goldhaber, Dan, and Michael Hansen. "Race, Gender, and Teacher Testing: How Informative a Tool Is Teacher Licensure Testing?" *American Educational Research Journal* 47, no. 1 (March 1, 2010): 218–51. https://doi.org/10.3102 /0002831209348970.

Green, Elizabeth. "Why Do Americans Stink at Math?" *New York Times*, July 23, 2014, sec. Magazine. https://www.nytimes.com/2014/07/27/magazine/why-do -americans-stink-at-math.html.

Green, Erica L. "New Biden Administration Rules for Charter Schools Spur Bipartisan Backlash." *New York Times*, May 13, 2022, sec. U.S. https://www .nytimes.com/2022/05/13/us/politics/charter-school-rules-biden.html.

Green, Erica L. "High Proportion of Maryland Students Continue to Meet Graduation Requirements." *Baltimore Sun*, October 30, 2013. https://www.baltimoresun.com/ education/bs-xpm-2013–10–30-bs-md-high-school-data-20131030-story.html.

Greene, Jay P. "The Moral and Religious Roots of Social and Emotional Learning." American Enterprise Institute, June 25, 2019. https://www.aei.org/wp-content /uploads/2019/06/The-Moral-and-Religious-Roots-of-Social-and-Emotional -Learning.pdf?x91208.

Greene, Maxine. "The Spaces of Aesthetic Education." *Journal of Aesthetic Education* 20, no. 4 (1986): 56–62. https://doi.org/10.2307/3332600.

Grier, Peter, and Chelsea Sheasley. "Public education, democracy, and the future of America." *The Christian Science Monitor*, June 8, 2022.

Gutmann, Amy. *Democratic Education*. Princeton, NJ: Princeton University Press, 1987.

Hambrick, David Z., and Christopher Chabris. "Yes, IQ Really Matters." *Slate*, April 15, 2014. https://slate.com/technology/2014/04/what-do-sat-and-iq-tests-measure -general-intelligence-predicts-school-and-life-success.html.

Hanushek, Eric A. "What Matters for Student Achievement: Updating Coleman on the Influence of Families and Schools." *Education Next* 16, no. 2 (April 2016). http://educationnext.org/what-matters-for-student-achievement/.

Hanushek, Eric A., and Ludger Woessman. "The High Cost of Low Educational Performance: The Long-Run Economic Impact of Improving PISA Outcomes." OECD Publishing, 2010. http://hanushek.stanford.edu/sites/default/files/ publications/Hanushek%2BWoessmann%202010%20OECD_0.pdf.

Hanushek, Eric A., and Ludger Woessmann. "Education and Economic Growth." In *International Encyclopedia of Education*, edited by Penelope Peterson, Eva Baker, and Barry McGaw, 2:245–52. Oxford: Elsevier, 2010. https://hanushek .stanford.edu/sites/default/files/publications/Hanushek%2BWoessmann%202010 %20IntEncEduc%202.pdf.

Hanushek, Eric A., Ludger Woessmann, and Lei Zhang. "General Education, Vocational Education, and Labor-Market Outcomes over the Life-Cycle." Working

Paper. National Bureau of Economic Research, October 2011. https://doi.org/10.3386/w17504.

Hanushek, Eric A., Paul E. Peterson, M. Danish Shakeel, Laura M. Talpey, and Ludger Woessman. "Closing the SES Achievement Gap: Trends in U.S. Student Performance," September 11, 2019. https://www.aeaweb.org/conference/2020/preliminary/paper/RkSbfi4T.

Harrison, Erin. "Are Interventions Promoting a Growth Mindset Effective in Raising Academic Achievement in School-Aged Pupils?" University College London Educational Psychology Group, n.d. https://www.ucl.ac.uk/educational-psychology/resources/CS1Harrison_19–22.pdf.

Hart Research Associates. "Public School Parents on the Value of Public Education: Findings from a National Survey of Public-School Parents Conducted for the AFT." September 2017. https://www.aft.org/sites/default/files/parentpoll2017_memo.pdf.

Hart, Ray, Michael Casserly, Renata Uzzell, Moses Palacios, Amanda Corcoran, and Liz Spurgeon. "Student Testing in America's Great City Schools: An Inventory and Preliminary Analysis." Washington, D.C.: Council of the Great City Schools, October 2015. https://files.eric.ed.gov/fulltext/ED569198.pdf.

Hattie, John. "We Aren't Using Assessments Correctly." *Education Week*, October 28, 2015, sec. Accountability. https://www.edweek.org/policy-politics/opinion-we-arent-using-assessments-correctly/2015/10.

Heidegger, Martin. *What Is Called Thinking?* Reprint ed. New York: Harper Perennial, 1976.

Heraclitus. In *Death by Philosophy: The Biographical Tradition in the Life and Death of the Archaic Philosophers Empedocles, Heraclitus, and Democritus*. Ann Arbor: University of Michigan Press, 2004.

Hess, Frederick M. "'Anti-Racist' Education Is Neither." *AEI | The American Mind* (blog), December 18, 2020. https://www.aei.org/articles/anti-racist-education-is-neither/.

Hess, Frederick M. "Oregon Democrats Resurrect the 'Soft Bigotry of Low Expectations.'" *The Dispatch* (blog), August 12, 2021. https://thedispatch.com/p/oregon-democrats-resurrect-the-soft.

Hess, Frederick M., and Michael Q. McShane. "OPINION | Few Students Take AP STEM Exams: Column." *USA TODAY*, October 9, 2014. https://www.usatoday.com/story/opinion/2014/10/09/stem-states-ap-exams-education-jobs-column/16823163/.

Hess, Rick. "5 Takeaways for Education from Virginia's Governor Race." *Education Week* (blog), November 5, 2021. https://www.edweek.org/policy-politics/opinion-5-takeaways-for-education-from-virginias-governor-race/2021/11.

Hippel, Paul T. von, and Laura Bellows. "Rating Teacher-Preparation Programs." *Education Next*, May 8, 2018. https://www.educationnext.org/rating-teacher-preperation-programs-value-added-make-useful-distinctions/.

Hirsch, E. D. *Cultural Literacy: What Every American Needs to Know*. Boston: Houghton Mifflin, 1987.

Hirsch, E. D. *The Making of Americans: Democracy and Our Schools*. New Haven, CT: Yale University Press, 2009.

Hirsch, E. D. *Validity in Interpretation.* New Haven, CT: Yale University Press, 1967.

Hirsch, E. D. *What Your Sixth Grader Needs to Know: Fundamentals of a Good Sixth-Grade Education.* 1st ed. The Core Knowledge Series. New York: Doubleday, 1993.

Hirsch, E. D. *Why Knowledge Matters: Rescuing Our Children from Failed Educational Theories.* Cambridge, MA: Harvard Education Press, 2016.

Hirsch, E. D., Marjorie Perloff, Elizabeth Fox-Genovese, John P. Sisk, and J. Mitchell Morse. "Responses to Robert Scholes." *Salmagundi,* no. 72 (1986): 118–63.

Hitchcock, David. "Critical Thinking." In *The Stanford Encyclopedia of Philosophy,* edited by Edward N. Zalta. Stanford, CA: Metaphysics Research Lab, Stanford University, 2020. https://plato.stanford.edu/archives/fall2020/entries/critical -thinking/.

Hitchens, Christopher. "Why We Don't Know What We Don't Know: Just Ask E. D. Hirsch." *New York Times,* May 13, 1990, sec. 6.

Hoffman, Nancy, and Robert Schwartz. "Gold Standard: The Swiss Vocational Education and Training System." International Comparative Study of Vocational Education Systems. Washington, D.C.: National Center on Education and the Economy, March 2015. https://ncee.org/wp-content/uploads/2015/03/ SWISSVETMarch11.pdf.

Hofstadter, Richard. *Anti-Intellectualism in American Life.* 1st ed. New York: Vintage, 1966.

Hollins, Etta R., and Connor K. Warner. "Evaluating the Clinical Component of Teacher Preparation Programs." National Academy of Education Committee on Evaluating and Improving Teacher Preparation Programs. Washington, D.C.: National Academy of Education, 2021. https://naeducation.org/wp-content/uploads /2021/11/2nd-pp-for-NAEd-EITPP-Paper-5-Hollins_Warner.pdf.

Honawar, Vaishali. "Gains Seen in Retooled Teacher Ed." *Education Week,* October 27, 2007, sec. Accountability. https://www.edweek.org/policy-politics/gains-seen -in-retooled-teacher-ed/2007/10.

Hoover Education Summit. "What Are the Stakes? A Global Perspective?" W/ Hanushek and Schleicher. Hoover Institution Education Summit 2022. https://www .youtube.com/watch?v=3cCfB6Dbdkc.

Hunter, James Davison. *The Death of Character: Moral Education in an Age without Good or Evil.* New York: Basic Books, 2000. https://www.basicbooks.com/titles/ james-davison-hunter/the-death-of-character/9780465011735/.

Ingersoll, Richard M., and Henry May. "The Minority Teacher Shortage: Fact or Fable?" *Kappan Magazine,* September 2011.

Innis, Gail. "Social Emotional Health; a Strong Indicator of Academic Success." *MSU Extension* (blog), May 24, 2013. https://www.canr.msu.edu/news/social_emotional _health_a_strong_indicator_of_academic_success.

Jackson, C. Kirabo, Shanette C. Porter, John Q. Easton, Alyssa Blanchard, and Sebastián Kiguel. "School Effects on Socio-Emotional Development, School-Based Arrests, and Educational Attainment." NBER Working Paper Series. Cambridge, MA: National Bureau of Economic Research, February 2020. https://www.nber.org /system/files/working_papers/w26759/w26759.pdf.

Jackson, C. Kirabo. "The Full Measure of a Teacher." *Education Next*, October 23, 2018. https://www.educationnext.org/full-measure-of-a-teacher-using-value-added -assess-effects-student-behavior/.

Jencks, Christopher, and Meredith Phillips. *The Black-White Test Score Gap*. Washington, D.C.: Brookings Institution Press, 1998.

Kandel, I. L. *The Impact of the War on American Education*. Chapel Hill: University of North Carolina Press, 1948.

Kane, Thomas. "Connecting to Practice: How We Can Put Education Research to Work." *Education Next*, February 23, 2016. http://educationnext.org/connecting-to -practice-put-education-research-to-work/.

Kant, Immanuel. *Grounding for the Metaphysics of Morals: With On a Supposed Right to Lie Because of Philanthropic Concerns*. Translated by James W. Ellington. 3rd ed. Indianapolis, IN: Hackett Publishing Company, Inc., 1993.

Kaufman, Julia H., John S. Davis, Elaine Lin Wang, Lindsey E. Thompson, Joseph D. Pane, Katherine Pfrommer, and Mark Harris. "Use of Open Educational Resources in an Era of Common Standards." Arlington, VA: RAND Corporation, 2017. https: //www.rand.org/pubs/research_reports/RR1773.html.

Kendi, Ibram X. *How to Be an Antiracist*. 1st ed. New York: One World, 2019.

Kimball, Roger. "Schiller's 'Aesthetic Education.'" *The New Criterion* 19, no. 7 (March 2001). https://newcriterion.com/issues/2001/3/schilleras-ldquoaesthetic -educationrdquo.

Kirp, David L. *Improbable Scholars: The Rebirth of a Great American School System and a Strategy for America's Schools*. Reprint ed. Oxford New York: Oxford University Press, 2015.

Kober, Nancy, and Diane Stark Rentner. "History and Evolution of Public Education in the US." Center on Education Policy, 2020. https://eric.ed.gov/?id=ED606970.

Koedel, Cory, Eric Parsons, Michael Podgursky, and Mark Ehlert. "Teacher Preparation Programs and Teacher Quality: Are There Real Differences Across Programs." American Institutes for Research/CALDER, July 2012. https://files.eric .ed.gov/fulltext/ED575350.pdf.

Koenig, Katherine A., Meredith C. Frey, and Douglas K. Detterman. "ACT and General Cognitive Ability." *Intelligence* 36, no. 2 (March 1, 2008): 153–60. https: //doi.org/10.1016/j.intell.2007.03.005.

Krachman, Sara Bartolino, and Bob Larocca. "The Scale of Our Investment in Social-Emotional Learning." Working Paper. Transforming Education, September 2017. chrome-extension://efaidnbmnnnibpcajpcglclefindmkaj/h ttps://transformingeducation.org/wp-content/uploads/2017/10/Inspire-Paper -Transforming-Ed-FINAL-2.pdf.

Kraemer, Jackie. "Statistic of the Month: Comparing Community College Completion Rates." *NCEE* (blog), May 9, 2013. http://ncee.org/2013/05/statistic-of-the-month -comparing-community-college-completion-rates/.

Kraft, Matthew A. "Interpreting Effect Sizes of Education Interventions." Providence, RI: Brown University Working Paper, December 2018. https://scholar.harvard.edu /files/mkraft/files/kraft_2018_interpreting_effect_sizes.pdf.

Kraut, Richard. "Aristotle's Ethics." In *The Stanford Encyclopedia of Philosophy*, edited by Edward N. Zalta, Fall 2022. Stanford, CA: Metaphysics Research Lab, Stanford University, 2022. https://plato.stanford.edu/archives/fall2022/entries/aristotle-ethics/.

Krugman, Paul. "Rip Van Skillsgap." *The Conscience of a Liberal: Paul Krugman Blog* (blog), February 22, 2015. https://krugman.blogs.nytimes.com/2015/02/22/rip-van-skillsgap/.

Ladson-Billings, Gloria. "From the Achievement Gap to the Education Debt: Understanding Achievement in U.S. Schools." *Educational Researcher* 35, no. 7 (October 2006): 3–12. https://doi.org/10.3102/0013189X035007003.

Langer Research Associates of New York. "51st Annual PDK Poll of the Public's Attitudes Toward the Public Schools." PDK Poll, September 2019. https://pdkpoll.org/wp-content/uploads/2020/05/pdkpoll51–2019.pdf.

Lemann, Nicholas. *The Big Test: The Secret History of the American Meritocracy.* 1st ed. New York: Farrar, Straus and Giroux, 2000.

Levanon, Gad, Layla O'Kane, Jennifer Burnett, Julia Nitschke, Frank Steemers, and Bledi Taska. "How Employers Combat Labor Shortages: Insights from Online Job Ads Data." Emsi Burning Glass & The Conference Board, 2021. https://www.conference-board.org/pdfdownload.cfm?masterProductID=38217.

Levin, Stephanie, and Kathryn Bradley. "Understanding and Addressing Principal Turnover: A Review of the Research." National Association of Secondary School Principals. Reston, VA: Learning Policy Institute, March 19, 2019. https://learningpolicyinstitute.org/product/nassp-understanding-addressing-principal-turnover-review-research-report.

Levine, Arthur. "Educating School Teachers." Washington, D.C.: The Education Schools Project, September 2006. http://edschools.org/pdf/Educating_Teachers_Report.pdf.

Lewis, Tyson E. "Rousseau and the Fable: Rethinking the Fabulous Nature of Educational Philosophy." *Educational Theory* 62, no. 3 (2012): 323–41. https://doi.org/10.1111/j.1741–5446.2012.00449.x.

Lexile. "What Does the Lexile Measure Mean?" MetaMetrics, 2008. https://doe.sd.gov/octe/documents/WhatDoestheLexileMeasureMean.pdf.

Leybold-Johnson, Isobel. "Can You Study after an Apprenticeship?" SWI swissinfo.ch - a branch of Swiss Broadcasting Corporation, August 29, 2019. https://www.swissinfo.ch/eng/society/your-education-questions--answered-_can-you-study-after-an-apprenticeship--/45120328.

Lindsay, Tom. "The 'Other' College Scandal: Grade Inflation Has Turned Transcripts into Monopoly Money." *Forbes*, March 30, 2019. https://www.forbes.com/sites/tomlindsay/2019/03/30/the-other-college-scandal-grade-inflation-has-turned-transcripts-into-monopoly-money/.

Lockhart, Paul. "A Mathematician's Lament." Edited by Keith Devlin. MAA Online, 2002. https://www.maa.org/external_archive/devlin/LockhartsLament.pdf.

Loewus, Liana. "Majority of Teachers Say Reforms Have Been 'Too Much.'" *Education Week*, December 20, 2017, sec. Teaching Profession. https://www

.edweek.org/teaching-learning/majority-of-teachers-say-reforms-have-been-too
-much/2017/12.

Los Angeles Times Editorial Board. "Opinion: What's behind LAUSD's Higher
Graduation Rates?" *Los Angeles Times*, August 12, 2016, sec. Opinion. https:
//www.latimes.com/la-ed-lausd-graduation-rates-credit-recovery-story-gallery
-storygallery.html.

Louisiana Believes. "Louisiana Innovative Assessment Program." Louisiana
Department of Education, n.d. https://www.louisianabelieves.com/docs/default
-source/key-initiatives/louisianas-key-initiatives---innovative-assessment-pilot.pdf
?sfvrsn=a6219f1f_18.

Louisiana Department of Education. "Believe and Prepare." Louisiana Believes, n.d.
https://www.louisianabelieves.com/teaching/believe-and-prepare.

Loveless, Tom. *Between the State and the Schoolhouse: Understanding the Failure of
Common Core*. Cambridge, MA: Harvard Education Press, 2021.

Lyons, Sean. "Rethinking the Way We Learn: UVA Psychologist Debunks Myths
about How the Brain Works." *Virginia Magazine*, Spring 2013. https://uvamagazine
.org/articles/rethinking_the_way_we_learn.

M. P. Foundation. "Nurturing the Whole Child." *Early Childhood Development
Initiatives - M.P. Foundation* (blog), May 2, 2019. https://www.mpfoundation.org
/nurturing-the-whole-child/.

MacIntyre, Alasdair. *After Virtue: A Study in Moral Theory*. 3rd ed. Notre Dame, IN:
University of Notre Dame Press, 2007.

Maguire, Larry. "What Is Resilience? The Definitive Guide To Coping." The
Performatist, June 4, 2020. https://theperformatist.com/what-is-resilience/.

Mark, Joshua J. "Agoge, the Spartan Education Program." In *World History
Encyclopedia*, June 15, 2021. https://www.worldhistory.org/article/342/agoge-the
-spartan-education-program/.

Markovits, Daniel. *The Meritocracy Trap: How America's Foundational Myth Feeds
Inequality, Dismantles the Middle Class, and Devours the Elite*. Illustrated ed. New
York: Penguin Press, 2019.

Maryland Commission on Innovation & Excellence in Education. "Blueprint for
Maryland's Future: Final Report." Annapolis, MD: Department of Legislative
Services, Office of Policy Analysis, December 2020. https://dls.maryland.gov/pubs
/prod/NoPblTabMtg/CmsnInnovEduc/2020-Final-Report-of-the-Commission.pdf.

Mattingly, Justin. "'This Is Just Outrageous': Richmond High Schools Plagued with
Course Credit Problems, State Investigation Finds." *Richmond Times-Dispatch*,
September 5, 2018. https://richmond.com/news/local/this-is-just-outrageous
-richmond-high-schools-plagued-with-course-credit-problems-state-investigation
-finds/article_34e79b01-f423-5e46-b570-7939a9a29505.html.

McCarthy, Kathryn S., and Danielle S. McNamara. "The Multidimensional Knowledge
in Text Comprehension Framework." *Educational Psychologist* 56, no. 3 (July 3,
2021): 196–214. https://doi.org/10.1080/00461520.2021.1872379.

McConnell, Michael W. "Education Disestablishment: Why Democratic Values Are
Ill-Served by Democratic Control of Schooling." *Nomos*, Moral and Political
Education, 43 (2002): 87–146.

McCormick, Meghan P., Elise Cappella, Erin E. O'Connor, and Sandee G. McClowry. "Do Intervention Impacts on Academic Achievement Vary by School Climate? Evidence from a Randomized Trial in Urban Elementary Schools." Society for Research on Educational Effectiveness, 2015. https://eric.ed.gov/?id=ED562123.

McGuffey, William Holmes. *McGuffey's Sixth Eclectic Reader*. Revised ed. McGuffey Readers. John Wiley & Sons, Inc., 1879. https://www.learn-to-read-prince-george.com/support-files/sixthelcreader.pdf.

Mcnally, Kate. "The New French Baccalaureat Changes in 2021." *Complete France* (blog), November 5, 2019. https://www.completefrance.com/living-in-france/integration/the-new-french-baccalaureat-changes-in-6305714/.

McPhail, Graham. "The Search for Deep Learning: A Curriculum Coherence Model." *Journal of Curriculum Studies* 53, no. 4 (July 4, 2021): 420–34. https://doi.org/10.1080/00220272.2020.1748231.

Mehta, Jal, and Sarah Fine. *In Search of Deeper Learning: The Quest to Remake the American High School*. Reprint ed. Cambridge, MA: Harvard University Press, 2020.

Mehta, Jal. "Less Schooling, More Learning: A Better Approach Is Hidden in Plain Sight." TED Talk presented at the TEDxMarin, n.d. https://www.ted.com/talks/jal_mehta_less_schooling_more_learning_a_better_approach_is_hidden_in_plain_sight.

Merriam-Webster Dictionary. "Metacognition." *Merriam-Webster.Com Dictionary*, n.d. https://www.merriam-webster.com/dictionary/metacognition.

Mill, John Stuart. *Utilitarianism*. Edited by Oskar Piest. Indianapolis, IN: Bobbs-Merrill, 1957.

Miller, Rann. "Why Charter Schools Are Failing Black Students." *The Progressive*, March 3, 2020. https://progressive.org/api/content/443600de-5d80-11ea-af0d-1244d5f7c7c6/.

Mischel, Walter, Ebbe B. Ebbesen, and Antonette Raskoff Zeiss. "Cognitive and Attentional Mechanisms in Delay of Gratification." *Journal of Personality and Social Psychology* 21, no. 2 (1972): 204–18. https://doi.org/10.1037/h0032198.

Moats, Louisa. "Reconciling the Common Core State Standards with Reading Research." *Perspectives on Language and Literacy*. Accessed August 21, 2022. http://www.onlinedigeditions.com/article/Reconciling+the+Common+Core+State+Standards+with+Reading+Research/1191904/128301/article.html.

Modan, Naaz. "What Does Carson v. Makin Mean for Ed Leaders?" *K-12 Dive* (blog), June 22, 2022. https://www.k12dive.com/news/what-does-carson-v-makin-mean-for-ed-leaders/625886/.

Morrison, Nick. "Creative, Flexible, Global: What Millennial Parents Want from Schools." *Forbes*, December 9, 2021. https://www.forbes.com/sites/nickmorrison/2021/12/09/creative-flexible-global-what-millennial-parents-want-from-schools/.

Munro, André. "Michael Oakeshott." In *Britannica Academic*. Britannica Digital Learning. Encyclopædia Britannica, 2022. https://academic-eb-com.proxy1.library.jhu.edu/levels/collegiate/article/Michael-Oakeshott/599866.

NAACP. "Calling for Moratorium on Charter School Expansion and Strengthening of Oversight in Governance and Practice | NAACP." January 1, 2016. https://naacp

.org/resources/calling-moratorium-charter-school-expansion-and-strengthening
-oversight-governance-and.

NAEP and IES. "School Composition and the Black–White Achievement Gap."
Washington, D.C.: National Assessment of Educational Progress and National
Center for Educational Statistics, June 2015. https://nces.ed.gov/nationsreportcard/
subject/studies/pdf/school_composition_and_the_bw_achievement_gap_2015.pdf.

National Assessment Governing Board. "Draft Reading Assessment Framework
for the 2025 National Assessment of Educational Progress." U.S. Department
of Education, June 12, 2020. https://www.federalregister.gov/documents/2020
/06/12/2020–12693/draft-reading-assessment-framework-for-the-2025-national
-assessment-of-educational-progress.

National Research Council. *Adding It Up: Helping Children Learn Mathematics.*
Edited by Jeremy Kilpatrick, Jane Swafford, and Bradford Findell. Mathematics
Learning Study Commitee, Center for Education, Division of Behavioral and
Social Sciences. Washington, D.C.: National Academy Press, 2001. https://doi.org
/10.17226/9822.

NCES. "Table 2.16. Social Studies Statewide Assessment Name/Title and Grade
Administered, by State: 2018." State Education Practices (SEP). National Center
for Education Statistics, 2018. https://nces.ed.gov/programs/statereform/tab2_16
.asp.

NCES. "Table 216.20. Number and Enrollment of Public Elementary and Secondary
Schools, by School Level, Type, and Charter and Magnet Status: Selected Years,
1990–91 through 2014–15." Digest of Education Statistics, 2020. National Center
for Education Statistics, 2020. https://nces.ed.gov/programs/digest/d16/tables/dt16
_216.20.asp.

NCTE, and NCATE. "NCTE/NCATE Standards for Initial Preparation of Teachers of
Secondary English Language Arts, Grades 7–12." October 2012. https://ncte.org/
app/uploads/2018/07/ApprovedStandards_111212.pdf.

NEA. "Great Teaching and Learning: Creating School Culture." Washington, D.C.:
National Education Association (NEA), July 2020. https://www.nea.org/resource
-library/great-teaching-and-learning-creating-school-culture.

New York State Education Department. "NY STATE - NEW YORK STATE REPORT
CARD [2017–18]." NYSED Data Site, 2019. https://data.nysed.gov/essa.php
?instid=800000081568&year=2018&createreport=1&regents=1.

New York Times. "Excerpts From Bush's Speech on Improving Education." *New York
Times, Late Edition (East Coast),* September 3, 1999, sec. A.

Next Generation Science Standards. "THE THREE DIMENSIONS OF SCIENCE
LEARNING." 2022. https://www.nextgenscience.org/.

Nichols-Barrer, Ira, Kate Place, Erin Dillon, and Brian P. Gill. "Testing College
Readiness." *Education Next,* May 17, 2016. https://www.educationnext.org/testing
-college-readiness-massachusetts-parcc-mcas-standardized-tests/.

NIH. "National Reading Panel Publications." Eunice Kennedy Shriver National
Institute of Child Health and Human Development (NIH), June 10, 2019. https://
www.nichd.nih.gov/about/org/der/branches/cdbb/nationalreadingpanelpubs.

Noguera, Pedro. *City Schools and the American Dream: Reclaiming the Promise of Public Education.* New York: Teachers College Press, 2003.

Nozick, Robert. *Anarchy, State, and Utopia.* Reprint ed. New York: Basic Books, 2013.

Nussbaum, Martha C. *Love's Knowledge: Essays on Philosophy and Literature.* Revised ed. New York: Oxford University Press, 1992.

O'Brien, Anne. "What Do Parents Want from Schools?" *Edutopia* (blog), October 13, 2017. https://www.edutopia.org/article/what-do-parents-want-schools.

Oakeshott, Michael. *The Voice of Liberal Learning.* Indianapolis, IN: Liberty Fund, 2001.

Oates, Tim. "Assessment - Perhaps It's Just about Good Questions . . . " *Assessment Network and Research from Cambridge University* (blog), May 13, 2021. https://www.cambridgeassessment.org.uk/blogs/view/assessment-its-about-good-questions/.

Oates, Tim. "Could Do Better: Using International Comparisons to Refine the National Curriculum in England." *The Curriculum Journal* 22, no. 2 (June 1, 2011): 121–50. https://doi.org/10.1080/09585176.2011.578908.

Oates, Tim. "England: England and PISA - The Long View." In *Improving a Country's Education: PISA 2018 Results in 10 Countries*, edited by Nuno Crato, 83–89. Switzerland: Springer Nature, 2021.

OECD. "International Student Assessment (PISA) - Mathematics Performance (PISA)." OECD Data, 2021. http://data.oecd.org/pisa/mathematics-performance-pisa.htm.

OECD. "PISA 2018: Sky's the Limit." 2021. https://www.oecd.org/pisa/growth-mindset.pdf.

OECD. "PISA 2021 Creative Thinking Framework (Third Draft)." April 2019. https://www.oecd.org/pisa/publications/PISA-2021-creative-thinking-framework.pdf.

Open Culture Staff. "The Summerhill School, the Radical Educational Experiment That Let Students Learn What, When, and How They Want (1966)." *Open Culture* (blog), March 9, 2020. https://www.openculture.com/2020/03/summerhill-school.html.

Oxford, Rebecca L. "Constructivism: Shape-Shifting, Substance, and Teacher Education Applications." *Peabody Journal of Education* 72, no. 1 (January 1, 1997): 35–66. https://doi.org/10.1207/s15327930pje7201_3.

Pangle, Lorraine Smith, and Thomas L. Pangle. *The Learning of Liberty: The Educational Ideas of the American Founders.* Lawrence: University Press of Kansas, 1993.

Passarella, Al. "The Necessary Components of an Effective Career and Technical Education (CTE) Program." Policy Brief. Baltimore: Johns Hopkins Institute for Education Policy, February 2018. https://drive.google.com/file/d/1y8eFyb7osSvd KicFN7r9QTWWVYCUnOWn/view.

PDK Poll. "49th Annual PDK Poll of the Public's Attitudes Toward the Public Schools." *Kappan Magazine*, September 2017. https://pdkpoll.org/wp-content/uploads/2020/05/pdkpoll51–2019.pdf.

Pelaez, Robert, and Steven Keehner. "School District Budgets Show Wide Disparity in Funding per Pupil - Featured." *The Island 360* (blog), May 25, 2022.

https://theisland360.com/featured/school-district-budgets-show-wide-disparity-in -funding-per-pupil/.

Peterson, Paul E. "How the 'Structural Racism' Talk Undermines Individual Agency." The Education Exchange with Paul E. Peterson. Accessed June 2, 2022. https://www.educationnext.org/education-exchange-how-structural-racism-talk -undermines-individual-agency-rowe/.

Plato, Minus. "Finding Nelson Mandela's Creon in Mark Rothko's Antigone." *The Minus Plato Archive* (blog), December 6, 2013. http://minusplato.com/2013/12/ finding-nelson-mandelas-creon-in-mark-rothkos-antigone-2.html.

Plato. "Perseus Under Philologic: Pl. Resp. 597e." In *Republic*, translated by University of Chicago. Perseus Project. Perseus Project Texts Loaded under PhiloLogi, 375 AD. https://anastrophe.uchicago.edu/cgi-bin/perseus/citequery3.pl ?dbname=GreekAug21&getid=1&query=Pl.%20Resp.%20597c.

Polikoff, Morgan. *Beyond Standards: The Fragmentation of Education Governance and the Promise of Curriculum Reform*. Cambridge, MA: Harvard Education Press, 2021.

Pondiscio, Robert. *How The Other Half Learns: Equality, Excellence, and the Battle over School Choice*. New York: Avery, 2020.

Pondiscio, Robert. "How US Schools Became Obsessed with Race." *American Enterprise Institute (AEI)* (blog), June 18, 2021. https://www.aei.org/op-eds/how-u -s-schools-became-obsessed-with-race/.

Pondiscio, Robert. "I Believe 'Antiracism' Is Misguided. Can I Still Teach Black Children?" *The Thomas B. Fordham Institute Flypaper* (blog), April 29, 2021. https://fordhaminstitute.org/national/commentary/i-believe-antiracism-misguided -can-i-still-teach-black-children.

Pondiscio, Robert. "Pondiscio: After 2 Years of Uncertainty and Shaken Trust, America's Relationship with Its Public Schools Is in Play Like Never Before." *The 74 Million* (blog), January 24, 2022. https://www.the74million.org/article /pondiscio-after-2-years-of-uncertainty-and-shaken-trust-americas-relationship -with-its-public-schools-is-in-play-like-never-before/.

Pondiscio, Robert. "Testing Alone Won't Make Good Readers." *The Thomas B. Fordham Institute Flypaper* (blog), April 20, 2016. https://fordhaminstitute.org/ national/commentary/testing-alone-wont-make-good-readers.

Pondiscio, Robert. "The Unexamined Rise of Therapeutic Education: How Social-Emotional Learning Extends K–12 Education's Reach into Students' Lives and Expands Teachers' Roles." American Enterprise Institute, October 13, 2021. https://www.aei.org/wp-content/uploads/2021/10/The-Unexamined-Rise-of -Therapeutic-Education.pdf?x91208.

Prather, Anika. "The Classics Are an Instrument of Freedom for Black People." *National Review* (blog), February 20, 2022. https://www.nationalreview.com/2022 /02/the-classics-are-an-instrument-of-freedom-for-black-people/.

Rabkin, Nick, and Robin Redmond. *Putting the Arts in the Picture: Reframing Education in the 21st Century*. 1st ed. Chicago, IL.: Columbia College Chicago Press, 2012.

Raths, Louis E., Merrill Harmin, and Sidney B. Simon. *Values And Teaching: Working with Values in the Classroom*. New York: Charles E. Merrill Publishing Company, 1973.

Ravitch, Diane. *Left Back: A Century of Battles over School Reform*. New York: Simon & Schuster, 2001.

Rawls, John. *A Theory of Justice*. 2nd ed. Cambridge, MA: Belknap Press: An Imprint of Harvard University Press, 1999.

Reardon, Sean F., Ericka Weathers, Erin Fahle, Heewon Jang, and Demetra Kalogrides. "Is Separate Still Unequal? New Evidence on School Segregation and Racial Academic Achievement Gaps." *Stanford CEPA: Center for Education Policy Analysis*, September 29, 2021. https://cepa.stanford.edu/content/separate -still-unequal-new-evidence-school-segregation-and-racial-academic-achievement -gaps.

Rebell, Michael A. "Preparation for Capable Citizenship: The Schools' Primary Responsibility." *Kappanonline.Org* (blog), October 22, 2018. https://kappanonline .org/rebell-preparation-capable-citizenship-schools-primary-responsibility/.

Reboot Foundation. "Critical Thinking Survey Report." November 2020. https: //reboot-foundation.org/wp-content/uploads/_docs/Critical_Thinking_Survey _Report_2020.pdf.

Redden, Elizabeth. "41% of Recent Grads Work in Jobs Not Requiring a Degree." Inside Higher Ed, February 18, 2020. https://www.insidehighered.com/quicktakes /2020/02/18/41-recent-grads-work-jobs-not-requiring-degree.

Relay Graduate School of Education. "Better Attendance, Fewer Suspensions, More Teachers of Color - Findings from Recent Research." *Relay/GSE* (blog), July 5, 2022. https://www.relay.edu/article/better-attendance-fewer-suspensions-more -teachers-of-color-findings-from-research.

Richardson, Virginia. "Constructivist Pedagogy." *Teachers College Record* 105, no. 9 (December 2003): 1623–40.

Rieger, Adam. "The Beautiful Art of Mathematics†." *Philosophia Mathematica* 26, no. 2 (June 1, 2018): 234–50. https://doi.org/10.1093/philmat/nkx006.

Rojstaczer, Stuart. "National Trends in Grade Inflation, American Colleges and Universities." GradeInflation.com, March 29, 2016. https://www.gradeinflation .com/.

Rotermund, Susan, and Amy Burke. "Elementary and Secondary STEM Education | Post-High School Transitions." NCSES | Science & Engineering Indicators, July 8, 2021. https://ncses.nsf.gov/pubs/nsb20211/post-high-school-transitions.

Rothstein, Jesse M. "College Performance Predictions and the SAT." *Journal of Econometrics*, Higher education (Annals issue), 121, no. 1 (July 1, 2004): 297–317. https://doi.org/10.1016/j.jeconom.2003.10.003.

Rothstein, Jesse, and Nathan Wozny. "Permanent Income and the Black-White Test Score Gap." NBER Working Paper Series. Cambridge, MA: National Bureau of Economic Research, November 2011. https://www.nber.org/system/files/working _papers/w17610/w17610.pdf.

Rothstein, Richard. *Class And Schools: Using Social, Economic, And Educational Reform to Close The Black-White Achievement Gap*. Illustrated ed. New York: Teachers College Press, 2004.

Rothstein, Richard. "Grading the Education Reformers." *Slate*, August 29, 2011. https://slate.com/culture/2011/08/steven-brill-s-class-warfare-what-s-wrong-with -the-education-reformers-diagnosis-and-cures.html.

Rothstein, Richard. "The Racial Achievement Gap, Segregated Schools, and Segregated Neighborhoods—A Constitutional Insult." *Race and Social Problems* 6, no. 4 (December 2014). https://www.epi.org/publication/the-racial-achievement -gap-segregated-schools-and-segregated-neighborhoods-a-constitutional-insult/.

Saavedra, Anna Rosefsky, and V. Darleen Opfer. "Nine Lessons on How to Teach 21st Century Skills and Knowledge." *The RAND Blog* (blog), October 19, 2012. https:// www.rand.org/blog/2012/10/nine-lessons-on-how-to-teach-21st-century-skills-and .html.

Sahlgren, Gabriel Heller. Press Regarding "Real Finnish Lessons: The true story of an education superpower," April 2015. https://cps.org.uk/research/real-finnish-lessons -the-true-story-of-an-education-superpower/.

Santens, Scott. "Stop Teaching Students What to Think. Teach Them How to Think." *Education Week*, September 27, 2017, sec. Education. https://www.edweek.org/ education/opinion-stop-teaching-students-what-to-think-teach-them-how-to-think /2017/09.

Saphier, Jon, Mary Ann Haley-Speca, and Robert Gower. *The Skillful Teacher: The Comprehensive Resource for Improving Teaching and Learning*. 7th ed. Acton, MA: Research for Better Teaching, 2017.

Sawchuk, Stephen. "What Is Critical Race Theory, and Why Is It Under Attack?" *Education Week*, May 18, 2021, sec. Equity & Diversity. https://www.edweek.org/ leadership/what-is-critical-race-theory-and-why-is-it-under-attack/2021/05.

Schaper, Eva. "Taste, Sublimity, and Genius: The Aesthetics of Nature and Art." In *The Cambridge Companion to Kant*, edited by Paul Guyer. Reprint ed. Cambridge: Cambridge University Press, 1992.

Schiller, Friedrich. *On the Aesthetic Education of Man*. Translated by Reginald Snell. 6th ed. New York: Frederick Ungar, 1981. https://www.biblio.com/book/aesthetic -education-schiller-friedrich/d/1278875917.

Schleicher, Andreas, and Qian Tang. "Editorial | Education Post-2015: Knowledge and Skills Transform Lives and Societies." Universal Basic Skills: What Countries Stand to Gain. OECD Publishing, 2015. https://read.oecd.org/10.1787 /9789264234833-en?format=read#page11.

Schleicher, Andreas. *Building a High-Quality Teaching Profession: Lessons from around the World*. Paris: OECD Publishing, 2011. https://www.oecd-ilibrary .org/education/building-a-high-quality-teaching-profession_9789264113046 -en;jsessionid=F9M_uTWUFWMr5IcTFY3OSReK.ip-10-240-5-16.

Schleicher, Andreas. "PISA 2018 Insights and Interpretations." Paris: OECD, 2019. https://www.oecd.org/pisa/PISA%202018%20Insights%20and%20Interpretations %20FINAL%20PDF.pdf.

Schmidt, W. H., Curtis C. McKnight, and S. Raizen, eds. *A Splintered Vision: An Investigation of U.S. Science and Mathematics Education*. Dordrecht: Springer, 1997.

Schmidt, William, Richard Houang, and Leland Cogan. "A Coherent Curriculum: The Case of Mathematics." *American Educator*, Summer 2002. https://www.aft.org/sites/default/files/periodicals/curriculum.pdf.

Schraw, Gregory, and Rayne Sperling Dennison. "Assessing Metacognitive Awareness." *Contemporary Educational Psychology* 19, no. 4 (October 1, 1994): 460–75. https://doi.org/10.1006/ceps.1994.1033.

Schwartz, Sarah. "Digging Deeper into the Stark Declines on NAEP: 5 Things to Know." *Education Week*, September 2 2022. https://www.edweek.org/leadership/digging-deeper-into-the-stark-declines-on-naep-5-things-to-know/2022/09.

Schwartz, Sarah. "Map: Where Critical Race Theory Is Under Attack." *Education Week*, June 11, 2021, sec. States. https://www.edweek.org/policy-politics/map-where-critical-race-theory-is-under-attack/2021/06.

Sennett, Richard. "The Troubled Craftsman." In *The Craftsman*. New Haven, CT: Yale University Press, 2008.

Shakeel, Danish, Patrick J. Wolf, and Kaitlin P. Anderson. "The Participant Effects of Private School Vouchers across the Globe: A Meta-Analytic and Systematic Review." Working Paper. Fayetteville: University of Arkansas, April 2016.

Silverstein, Jake. "An Update to the 1619 Project." *New York Times Magazine*, March 11, 2020, sec. Magazine. https://www.nytimes.com/2020/03/11/magazine/an-update-to-the-1619-project.html.

Silverstein, Jake. "The 1619 Project." *New York Times Magazine*, August 14, 2019, sec. Magazine. https://www.nytimes.com/interactive/2019/08/14/magazine/1619-america-slavery.html, https://www.nytimes.com/interactive/2019/08/14/magazine/1619-america-slavery.html.

Sisk, Victoria F., Alexander P. Burgoyne, Jingze Sun, Jennifer L. Butler, and Brooke N. Macnamara. "To What Extent and Under Which Circumstances Are Growth Mind-Sets Important to Academic Achievement? Two Meta-Analyses." *Psychological Science* 29, no. 4 (April 1, 2018): 549–71. https://doi.org/10.1177/0956797617739704.

Slavin, Robert, and David Steiner. "Tutoring as an Effective Strategy in Our Troubled Times." *The Thomas B. Fordham Institute Flypaper* (blog), July 22, 2020. http://fordhaminstitute.org/national/commentary/tutoring-effective-strategy-our-troubled-times.

Slavin, Robert. "Tutoring Could Change Everything." *Robert Slavin's Blog* (blog), January 14, 2021. https://robertslavinsblog.wordpress.com/2021/01/14/tutoring-could-change-everything/.

Smith, Kara, Sanja Jagesic, Jeff Wyatt, and Maureen Ewing. "AP® STEM Participation and Postsecondary STEM Outcomes: Focus on Underrepresented Minority, First-Generation, and Female Students." The College Board, 2018. https://files.eric.ed.gov/fulltext/ED581514.pdf.

Smith, Reid, Pamela Snow, Tanya Serry, and Lorraine Hammond. "The Role of Background Knowledge in Reading Comprehension: A Critical Review." *Reading*

Psychology 42, no. 3 (April 3, 2021): 214–40. https://doi.org/10.1080/02702711 .2021.1888348.

Smith, Ryan. "Advancing Racial Equity in Career and Technical Education Enrollment." *Center for American Progress* (blog), August 28, 2019. https://www .americanprogress.org/article/advancing-racial-equity-career-technical-education -enrollment/.

Social Security Administration. "Research Summary: Education and Lifetime Earnings." Social Security Administration Research, Statistics, and Policy Analysis, November 2015. https://www.ssa.gov/policy/docs/research-summaries/education -earnings.html.

St. George, Donna. "Maryland Investigates Claim of Inappropriate Help on Diploma-Related Projects." *Washington Post*, January 20, 2020, sec. Education. https://www.washingtonpost.com/local/education/maryland-investigates-claim-of -inappropriate-help-on-diploma-related-projects/2020/01/20/6df0cbc2–322c-11ea -a053-dc6d944ba776_story.html.

Steiner, David M. "Commencement Address to the Hunter College School of Education." Presented at the Graduation, Hunter College School of Education at the City University of New York, 2009, 2012–2015, 2005. [AQ]

Steiner, David M. "Fair Copy Book." Perse School, 1970.

Steiner, David M. *Rethinking Democratic Education: The Politics of Reform.* Baltimore: Johns Hopkins University Press, 1994.

Steiner, David, and Ashley Berner. "Chicago's Use of the International Baccalaureate: An Education Success Story That Didn't Travel." Johns Hopkins Institute for Education Policy, October 2015. https://drive.google.com/file/d/1W7FTH0C23rj W3x4sjkJ2wdP4nW6xtQSa/view.

Steiner, David, and Daniel Weisberg. "When Students Go Back to School, Too Many Will Start the Year Behind. Here's How to Catch Them Up—in Real Time." *The 74 Million* (blog), April 26, 2020. https://www.the74million.org/article/steiner -weisberg-when-students-go-back-to-school-too-many-will-start-the-year-behind -heres-how-to-catch-them-up-in-real-time/.

Steiner, David, and Mark Bauerlein. "A Feel-Good Report Card Won't Help Children." *City Journal* (blog), October 13, 2020. https://www.city-journal.org/ naep-proposes-changes-to-reading-tests.

Steiner, David, Ben Jensen, and Jacqueline Magee. "Curriculum Literacy in Schools of Education? The Hole at the Center of American Teacher Preparation." Collingwood, Australia: Johns Hopkins Institute for Education Policy and Learning First, November 2018. https://drive.google.com/file/d/1IeFssCpRxWs-I __FqeIoFKcgzzfSypTM/view.

Steiner, David. "Make Sense of the Research: A Primer for Educational Leaders." *Phi Delta Kappan* 103, no. 3 (November 1, 2021): 43–47. https://doi.org/10.1177 /00317217211058524.

Steiner, David. "The Common Core: Let the Light Sing." *PMLA* 130, no. 3 (2015): 704–10.

Steiner, David. "The New Common Core Assessments: How They Could Stop Patronizing Our Students." *The Huffington Post*, February 21, 2014. http://www

.huffingtonpost.com/david-m-steiner/the-new-common-core-asses_b_4809973 .html.

Stolp, Stephen. "Leadership for School Culture." *ERIC Digest*. Eugene, OR: ERIC Clearinghouse on Educational Management, June 1994. https://eric.ed.gov/?id =ED370198.Stringer, Kate. "Bored in Class: A National Survey Finds Nearly 1 in 3 Teens Are Bored 'Most or All of the Time' in School, and a Majority Report High Levels of Stress." *The 74 Million* (blog), January 16, 2019. https:// www.the74million.org/bored-in-class-a-national-survey-finds-nearly-1-in-3-teens -are-bored-most-or-all-of-the-time-in-school-and-a-majority-report-high-levels-of -stress/.

Sun Sentinel Editorial Board. "DeSantis Weaponizes the Anguish of Children | Editorial." *South Florida Sun Sentinel*, March 29, 2022. https://www.sun -sentinel.com/opinion/editorials/fl-op-edit-dont-say-gay-desantis-20220329 -kcicveb4wvco5n2kdahuiynfbi-story.html.

Suto, Irenka, and Tim Oates. "High-Stakes Testing after Basic Secondary Education: How and Why Is It Done in High-Performing Education Systems?" Cambridge Assessment Research Report. Cambridge, UK: Cambridge Assessment, February 2021. https://www.cambridgeassessment.org.uk/Images/610965-high-stakes -testing-after-basic-secondary-education-how-and-why-is-it-done-in-high -performing-education-systems-.pdf.

Taylor, Kate. "Regents Drop Teacher Literacy Test Seen as Discriminatory." *New York Times*, March 13, 2017, sec. N.Y. / Region. https://www.nytimes.com/2017 /03/13/nyregion/ny-regents-teacher-exams-alst.html.

Terada, Youki. "How Metacognition Boosts Learning." *Edutopia* (blog), November 21, 2017. https://www.edutopia.org/article/how-metacognition-boosts-learning.

The Century Foundation. "Closing America's Education Funding Gaps." July 22, 2020. https://tcf.org/content/report/closing-americas-education-funding/?agreed=1 &agreed=1&agreed=1.

The Century Foundation. "The Benefits of Socioeconomically and Racially Integrated Schools and Classrooms." *The Century Foundation* (blog), April 29, 2019. https: //tcf.org/content/facts/the-benefits-of-socioeconomically-and-racially-integrated -schools-and-classrooms/.

The Core Knowledge Foundation. "CKLA Grade 1: Domain 1—Fables and Stories (10 Daily Lessons)." *Core Knowledge Foundation* (blog), n.d. https://www .coreknowledge.org/free-resource/ckla-domain-01-fables-stories/.

The Gettysburg Address: An Exemplary Curricular Module in Literacy. Common Core Video Series. PBS Learning Media, 2011. https://www.pbslearningmedia .org/resource/engny.pd.ccvs.ela9/the-gettysburg-address-an-exemplary-curricular -module-in-literacy/.

The Glossary of Education Reform. "21st Century Skills Definition." May 15, 2013. https://www.edglossary.org/21st-century-skills/.

The Nation's Report Card. "NAEP Mathematics 2019 Highlights Grade 12." The Nation's Report Card: National Assessment of Educational Progress, 2019. https:// www.nationsreportcard.gov/highlights/mathematics/2019/g12/.

The Nation's Report Card. "NAEP Mathematics: Mathematics Results, Grade 4." The Nation's Report Card: National Assessment of Educational Progress, 2019. https://www.nationsreportcard.gov/mathematics/?grade=4.

The Nation's Report Card. "NAEP Mathematics: Mathematics Results, Grade 12." The Nation's Report Card: National Assessment of Educational Progress, 2019. https://www.nationsreportcard.gov/mathematics/nation/achievement/?grade=12.

The Nation's Report Card. "NAEP Reading: Reading Results, Grade 4." The Nation's Report Card: National Assessment of Educational Progress, 2019. https://www.nationsreportcard.gov/reading/?grade=4.

The Nation's Report Card. NAEP Report Card: Civics: Achievement-Level Results. https://www.nationsreportcard.gov/civics/results/achievement/.

The Nation's Report Card. "Results from the 2019 NAEP High School Transcript Study." The Nation's Report Card, 2019. https://www.nationsreportcard.gov/hstsreport/#home.

The Nation's Report Card. NAEP Long-Term Trend Assessment Results: Reading and Mathematics. https://www.nationsreportcard.gov/ltt/?age=9.

The National Commission on Excellence in Education. "A Nation at Risk: The Imperative for Educational Reform." U.S. Department of Education, April 1983. https://edreform.com/wp-content/uploads/2013/02/A_Nation_At_Risk_1983.pdf.

The National Council of Teachers of English. "Beliefs about Methods Courses and Field Experiences in English Education." The National Council of Teachers of English (NCTE), May 22, 2020. https://ncte.org/about/.

Thornton, Bruce. "America's Problem of Assimilation." *Defining Ideas from the Hoover Institution* (blog), May 24, 2012. https://www.hoover.org/research/americas-problem-assimilation.

The New Teacher Project. "Greenhouse Schools: Executive Summary." New York: TNTP, 2012. https://tntp.org/assets/documents/TNTP_Greenhouse_Schools_ExecSum_2012.pdf.

The New Teacher Project. "The Opportunity Myth: What Students Can Show Us About How School Is Letting Them Down—and How to Fix It." New York: TNTP, September 25, 2018. https://tntp.org/publications/view/student-experiences/the-opportunity-myth.

Tosh, Katie, Sy Doan, Ashley Woo, and Daniella Henry. "Digital Instructional Materials: What Are Teachers Using and What Barriers Exist?" Insights from the American Education Panels. Arlington, VA: RAND Corporation, 2020. https://www.rand.org/pubs/research_reports/RR2575z17.html.

Tucker, Marc. "Differences in Performance WITHIN Schools: Why So Much Greater Than in Other Countries?" *Education Week*, September 6, 2017, sec. Equity & Diversity. https://www.edweek.org/leadership/opinion-differences-in-performance-within-schools-why-so-much-greater-than-in-other-countries/2017/09.

Tyack, David B. *Seeking Common Ground: Public Schools in a Diverse Society*. Cambridge, MA: Harvard University Press, 2007.

Tyner, Adam, and Nicholas Munyan-Penney. "Gotta Give 'Em Credit: State and District Variation in Credit Recovery Participation Rates." Thomas B. Fordham

Institute, November 29, 2018. https://fordhaminstitute.org/national/research/gotta
-give-em-credit.

U.S. Bureau of Labor Statistics. "Occupational Outlook Handbook: Computer
Programmers." April 18, 2022. https://www.bls.gov/ooh/computer-and-information
-technology/computer-programmers.htm.

U.S. Bureau of Labor Statistics. "Occupational Outlook Handbook: Most New Jobs."
April 18, 2022. https://www.bls.gov/ooh/most-new-jobs.htm.

U.S. Department of Education. "Innovative Assessment Demonstration Authority."
Application Materials; Indexes; Letters (Correspondence). U.S. Department of
Education (ED), January 17, 2020. https://www2.ed.gov/admins/lead/account/iada
/index.html.

Urmson, J. O. "9. Aristotle's Doctrine of the Mean." In *Essays on Aristotle's Ethics*,
edited by Amélie Oksenberg Rorty, 2:157–70. Major Thinkers Series. Berkeley:
University of California Press, 1980. https://doi.org/10.1525/9780520340985–012.

Valant, Jon. "The Banality of Racism in Education." *Brookings* (blog), June 4,
2020. https://www.brookings.edu/blog/brown-center-chalkboard/2020/06/04/the
-banality-of-racism-in-education/.

Wagner, Jennifer. "Two Polls Diverged on The Issue Of School Choice: An Explainer."
EdChoice (blog), September 7, 2021. https://medium.com/educationchoice/two
-polls-diverged-on-the-issue-of-school-choice-an-explainer-5632abd0130a.

Walsh, Bryan. "Major Harvard Change Underscores the Decline of Standardized
Testing." Axios, December 18, 2021. https://www.axios.com/2021/12/18/decline
-of-sat-tests-harvard.

Warden, Bryce. "Knowing Better, Doing Better: Mississippi's Story In Literacy
Success." SCORE, March 12, 2020. https://tnscore.org/knowing-better-doing
-better-mississippis-story-in-literacy-success/.

Watts, Tyler W., Greg J. Duncan, and Haonan Quan. "Revisiting the Marshmallow
Test: A Conceptual Replication Investigating Links Between Early Delay of
Gratification and Later Outcomes." *Psychological Science* 29, no. 7 (July 2018):
1159–77. https://doi.org/10.1177/0956797618761661.

Webster, John. *The Duchess of Malfi*. Project Gutenberg, 1613. https://www
.gutenberg.org/ebooks/2232.

West, Martin R. "Schools of Choice: Expanding Opportunity for Urban Minority
Students." *Education Next*, Spring 2016. https://www.educationnext.org/schools-of
-choice-expanding-opportunity-urban-minority-students/.

West, Martin R., Matthew A. Kraft, Amy S. Finn, Rebecca E. Martin, Angela L.
Duckworth, Christopher F. O. Gabrieli, and John D. E. Gabrieli. "Promise and
Paradox: Measuring Students' Non-Cognitive Skills and the Impact of Schooling."
Educational Evaluation and Policy Analysis 38, no. 1 (March 1, 2016): 148–70.
https://doi.org/10.3102/0162373715597298.

What Works Clearinghouse. "WWC SUMMARY OF EVIDENCE FOR THIS
INTERVENTION | Growth Mindset." January 2022. https://ies.ed.gov/ncee/wwc/
Intervention/1629.

Wiggins, David. "13. Deliberation and Practical Reason." In *Essays on Aristotle's
Ethics*, edited by Amélie Oksenberg Rorty, 2:221–40. Major Thinkers Series.

Berkeley: University of California Press, 1980. https://doi.org/10.1525 /9780520340985–016.

Wikipedia. "Grit (Personality Trait)." In *Wikipedia*, February 9, 2022. https://en .wikipedia.org/w/index.php?title=Grit_(personality_trait)&oldid=1070873783.

Wilkes, Kathleen V. "18. The Good Man and the Good for Man in Aristotle's Ethics." In *Essays on Aristotle's Ethics*, 2:341–58. Major Thinkers Series. Berkeley: University of California Press, 1980. https://doi.org/10.1525/9780520340985–021.

Will, Madeline. "Fewer People Are Getting Teacher Degrees. Prep Programs Sound the Alarm." *Education Week*, March 22, 2022, sec. Teacher Preparation. https: //www.edweek.org/teaching-learning/fewer-people-are-getting-teacher-degrees -prep-programs-sound-the-alarm/2022/03.

Will, Madeline. "Teacher-Preparation Programs Make Gains in the 'Science of Reading,' Review Finds." *Education Week*, January 28, 2020, sec. Reading & Literacy. https://www.edweek.org/teaching-learning/teacher-preparation-programs -make-gains-in-the-science-of-reading-review-finds/2020/0.

Willingham, Daniel T. "Critical Thinking: Why Is It So Hard to Teach?" *American Educator*, Summer 2007. https://www.aft.org/sites/default/files/periodicals/Crit _Thinking.pdf.

Willingham, Daniel. "Critical Thinking: Why Is It So Hard to Teach?" *Reading Rockets* (blog), April 24, 2013. https://www.readingrockets.org/article/critical -thinking-why-it-so-hard-teach.

Willis, George, William H. Schubert, Robert V. Bullough, Craig Kridel, and John T. Holton, eds. *The American Curriculum: A Documentary History*. Westport, CT: Praeger, 1994.

Willms, J. Douglas. "Catholic-School Effects on Academic Achievement: New Evidence from the High School and Beyond Follow-Up Study." *Sociology of Education* 58, no. 2 (1985): 98–114. https://doi.org/10.2307/2112250.

Wilson, Andrew. "Antigone: Nelson Mandela Plays Creon." The Classics Pages, 2011. http://www.users.globalnet.co.uk/~loxias/mandela.htm.

Wineburg, Sam. "Crazy for History." *The Journal of American History* 90, no. 4 (2004): 1401–14. https://doi.org/10.2307/3660360.

Winthrop, Rebecca. "The need for civic education in 21st-century schools," Brookings, June 4, 2020. https://www.brookings.edu/policy2020/bigideas/the-need -for-civic-education-in-21st-century-schools/.

Wolf, Patrick J., ed. *School Choice: Separating Fact from Fiction*. 1st ed. London: Routledge, 2018.

Wolpert, Stuart. "Why so Many U.S. Students Aren't Learning Math." *UCLA Newsroom* (blog), October 15, 2018. https://newsroom.ucla.edu/stories/why-so -many-u-s-students-arent-learning-math.

Wooldridge, Adrian. "Kissinger Knows Why the Global Leadership Deficit Is Getting Worse." *Bloomberg.Com*, July 25, 2022. https://www.bloomberg.com/opinion/ articles/2022–07–25/kissinger-knows-why-the-global-leadership-deficit-is-getting -worse.

Yeats, W. B. "Among School Children." In *The Poems of W. B. Yeats: A New Edition*, edited by Richard J. Finneran. New York: Macmillan Publishing Company, 1933. https://www.poetryfoundation.org/poems/43293/among-school-children.

Zernike, Kate. "Testing for Joy and Grit? Schools Nationwide Push to Measure Students' Emotional Skills." *New York Times*, March 1, 2016, sec. U.S. https://www.nytimes.com/2016/03/01/us/testing-for-joy-and-grit-schools-nationwide-push-to-measure-students-emotional-skills.html.

Index

Abitur test, 73, 126

academic, engagement, 108, 124–26

academic achievement, 3, 15–16, 26

academic content: aptitude tests and, 85, *85*; focus on, 76; lowered expectations for, 103, 105, 125; rigorous, 57, 58–59, 130; in teacher training programs, 68

academic core, 59–60

academic potential, psychological stance and, 37

academic preparation, as highest aim, 31

academics: creative thinking subjects in, 53; distractions from, 31–54; lack of emphasis on, 7–8, 105

achievement: gaps between races, 2, 10–11, 17–18, 65; metrics as white, 23

ACT scores, 5, 84–85, *85*

administrators, departure of, 55

adults: labeling of children and, 40; virtuous behavior and, 111

AEI. *See* American Enterprise Institute

aerospace training, 12

Aesop's Fables, 113

aesthetics, 108, 118, 153n38; cognition and, 131–32; judgements in, 119–22; observations in, 122–23; sensibilities

of students of, 122–23; synthesis of experience of, 123–24, 132

African American students, 18

AFT. *See* American Federation of Teachers

After Virtue (McIntyre), 108

agogê (Spartan education program), 99

air conditioning, of Baltimore public schools, 19

AIT. *See* Anderson Institute of Technology

A-Level exams, 73, 126–27

algebra, 101

alternative factors, study outcomes and, 35

American college degree, career prospects of, 14

The American Curriculum (Willis et al.), 62

American dream, as portrayed in *The Great Gatsby*, 98–99

American education. *See specific topics*

American Enterprise Institute (AEI), xxiv, 23

American Federation of Teachers (AFT), xxiv

American identity, as variable, 64

American public, xxiii–xxiv

American reading tests: reform of, 73; vocabulary of, 73

American University School of Education, 40

Anderson Institute of Technology (AIT), 12, 14

Antigone (Sophocles), 132

AP tests, 70

aptitude tests, 63, 69, 84

Arendt, Hannah, 92, 107, 117

Aristotle, 94, 106, 107, 109–12, 115–17; highest good and, 152n36

Arizona state department, 25

art: education in, 118–19; reaction to, 119–22; response as cognition, 121

assessments, 57, 69, 76–77

authentic learning, 65

author meaning, Hirsch on, 92–93

background knowledge: decoding texts and, 89–91; reading tests and, 73–74

backgrounds of minority students, inequalities in, 18–19, 21

Balfanz, Robert, 44, 45, 46

Ball, Deborah, 102

Baltimore City Community College, 6–7

Baltimore public schools, 18

Bashant, Jennifer, 41

battlefield address, as genre, 98

Battle of Gettysburg, 34

behavior index, of Jackson, 47

Berner, Ashley, 80

Beyond Good and Evil, 128–29

biserial correlation, 70–71

bookish learning, commitment to, 9

Bridge Project, 4

Bruner, Jerome, 127

Bryk, Tony, 56, 80

Bureau of Labor statistics, on new jobs, 15–16

Burnyeat, Myles, 114–15

Bush, George W., 8

Byrnes, Vaughan, 44, 45, 46

CAEP. *See* Council for the Accreditation of Educator Preparation

California Department of Education, 109

Cambridge Assessments, 59

capacity to think, education and, 106–7

career and technical (CTE) programs, 11–12, 13; academic skills needed for, 14–15; high school completion and, 14

career prospects, of high school graduates, 2

CASEL. *See* Collaborative for Academic, Social, and Emotional Learning

Catholic schools, public schools contrasted with, 79

causation, correlation and, 35, 38

CCSO. *See* the Council for Chief State School Office (CCSO)

CCSS. *See* Common Core State Standards

CEDEFOP. *See* European Centre for the Development of Vocational Training

Center for Civic Education, 28

Center for Critical Thinking, 48–49

Center for Global Education, 48–49

Central Park East School, 66

challenging curriculum, high-performing students and, 63

chaotic school environments, SEL programs and, 44

charter schools, 21–22, 45

Chenoweth, Karin, 56

Chicago, 76

child psychology, Kirkpatrick on, 62

choice, of parents, xx

Christodoulou, Daisy, 49–50

City Schools and the American Dream (Noguera), 17–18

City University of New York, 132–33

City Year volunteers, 45–46

civics: class cognitive requirements for, 28–29; disagreement on values in, 28; education lack of emphasis on, 27; knowledge of, 3, 140n110; K-12 system and, 29; participation in, 27; subject matter lack of consensus on, 27

classical education, activism and, 26

Cleveland public schools, 63

clinical preparation, of teachers, 68

cognitive engagement, 127

cognitive processes, codifying of, 50

cognitive skills, 83; Aristotle on, 94

Coleman, David, 86–88, 90–91, 93, 94, 97; on expected learning, 100

Coleman, James, 79

Coleman-Hirsch model, of reading, 96–99

Collaborative for Academic, Social, and Emotional Learning (CASEL), 43

college: earnings and, 13; performance SAT score and, 84–85, *85*; insufficient preparation for, 6–7

College Board, 33

Common Core State Standards (CCSS), 74, 86, 88; lack of change through grade levels of, 87, 100, 105; math, 100–102; texts required by, 89

common experience, knowledge and, 60

common sense concepts, new terms for, 53–54

community colleges, 6; economic prospects of students of, 13–14

competence, creative thinking and, 51–52

competitive advantage of America, as shrinking, 9–10

complex texts, discouragement from, 72

"conceived," multiple meanings of, 97

conceptual frameworks, 128

confidence, accuracy and, 50

conflicting sources, understanding of material in, 29

consensus, on standards, 1–2, 64

conservative commentators, antiracist activists and, 23–24

Consortium on Chicago School Research, 56

constructivism, 65–66

constructivist pedagogy, 65–66

consummatory moment, 123

content, creative thinking and, 34

contexts, of schools, 2

control group, 35–36

core aims, of American education, 31

core five subjects, 1

Core Knowledge, of Hirsch, 100

correlational studies, 35

Council for Chief State School Office (CCSO), 75

Council for the Accreditation of Educator Preparation (CAEP), 67

The Council of the Great City Schools, 69–70

COVID-19, xxiii, 55

The Craftsman (Sennett), 94

craftsmen (*technê*), 94, 95, 98

creative ideas, outcome of, 52

creative thinking, 32, 51–52

creativity, types of, 52

Credé, Martin, 41–42

credit recovery, 4

CREDO 2015 report, 21

cricket example, 90

Crisis (magazine), 70

critical race theory (CRT), 22, 25

critical thinking, 32, 33; confusion about, 34–35

criticism, of American education system, 26–27

CRT. *See* critical race theory

CTE. *See* career and technical programs

CTE pathways, 12

cultural discord, 28

cultural heterogeneity, 59–60

cultural literacy, 91

curriculum: autonomy, 59; of Chicago schools, 62; as fixed, 62; fragmented, 64–65, 83

Daisy (fictional character, *The Great Gatsby*), 98–99, 114

Deans for Impact, 75

debate skills, xx, xxi
de Bolla, Peter, 120–22
decoding skills, 86–87, 96
deep learning, 128
degree-requiring jobs, 16–17
Delaware, 14, 72
deliberation skills, xx
"delicate," use of in Gettysburg
    address, 97
democracy: skills of citizens and, xx;
    wide spans of knowledge and, 90
democratic citizenship, 3, 27
Denmark, 13
detectives, reader, 87–88, 93
development, arts education
    and, 118–19
Devereux Student Strengths Assessment
    (DESSA), 45
Dewey, John, 59–60, 62, 116, 121,
    152n30; on observations, 123
diagnostic tests, 70
DiAngelo, Robin, 23, 24
Diploma Program of the International
    Baccalaureate, 76
"discovery and conjecture," math as
    (Lockhart), 102
disposition (*hexix*), 112
distractions, from academics,
    31–54, 105
Districts that Succeed (Chenoweth), 56
Douglass, Frederick, 26
Duckworth, Angela, 41, 42
Duncan-Andrade, Jeff, 24
Dweck, Carole, 38, 39–40, 42

early American public education, 60, 62
earnings, gap in, 13
economic growth, learning
    levels and, *10*
economic outcomes, cognitive
    skills and, 9
economic prospects, of community
    college students, 13–14
economy of countries, schooling and, 13

Educating American Democracy
    Project, 29
education: in arts, 118–19; for black
    children, 24; effective systems of,
    81; expectations for, 1; goals for, xxi,
    2; governance of, 64; outcomes in,
    xxiv, 7; as public interest, xix, xxiii;
    slow reform of, 20–21; U.S. quality
    of, 29–30, 124–25, 129. *See also
    specific topics*
Education Week (trade publication), 48
education work, conditions for, 55–56
effect size, 36
Eisner, Elliot, 131–32
ELA. *See* English language arts
ELA assessments, 71–72, 76
elementary education, secondary
    education contrasted with, 86
Elliot, Charles, 62
Eluard, Paul, 133
Emile (Rousseau), 112–13
emotivism, 108–9
employment, in (U.S.), *16*
engagement: academic, 108, 124–29;
    cognitive, 127
EngageNY, 75
England, 58, 69, 75, 126–27
English language arts (ELA), 6, 83,
    86, 126, 132
ESSA. *See* Every Student Succeeds Act
Estonia, 57
Estonian Basic Schools and Upper
    Secondary Schools Act, 57
ethical judgement (*phronesis*), 110–11,
    114–15, 117, 119
ethics: behavior of children and, 109;
    education in, 108–17; lasting beliefs
    and, 109; practice as children
    of, 111–12
eudaimonia, 106, 109–10, 151n13
European Centre for the Development of
    Vocational Training (CEDEFOP), 17
European countries, career
    courses in, 12–13
Evers, Williamson, 23

Every Student Succeeds Act (ESSA), xxiii, 3, 76
exit exams, selection of less challenging subjects for, 11
external measure, of learning, 8

fables, children and, 112–13
factory model, of education, 48–49
faculties of imagination, Kant on, 120
Federal Reserve Bank of New York, 17
federal vocational baccalaureate, 14
Felski, Rita, 95–96, 132
fictional text, Coleman/Hirsch method on, 98–99
fields of study, ranking in, 125–26
Fine, Sarah, 127–28
Finland, 58–59
Finn, Chester, 29
Fitzgerald, F. Scott, 98
Florida, xxii, 25, 79
foreign language instruction, attention given to, 126
forensic approach, to reading, 88–89
founding documents, study of, 27
France, 58
Fry, Meredith, 84, 148n4
funding: advantages for affluent area charter schools, 21; for publics schools, 2

G. *See* general intelligence level
Gadamer, Hans Georg, 95–96, 121
Galston, William, xxii, 28
gap, in earnings, 13
Gatsby (fictional character, *The Great Gatsby*), 98–99, 114
General Baccalaureate test, 126
general intelligence level (G), 84
Germany, 13, 73, 78
Gettysburg Address (Lincoln), 97
Giroux, Henry, 91–92
The Glossary of Education Reform, 49
GMS. *See* Growth Mindset
grade-level assignments, minority students and, 18–20

grade point averages: inflation of, 5–6; Jackson study and, 47
graduation: alternative pathways for, 4; rates of, 5, 7–8; tests and, 3–4
gratification delay, SAT scores and, 41
The Great Gatsby (Fitzgerald), 98, 114, 132
green, as used in *The Great Gatsby*, 98
Greene, Jay, 47
Greene, Maxime, 122
grit, 32, 41–42
growth, progressivists on, 63
Growth Mindset (GMS), 32, 37–39; misuse of, 39–40; simplicity of, 40–41; studies of, 39
Gutmann, Amy, xix-xxii, 90

Hall, G. Stanley, 62
Hannah-Jones, Nikole, 23–24
Hanushek, Rick, 9–10, 13
Hardy, Harold, 89
Harrison, Erin, 37
Harvard University, 62
Heidegger, Martin, 94, 131
hermeneutics, 92, 95
Hess, Frederick, 23
hexix (disposition), 112
higher education, grade inflation in, 6
high-performing schools, student expectations and, 44–45
high-performing students, challenging curriculum for, 63
high quality content-rich instructional materials (HIQM), 75
high school, graduation low standards for, 8, 11
"High School and Beyond" (Coleman), 79
high-skill jobs, in the United States, 17
high stakes tests, district intervention and, 71
HIQM. *See* high quality, content-rich instructional materials
Hirsch, E. D., 57–58, 89–91, 94, 95, 100; criticism of, 92–93

Hofstadter, Richard, 63
Homer, 98
"How Metacognition Boosts Learning"
    (Terada), 50
How to Be an Antiracist (Kendi), 22–23
"How to Measure Metacognition"
    (study), 50
Hunter, James, 109, 113, 152n23
Hunter College School of
    Education, 132–33

The Iliad (Homer), 98
imaginary worlds, ethics
    lessons and, 113
imagination, as cognitive power, 120
IMPD. *See* Instructional Materials and
    Professional Development Network
income levels, racial gap and, 18
information, processing of, 48–49
In Search of Deeper Learning (Fine and
    Mehta), 127–28
instincts: nurturing of, 65;
    reliance on, 131
instructional culture, 81
instructional guidance, 56
Instructional Materials and Professional
    Development (IMPD) Network, 75
intellectual skills, 52
intervention group, 35–36
introspection, 50
IQ tests, 63, 69, 84
iReady test, 70

Jackson, Kirabo, 46–47
jobs, requiring degrees, 16–17
Johns Hopkins University, 20, 44–45;
    Institute for Education Policy, 12
journeyman, in *Republic*, 93
Journeys (ELA curriculum),
    130, 130–31

Kane, Tom, 68
Kant, Immanuel, 116–17, 119–23
Kendi, Ibram X., 22–23, 24
Kimball, Roger, 132

King, Martin Luther, Jr., 26
King Creon (fictional character,
    Antigone), 132
Kirkpatrick, William H., 62
Kirp, David, 56–57
knowledge: accumulation of, 89–90, 92;
    as fluid, 62, 64; necessity of, 54, 125
Koffler, Steven, 71
Kraut, Richard, 107

labeling of children by adults, 40
labor market, of America, 9
Lampert, Magdalene, 102
language, ambiguity of, 88
The Laws (Plato), 106
leadership, from principal, 56, 144n15
learning: economic growth levels and,
    10; external measure of, 8; Giroux
    on, 92; Hirsch on, 91; to learn, 53–54
Lee, Robert E., 34
lessons, curation of, 64–65, 81–82
"Letter from Birmingham Jail"
    (King), 26
Levine, Arthur, 68
Lewis, William D., 63
Lexile rating, of texts, 87
life narrative, feeling of control in, 110
Lincoln, Abraham, 97
literacy program, as strong, 19–20
literary theory, Coleman and, 88
literature, aesthetic elements of, 132
Lockhart, Paul, 102
long term memory, reading and, 90
Los Angeles, 63
Louisiana, 20, 76
Loveless, Tom, 101
low-income African American
    students, 80
low-income students, growth mindset
    and, 38–40
low-wage workers, demand for, 17

Macbeth (fictional character,
    Macbeth), 114
Macbeth (Shakespeare), 93, 114

MacIntyre, Alasdair, 111, 112, 152n34

MAI. *See* The Metacognitive Awareness Inventory

main idea: art appreciation contrasted with, 121–22; of state test passages, 71–72

Malcolm X, 26

Mandela, Nelson, 132

Mann, Horace, 17

MAP test, 70

marshmallow test, 41

Maryland, 4; Commission on Innovation and Excellence, 14–15

Massachusetts, 76, 84

mathematical pathways, exploration of, 102

mathematics: Common Core procedures and, 102; inflexible standards of, 100, 102; pedagogy, Ball on, 102; ranking of in study fields, 126; scores of African American students, 18; skill in, 89

math teaching, race and, 23

MCAS test, 84

McConnell, Michael, xx-xxii, xxiv

McGuffey Readers, 60, *61*, 62, 64

McIntyre, Alasdair, 108

McPhail, Graham, 54, 128

meaning, interpretation contrasted with, 95

mechatronics, 14

Mehta, Jal, 127–28

Meier, Deborah, 66

melting pot, salad bowl contrasted with, 64, 145n41

memorization, overemphasis on, 103

mentors: academic achievement and, 45–47; for novice teachers, 130

meta-analyses: of Coleman study, 79–80; of Growth Mindset, 38–39; on Social and Emotional Learning, 43–44

metacognition, 48–51, 54; Terada on, 50

Metacognitive Awareness Inventory (MAI), 49

metacognitive skills, 48–50

methods courses, 67

metrics, devaluation of, 8–9

Michigan State University, 57

Minor, Cornelius, 23

minority students, inequalities in backgrounds of, 18–19, 21

Mississippi, 19, 86

Missouri, 67–68

Morrison, Nick, xxiv

"Much Ado about Grit" (Credé), 42

multicheck assessment, 13

NAEP math results, 101

National Assessment for Educational Progress (NAEP), 5, 27, 73, 136n18

National Center for Education Statistics, 6

National Center for Teacher Quality (NCTQ), 75

National Center on Education and the Economy, 33

National Council for the Teachers of English (NCTE), 67

national curriculum: in American education, 60, 62, 64; high performing countries and, 57–58

National Reading Panel, 86

NCLB. *See* No Child Left Behind

NCQT. *See* National Center for Teacher Quality

NCTE. *See* National Council for the Teachers of English

Netherlands, 79–80

neutral approach, of public school system, xx

new jobs, as low-paying, 15–17

new learning, 54

Newman, Barnett, 120–21, 132

The New Teacher Project, 18, 80–81

new terms, for common sense concepts, 53–54

New York, 21, 25, 71, 74–75

New York Times, 22, 23–24

Nietzsche, Friedrich, 128–29

9/11 attacks lesson, 29
No Child Left Behind (NCLB), xxiii, 3
Noguera, Pedro, 17–18
noncognitive measures, of Jackson, 47
nonfiction text, Coleman
    method on, 96–98
normed-based assessments, 70–71
Nozick, Robert, 117
Nussbaum, Martha, 115–16

Oakeshott, Michael, 107, 108, 110
Oates, Tim, 59, 69–70
OECD. *See* Organisation for Economic
    Co-operation and Development
opinion, analysis of, 117
opportunity gap, 18, 79
Oregon policy, 7, 137n26
Organisation for Economic
    Co-operation and Development
    (OECD), 38, 51–53

PARCC assessment, 84
parental choice, xx-xxiv
parent-community ties, 56
parents, disagreement between
    teachers and, 2
passion, successful teaching and,
    128–29, 133
past, lack of guidance from, 24
"A Pathway to Equitable Math
    Instruction" (education policy
    document), 23
PDK 2017 poll, xxiii
Pearson testing company, 72, *72*, 73
pedagogy, change in conception
    of, 129–30
percentage, results in, 36–37
performance curves, standardized
    tests and, 71
performing arts, 132
The PE Specialist (YouTube
    creator), 144n28
Peter Rabbit stories, 113
phronesis (ethical judgement), 110–11,
    114–15, 117, 119

Piano, Renzo, 94
PISA. *See* Program for International
    Student Assessment
Plato, 60, 93, 106
plausible cause, 36
pluralist education system, xxii
political structures, school content
    and, xix-xx
Poll of the Public's Attitudes Toward the
    Public Schools, 14
Pondiscio, Robert, 48
postracial language, 24
practicum, of student teachers, 67
Praether, Anika, 26
pragmatism, 8–9
pre-K, emphasis on, 20
principals, high turnover rate
    of, 55, 81–82
private schools, xxii, 2
professional capacity, 56
Program for International Student
    Assessment (PISA), 7, 9, 33, 38,
    58–59; creative thinking test of,
    52–53; Dutch system and, 80;
    in U.S., 66
progress, impossibility of, 20–21, 24
progressivism, 59–65, 128; in teacher
    training programs, 68
progressivists, 63
The Project Method (Kirkpatrick), 62
psychological well-being, of
    children, 109
public interest, education as, xix, xxiii
public knowledge, base of, 92
public-school performance, 56
public school system: declining interest
    in, xxiii; neutral approach of, xx
published curricular materials,
    use of, 75

quasi-experimental research, 36

"Race to the Top" competition, 74–75
racial content teaching bills, 28
racial disparities, in K-12 education, 22

racial equity, social justice and, 17–18
racism, 7, 19–25
RAND corporation, 48–49
randomized control trials (RCT), 35–36, 44
RAND survey, 64
range of subjects, support for, 127
Rawls, John, 117
RCT. *See* randomized control trials
reaction, to art object, 119–22
reading: choice ethical education and, 113; comprehension skills, 90; forensic approach to, 88–89; Gadamer on, 96; to learn, 86–87, 96, 99; material as overly simple, 20; McGuffey Readers, *61*; science lack of emphasis on, 67, 86
reading skills: as taught, 83–84, 86; young children and, 86
Rebell, Michael, 28
rebirth, in Gettysburg Address, 97
Reboot Foundation, 33
reflective thinking, 106
reform, within existing system, 24
Regents exam, 10–11
religious schools, funding of, xxi, xxii
Remainder Theorem, 101
remediation, 20, 40, 65, 130
Report of the Committee of Ten on Secondary School Studies, 62
"Report of the National Reading Panel," 67
reproduction, of skill, 94
Republic (Plato), 93
research groups, as similar, 36
research terminology, 35–36
resilience, 41
Romeo and Juliet (Shakespeare), 91
Roosevelt, Franklin Delano, 28
Rothstein, Richard, 21
Rousseau, Jean-Jacques, 112–13
Rowe, Ian, 24
rowing, as used in *The Great Gatsby*, 98–99

safe environment, school performance and, 80
salad bowl, melting pot contrasted with, 64
Saphier, Jon, 66–67
SAT, 33, 69, 70, 83, 84; prep work and, 84
Schleicher, Andreas, 9–10, 59
Schmidt, Bill, 57, 100–101
school: choice bills, xxiii; content political structures and, xix-xx; culture of, 79–80; district policies as consistent, 57; districts as varied, 64
school boards, authority of, 21
"School Effects on Socio-Emotional Development, School-Based Arrests, and Educational Attainment" (Jackson), 46
schooling, alternative purposes for, 54
school interventions, of CASEL program, 43–44
schools, 77; effectiveness of, *78*
schools of education: creation of curricula and, 65–67; lack of difference between, 68; low requirements for, 68
school system, state and, xx
Science, Technology, Engineering and Mathematics (STEM): AP exams in, 10–11, 137n36; earnings for students of, 10
SEL. *See* Social and Emotional Learning
self-discipline, 41, 142n40
self-fulfilling prophecy, academic progress beliefs as, 40, 65
self-reporting studies, problems with, 44–45
Sennett, Richard, 94
sentence length, as metric for text difficulty, 87
Seven Myths About Education (Christodoulou), 49–50
significance of text, attribution of, 95
Simon, Hebert, 54

1619 Project (*New York Times*), 22, 23–24
The Skillful Teacher (Saphier), 66–67
skills of citizens, democracy and, xx-xxi
Slavin, Robert, 20
Social and Emotional Learning (SEL), 3, 32; as distractor, 42–43, 48; implementation in underperforming school of, 45–47
social inequalities, 65
social justice, racial equity and, 17–18
social skills, academics contrasted with, 3–4
social studies assessments, 72, *72*, 126; lack of historical knowledge required for, 73
socioeconomic inequalities, 25–26, 77
socioeconomic integration, attempt at, 79
socioeconomic segregation, in American schools, 79
Socrates, 93
Sophocles, 132
South Carolina, 14
Spartan education program (*agogê*), 99
Standard Encyclopedia of Philosophy, 33
standardized tests: consequences for students of, 73, 81, 126; lack of connection to curriculum of, 69; number of in U.S., 69–70; passing standards of, 71
standards, abolition of, 7
standards, school practices and, 101
Stanford University, 21, 80
state assessments, xxiii, 24, 69, 70–71; SEL studies and, 44
state authority, xxiv-xxv
state-mandated testing, entry into higher education and, 126
state-run school system, xx
STEM. *See* Science, Technology, Engineering and Mathematics
Stigler, James, 103

stories: childhood and, 113–14; ethical lessons from, 114
strong curriculum, *130*, 130–31
student-centered curriculum, 59; PISA results and, 65
student learning climate, 56
student-made art, 123
student mental health, teacher skill for, 43
students, as detectives, 87–88
student teachers, practicum of, 67
study techniques, 50
Summerhill School, 65–66
Supreme Court, choice laws and, xxiii
Swiss model, 13
Switzerland, 13
Switzerland, AIT model of, 13
systemic racism: acknowledgment of, 22; conservatives on, 25

taste, aesthetic judgement contrasted with, 119–20
Tbilisi, Georgia, 132
teacher-designed curriculum, 58–59, 65
teacher education programs: quality of graduates of, 67–68, 105–6; references to state curriculum of, 67; reforms to, 75–76; strong curriculum and, *130*, 130–31
teachers: preparation of, 2, 19–20, 65–66, 81–82, 83; preparation program graduates decline in, 55; recruitment of, 55; skill sets of, 129
Teach for America, 24
teaching: changing methods in Finland, 59; effective, 127–28; from memory, 132
"Teaching Tips" (YouTube video), 144n28
technê (craftsmen), 94, 95, 98
technical education, 9
tenth grade assessment, in Maryland, 15
Terada, Youki, 50
test design, 70–73
testing, conflicting information from, 70

test scores: career outcomes and, 4–5; drop in, 5; inequality statistics and, 24

Texas, xxii

texts: Hirsch on, 92–93; interpretive layers of, 96; multiple reading of, 95, 97

thinking: as silent dialogue, 107–8; about thinking, 48, 50

thought, emotions and, 123

threat: appropriate response to, 112; charter schools as, 21

TIMSS international assessment, 57

TNTP. *See* The New Teacher Project

Tom Buchanan (fictional character, *The Great Gatsby*), 98–99, 114

"To What Extent and Under Which Circumstances Are Growth Mind-Sets Important to Academic Achievement?," 38–39

training, American education system as, 99–100

transmission model of learning, 49

tutoring, academic achievement and, 45–47, 80

tutoring, SEL contrasted with, 45–47

twenty-first century skills, 31–32, 48–50

Tyack, David, 64

underprivileged students: assumed poor performance of, 77; career tracks and, 12, 63

Union City, 56–57

United Kingdom, 59, 65–66

United States (U.S.): employment in, *16*; support for pluralist model in, xxii

university acceptance, shift in requirements for, 129–30

upbringing, ethical behavior and, 111

urban charter schools, 80

urban public schools, 4, 21–22

Urmson, J. O., 112

U.S. *See* United States

utilitarianism, 116

Valent, John, 19

Validity in Interpretation (Hirsch), 92, 95

value judgements, in civics, 29

values clarification, 109

Vanderbilt University, 50

variable curriculum, in American education system, 58

Virginia, 25

Vir Heroicus Sublimis (painting), 120–21

virtue (*aretê*), 115

vocabulary gap, of minority students, 19

vocational training, 13

Watts, Tyler, 42

Webster, Daniel, 105, 106

Western philosophy, Dewey on, 59–60

What Your Sixth Grader Needs to Know (Hirsch), 93

White, John, 76

White Fragility (DiAngelo), 23

whole child teaching, 31–32

Why Knowledge Matters (Hirsch), 58

Willingham, Daniel, 33, 34

Wineberg, Sam, 70

wisdom, 124–25, 133

within-school variation, in the US, 77–79, *78*

Wolf, Patrick, xxiv

Wood, Ellen, 96–97

Woodrow Wilson National Fellowship, 6

word frequency, as metric for text difficulty, 87

words, as facts, 93

Works Clearinghouse, 37–38

Wurman, Ze'Ev, 23

yearlong clinical experience, 75

Yeats, William Butler, 124

young adults, low wage jobs done by, 17

About the Author

David Steiner is executive director of the Johns Hopkins Institute for Education Policy and professor of education at Johns Hopkins University. He served as a member of the Maryland State Board of Education and the Maryland Commission for Innovation and Excellence in Education. Prior to moving to Johns Hopkins, Dr. Steiner was commissioner of education for New York State and was for eight years the Klara and Larry Silverstein Dean at the Hunter College School of Education. Before his work in New York, he was director of arts education at the National Endowment for the Arts. Additionally, Dr. Steiner is currently a board member of The Relay Graduate School of Education and serves on the Practitioner Council of the Hoover Institution at Stanford University.

As New York State education commissioner, Dr. Steiner took a lead role in the state's successful $700 million Race to the Top application to support the redesign of state standards, assessments, and teacher certification requirements. His insistence on including major funding for curricula in that grant led to the launch of EngageNY, which become the nation's most consulted online curriculum resource. Dr. Steiner consults with state education leaders, school superintendents, educational reform organizations, and universities. He has addressed audiences on both side of the Atlantic and has authored or edited books, book chapters, and more than fifty articles. He holds degrees from Balliol College, Oxford University (BA and MA), and Harvard University (PhD in political science).

Made in the USA
Middletown, DE
17 July 2023

35259556R00135